The AMAZING SPIDER-MAN

The AMAZING SPIDER-MAN

WORLDWIDE

DAN SLOTT
WRITER

MATTEO BUFFAGNI
ARTIST, #6-8

GIUSEPPE CAMUNCOLI
PENCILER, #9-11

CAM SMITH
INKER, #9-11

MARTE GRACIA
COLORIST

VC'S JOE CARAMAGNA (#1-2 & #4-5) & CHRIS ELIOPOULOS (#3)
LETTERERS

ALEX ROSS
COVER ART

DEVIN LEWIS
ASSISTANT EDITOR

NICK LOWE
EDITOR

SPIDER-MAN CREATED BY
STAN LEE & STEVE DITKO

COLLECTION EDITOR: **JENNIFER GRÜNWALD**
ASSOCIATE EDITOR: **SARAH BRUNSTAD**
ASSOCIATE MANAGING EDITOR: **ALEX STARBUCK**
EDITOR, SPECIAL PROJECTS: **MARK D. BEAZLEY**

VP, PRODUCTION & SPECIAL PROJECTS: **JEFF YOUNGQUIST**
SVP PRINT, SALES & MARKETING: **DAVID GABRIEL**
BOOK DESIGNER: **ADAM DEL RE**

EDITOR IN CHIEF: **AXEL ALONSO**
CHIEF CREATIVE OFFICER: **JOE QUESADA**
PUBLISHER: **DAN BUCKLEY**
EXECUTIVE PRODUCER: **ALAN FINE**

AMAZING SPIDER-MAN: WORLDWIDE VOL. 2. Contains material originally published in magazine form as AMAZING SPIDER-MAN #6-11. First printing 2016. ISBN# 978-0-7851-9943-4. Published by MARVEL WORLDWIDE, INC., a subsi of MARVEL ENTERTAINMENT, LLC. OFFICE OF PUBLICATION: 135 West 50th Street, New York, NY 10020. Copyright © 2016 MARVEL No similarity between any of the names, characters, persons, and/or institutions in this magazine with th any living or dead person or institution is intended, and any such similarity which may exist is purely coincidental. **Printed in Canada.** ALAN FINE, President, Marvel Entertainment; DAN BUCKLEY, President, TV, Publishing & Brand Manage JOE QUESADA, Chief Creative Officer; TOM BREVOORT, SVP of Publishing; DAVID BOGART, SVP of Business Affairs & Operations, Publishing & Partnership; C.B. CEBULSKI, VP of Brand Management & Development, Asia; DAVID GABRIEN of Sales & Marketing, Publishing; JEFF YOUNGQUIST, VP of Production & Special Projects; DAN CARR, Executive Director of Publishing Technology; ALEX MORALES, Director of Publishing Operations; SUSAN CRESPI, Production Manager; LEE, Chairman Emeritus. For information regarding advertising in Marvel Comics or on Marvel.com, please contact Vit DeBellis, Integrated Sales Manager, at vdebellis@marvel.com. For Marvel subscription inquiries, please call 888-511- **Manufactured between 5/13/2016 and 6/20/2016 by SOLISCO PRINTERS, SCOTT, QC, CANADA.**
10 9 8 7 6 5 4 3 2 1

WHEN PETER PARKER WAS BITTEN BY A RADIOACTIVE SPIDER, HE GAINED THE PROPORTIONAL SPEED, STRENGTH AND AGILITY OF A SPIDER; ADHESIVE FINGERTIPS AND TOES; AND THE UNIQUE PRECOGNITIVE AWARENESS OF DANGER CALLED "SPIDER-SENSE"! AFTER LEARNING THAT WITH GREAT POWER THERE MUST ALSO COME GREAT RESPONSIBILITY, HE BECAME THE CRIMEFIGHTING SUPER HERO CALLED...

The AMAZING SPIDER-MAN

PETER PARKER'S COMPANY, PARKER INDUSTRIES, IS CHANGING THE WORLD WITH CUTTING-EDGE TECHNOLOGY, HIS DESIGNS AND INNOVATIONS ARE HELPING EQUIP S.H.I.E.L.D. AND HE HAS EVEN STARTED HIS OWN NON-PROFIT CHARITY TO PROVIDE HUMANITARIAN AID ACROSS THE PLANET.

BUT PETER PARKER'S GLOBAL PRESENCE HAS ALSO PUT HIS ALTER EGO THE AMAZING SPIDER-MAN FACE-TO-FACE WITH NEW AND DEADLY THREATS FROM ACROSS THE WORLD. THE WEB-SLINGER HAS BEEN SPOTTED SAVING LIVES IN SAN FRANCISCO, LONDON AND EVEN SHANGHAI!

AMIDST ALL OF THESE NEW THREATS, SPIDEY'S OLDEST AND DEADLIEST FOES HAVE ALSO COME CRAWLING OUT OF THE WOODWORK...

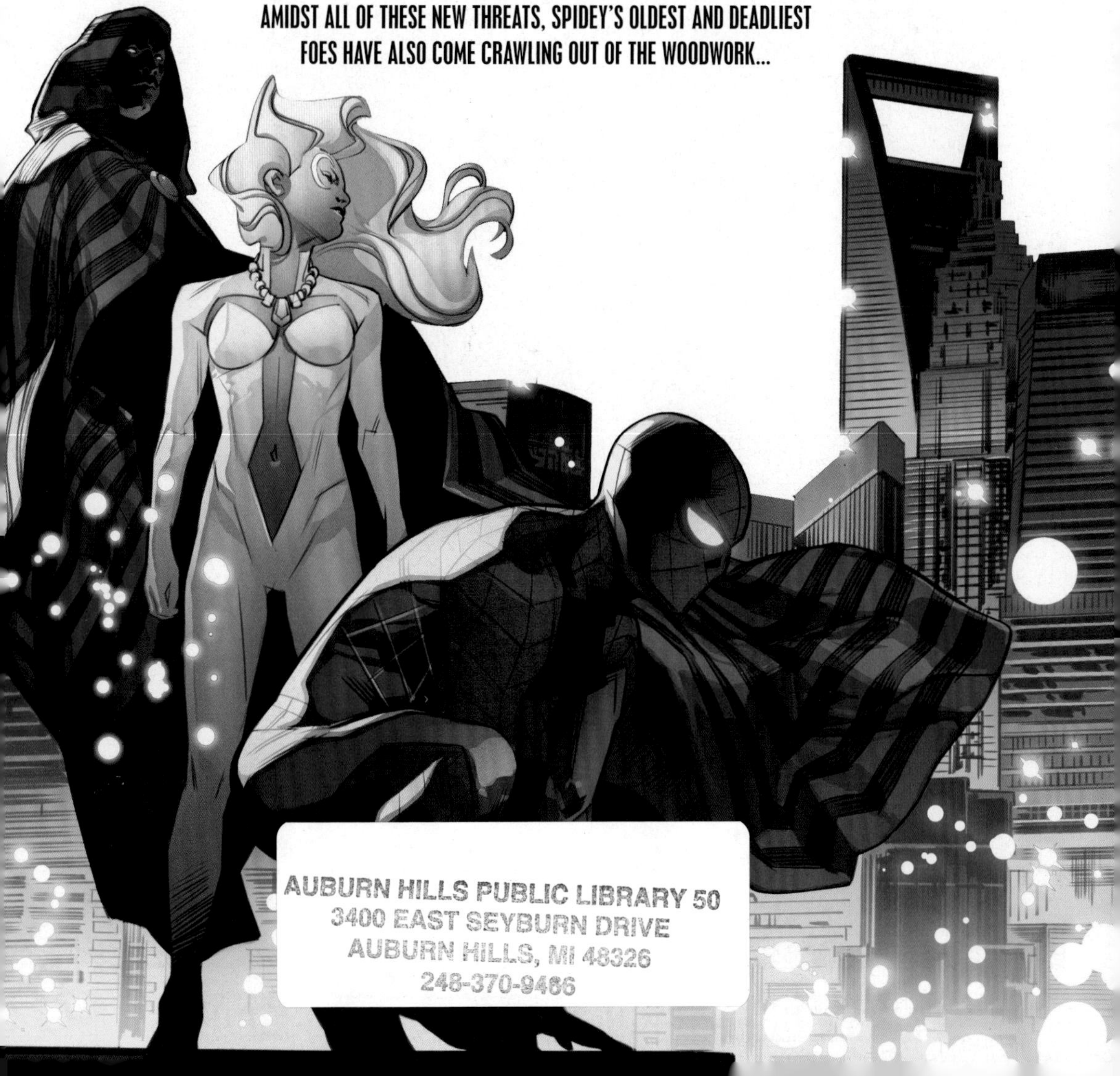

6

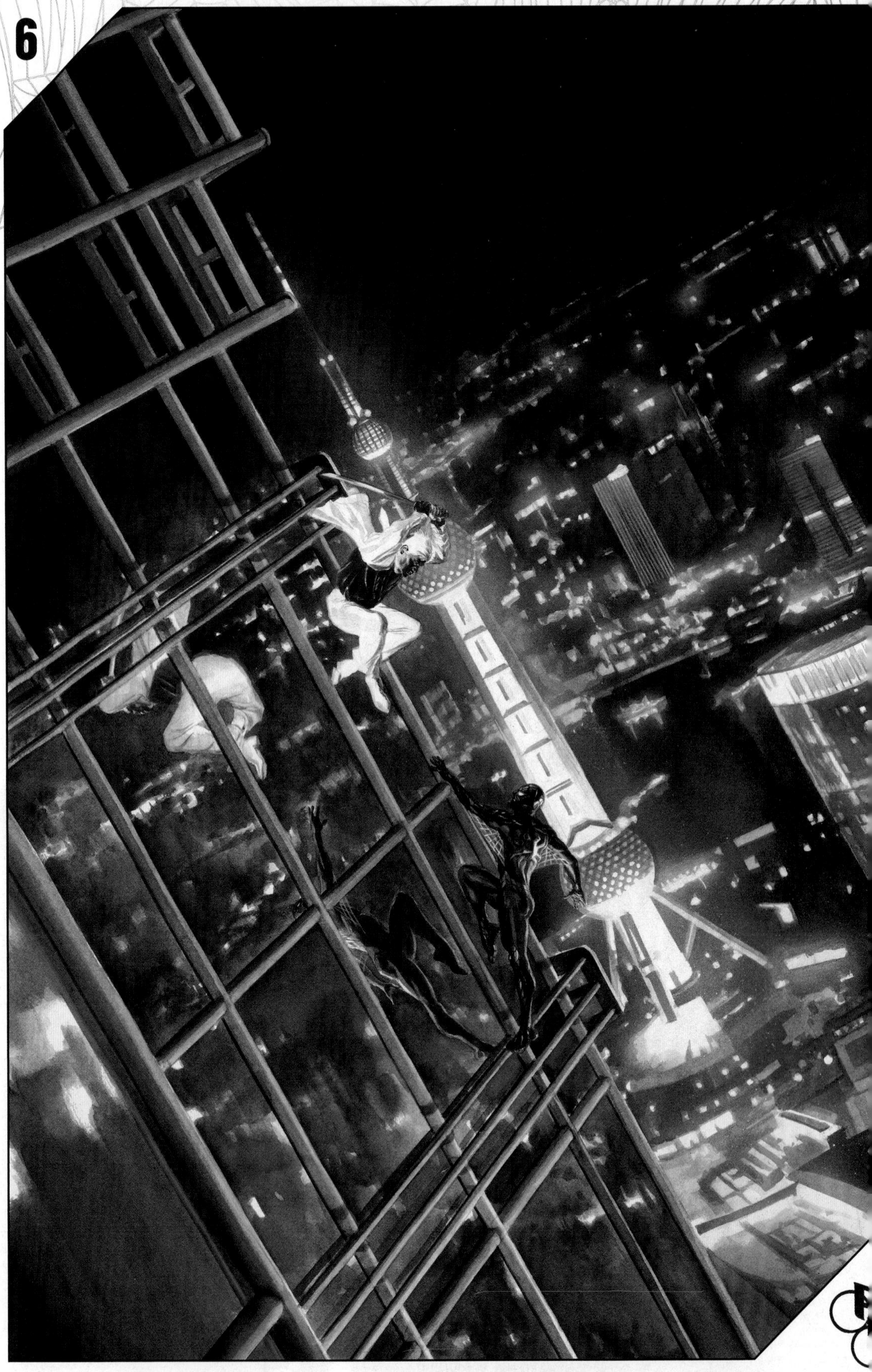

THE DARK KINGDOM - PART 1: "TURNABOUT"

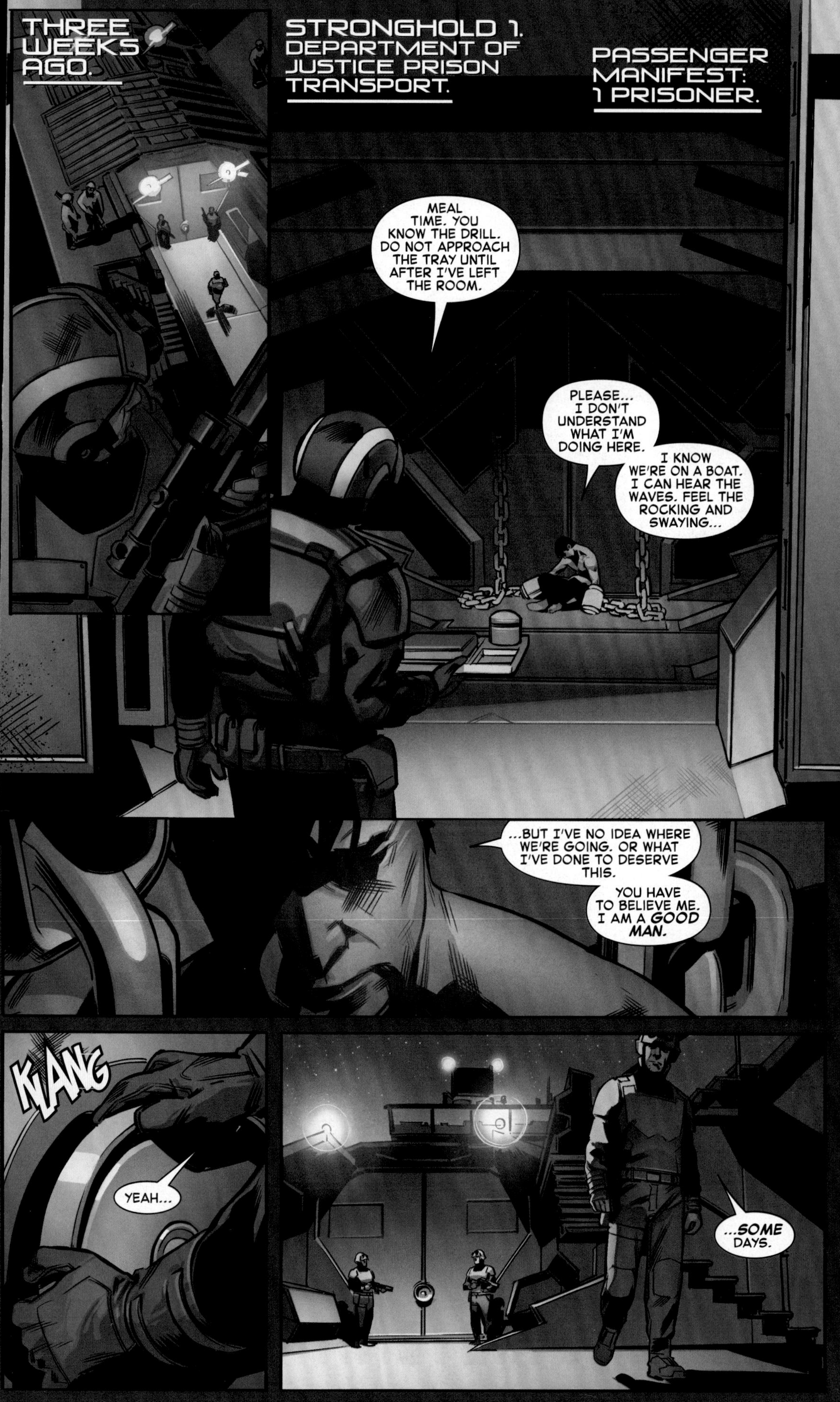
THREE WEEKS AGO.
STRONGHOLD 1. DEPARTMENT OF JUSTICE PRISON TRANSPORT.
PASSENGER MANIFEST: 1 PRISONER.
MEAL TIME. YOU KNOW THE DRILL. DO NOT APPROACH THE TRAY UNTIL AFTER I'VE LEFT THE ROOM.
PLEASE... I DON'T UNDERSTAND WHAT I'M DOING HERE.
I KNOW WE'RE ON A BOAT. I CAN HEAR THE WAVES. FEEL THE ROCKING AND SWAYING...
...BUT I'VE NO IDEA WHERE WE'RE GOING. OR WHAT I'VE DONE TO DESERVE THIS.
YOU HAVE TO BELIEVE ME. I AM A GOOD MAN.
KLANG
YEAH...
...SOME DAYS.

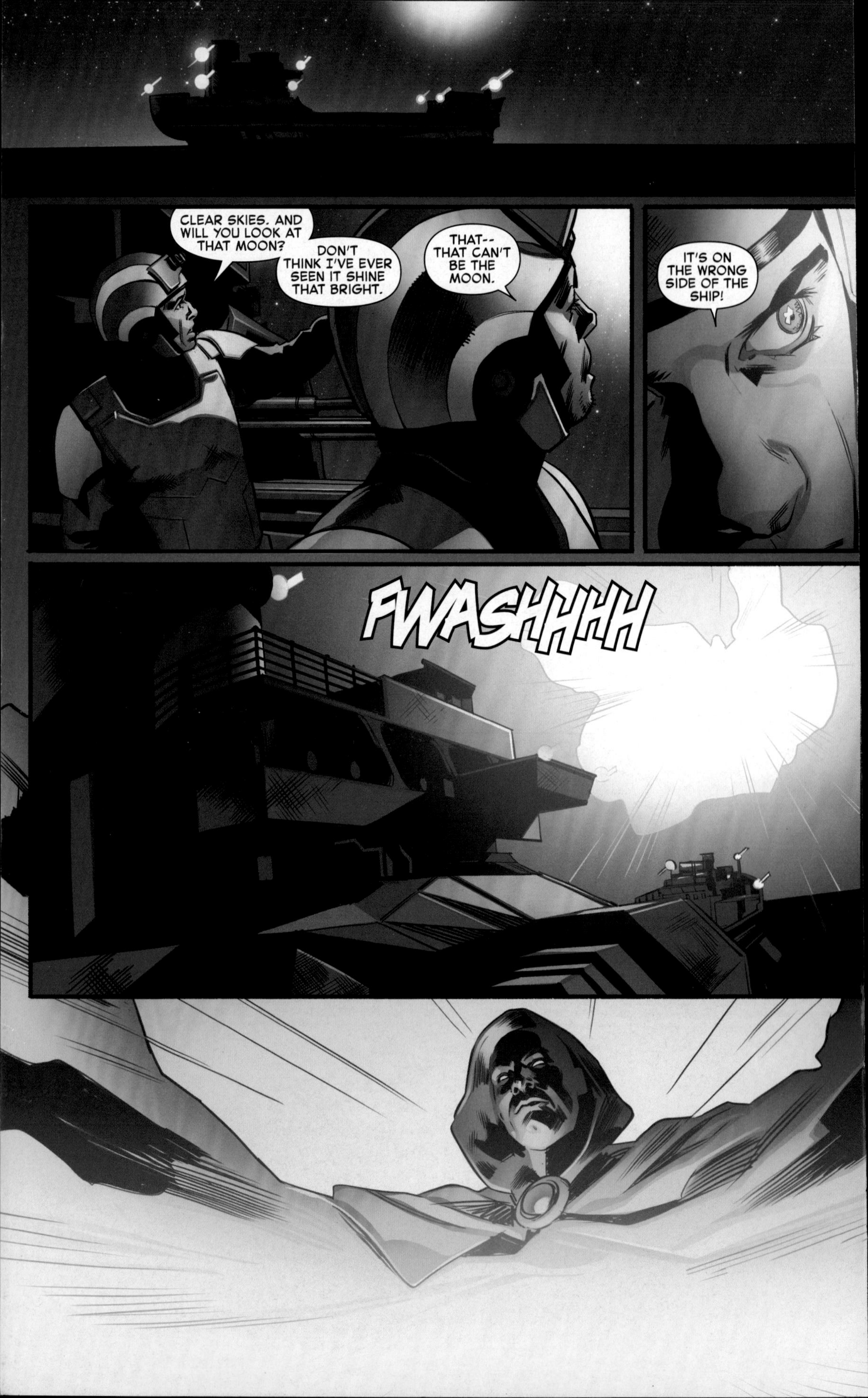
CLEAR SKIES. AND WILL YOU LOOK AT THAT MOON?
DON'T THINK I'VE EVER SEEN IT SHINE THAT BRIGHT.
THAT-- THAT CAN'T BE THE MOON.
IT'S ON THE WRONG SIDE OF THE SHIP!
FWASHHHH

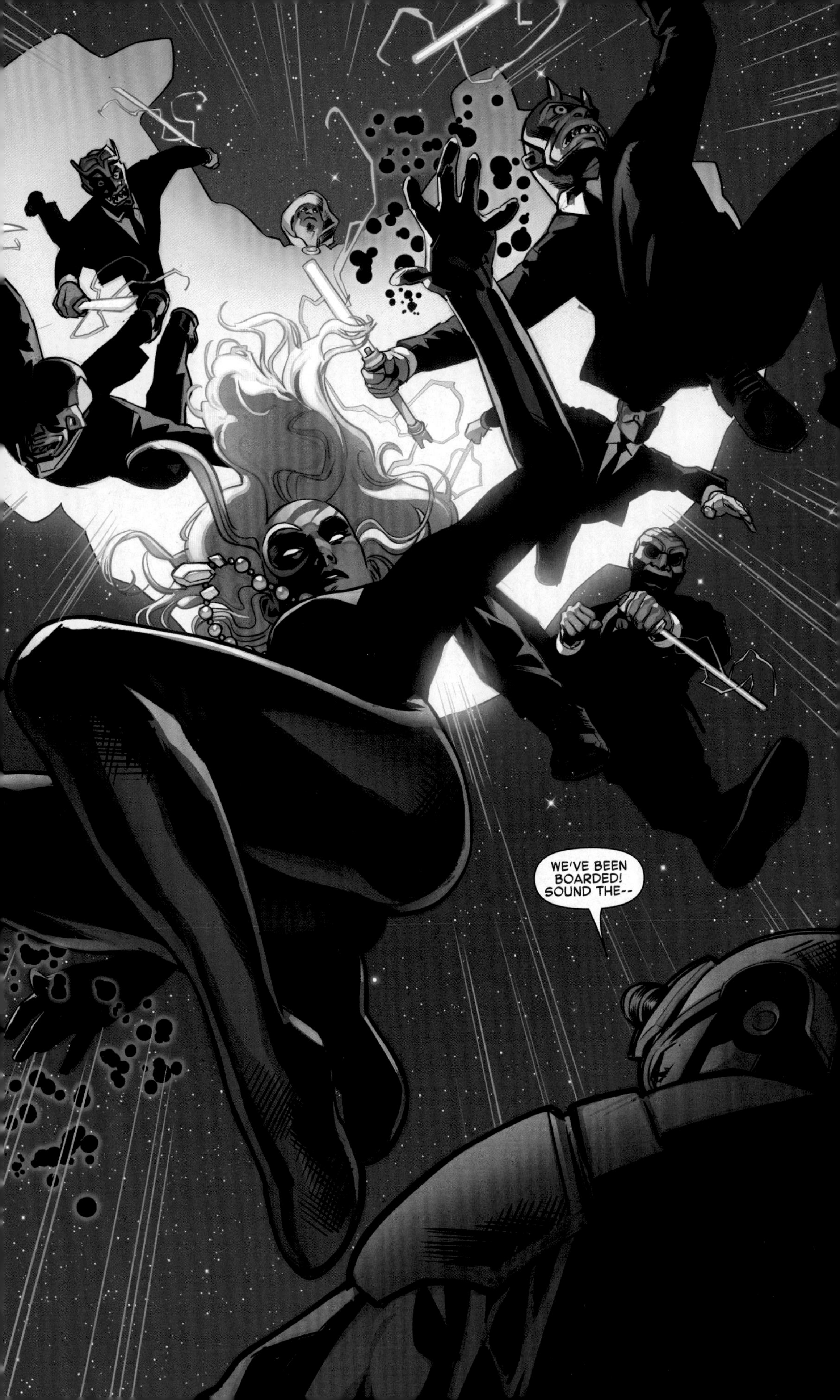
WE'VE BEEN BOARDED! SOUND THE--

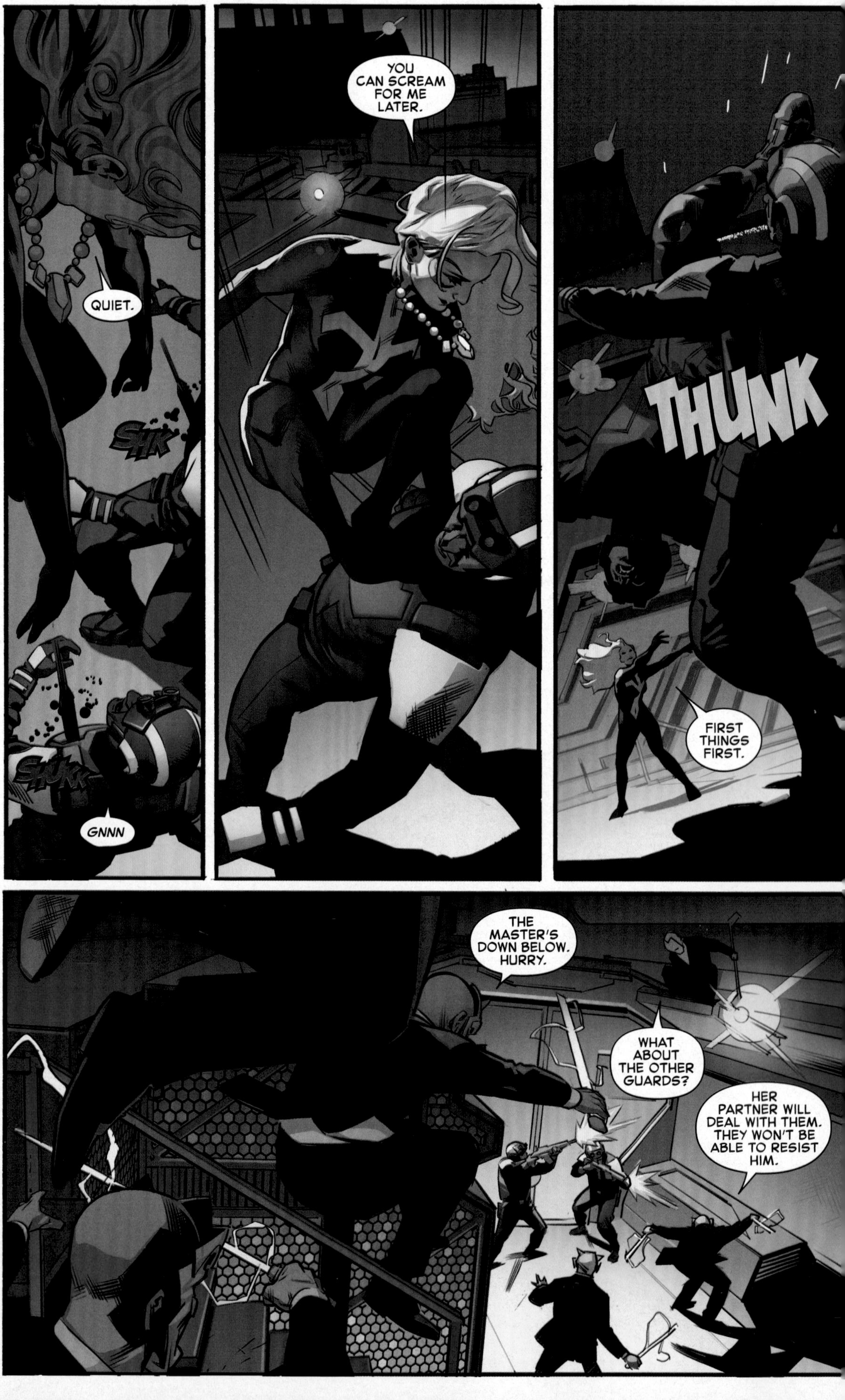
QUIET.
SHK
SHUKK
GNNN
YOU CAN SCREAM FOR ME LATER.
THUNK
FIRST THINGS FIRST.
THE MASTER'S DOWN BELOW. HURRY.
WHAT ABOUT THE OTHER GUARDS?
HER PARTNER WILL DEAL WITH THEM. THEY WON'T BE ABLE TO RESIST HIM.

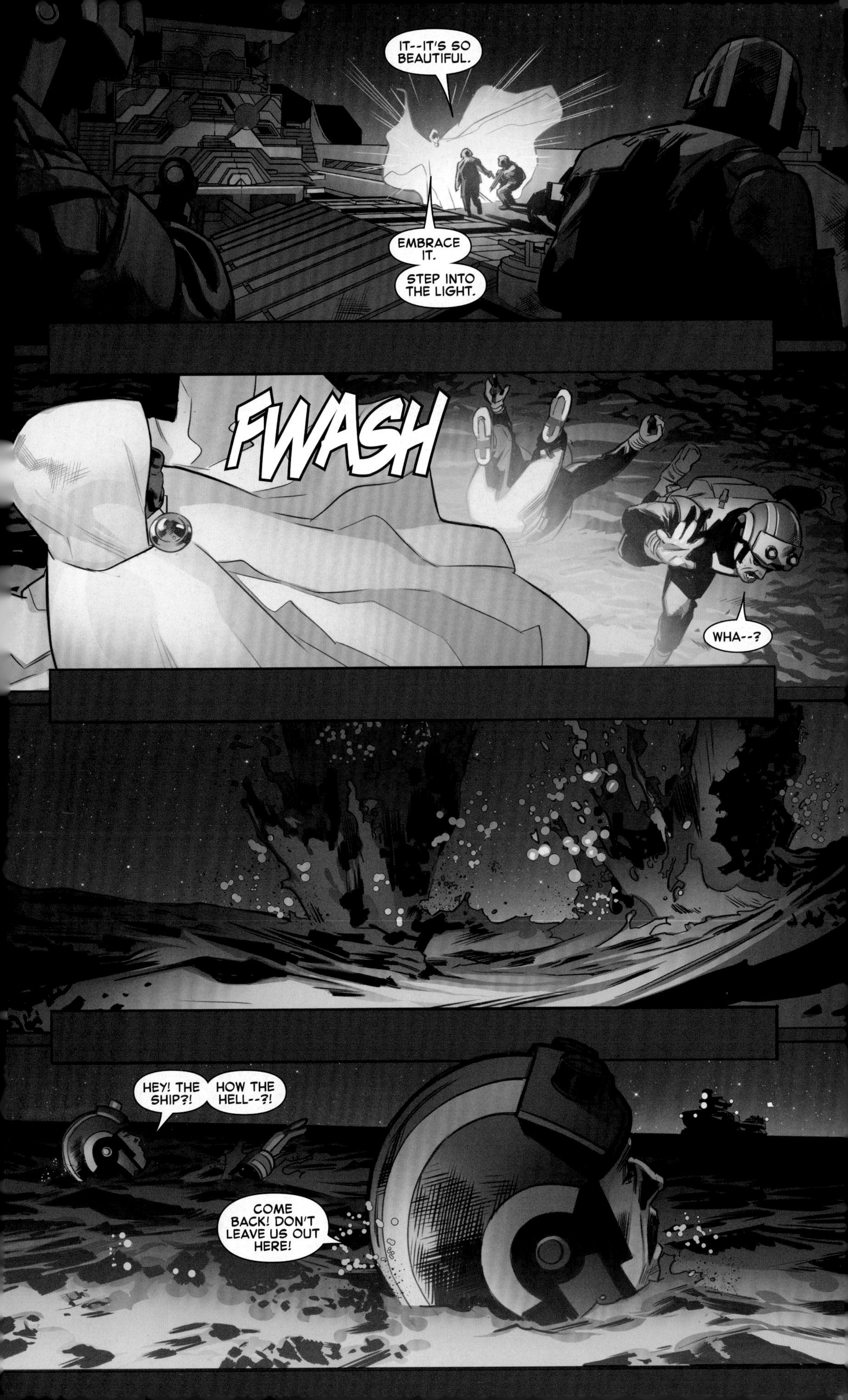
IT--IT'S SO BEAUTIFUL.
EMBRACE IT.
STEP INTO THE LIGHT.
FWASH
WHA--?
HEY! THE SHIP?!
HOW THE HELL--?!
COME BACK! DON'T LEAVE US OUT HERE!

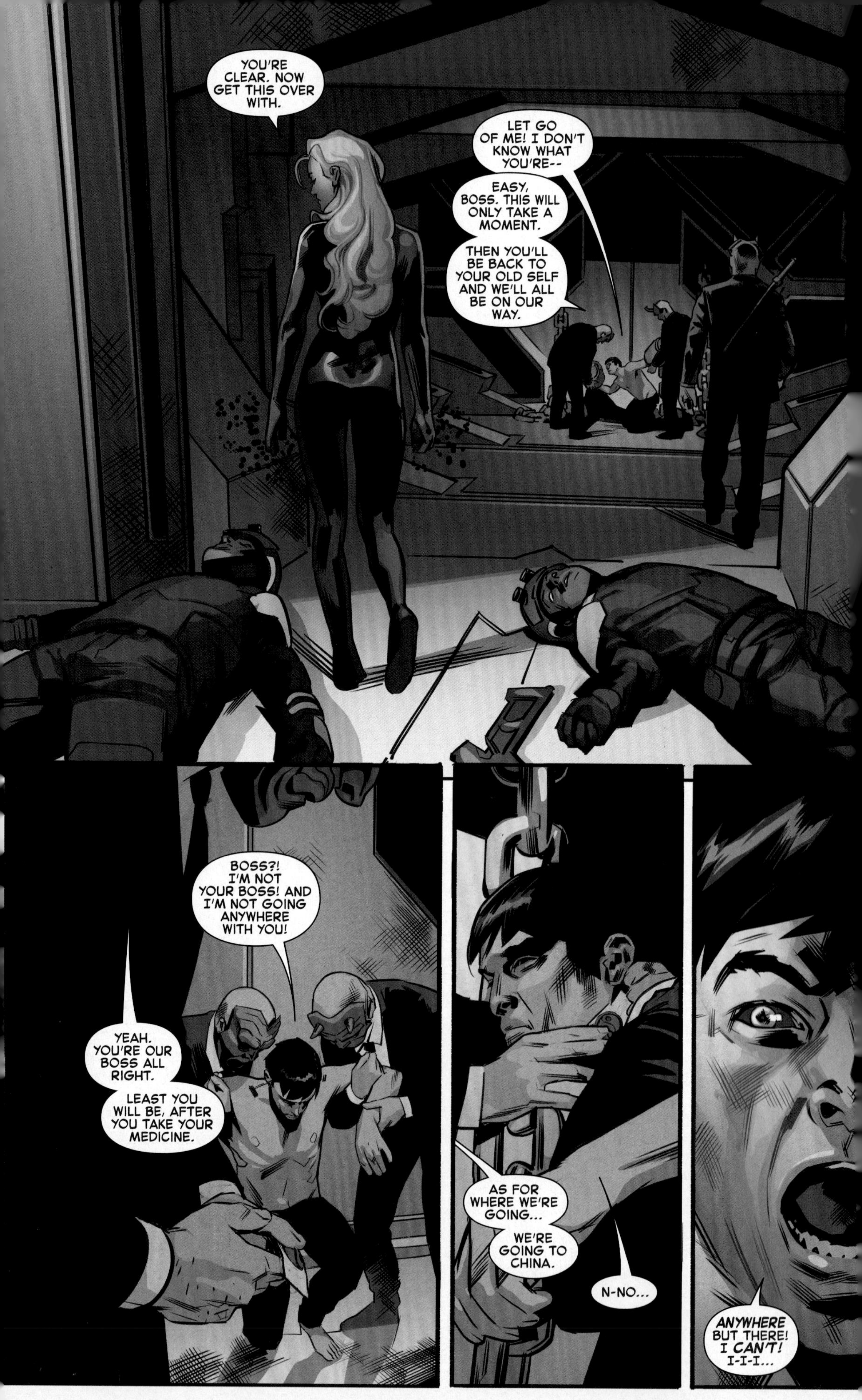
YOU'RE CLEAR. NOW GET THIS OVER WITH.
LET GO OF ME! I DON'T KNOW WHAT YOU'RE--
EASY, BOSS. THIS WILL ONLY TAKE A MOMENT.
THEN YOU'LL BE BACK TO YOUR OLD SELF AND WE'LL ALL BE ON OUR WAY.
BOSS?! I'M NOT YOUR BOSS! AND I'M NOT GOING ANYWHERE WITH YOU!
YEAH. YOU'RE OUR BOSS ALL RIGHT.
LEAST YOU WILL BE, AFTER YOU TAKE YOUR MEDICINE.
AS FOR WHERE WE'RE GOING...
WE'RE GOING TO CHINA.
N-NO...
ANYWHERE BUT THERE! I *CAN'T!* I-I-I...

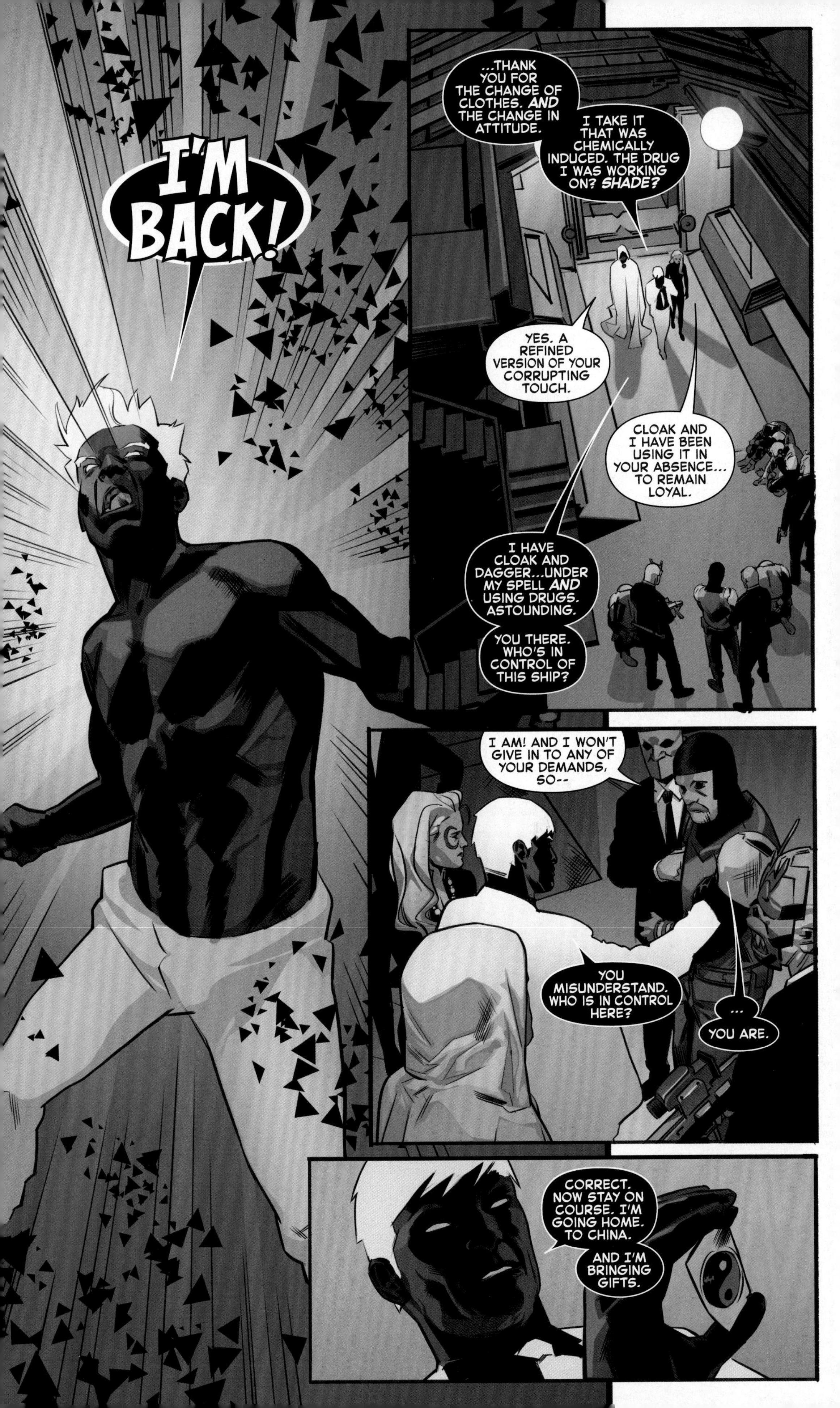
I'M BACK!
...THANK YOU FOR THE CHANGE OF CLOTHES. AND THE CHANGE IN ATTITUDE.
I TAKE IT THAT WAS CHEMICALLY INDUCED. THE DRUG I WAS WORKING ON? SHADE?
YES. A REFINED VERSION OF YOUR CORRUPTING TOUCH.
CLOAK AND I HAVE BEEN USING IT IN YOUR ABSENCE... TO REMAIN LOYAL.
I HAVE CLOAK AND DAGGER...UNDER MY SPELL AND USING DRUGS. ASTOUNDING.
YOU THERE. WHO'S IN CONTROL OF THIS SHIP?
I AM! AND I WON'T GIVE IN TO ANY OF YOUR DEMANDS, SO--
YOU MISUNDERSTAND. WHO IS IN CONTROL HERE?
...
YOU ARE.
CORRECT. NOW STAY ON COURSE. I'M GOING HOME. TO CHINA.
AND I'M BRINGING GIFTS.

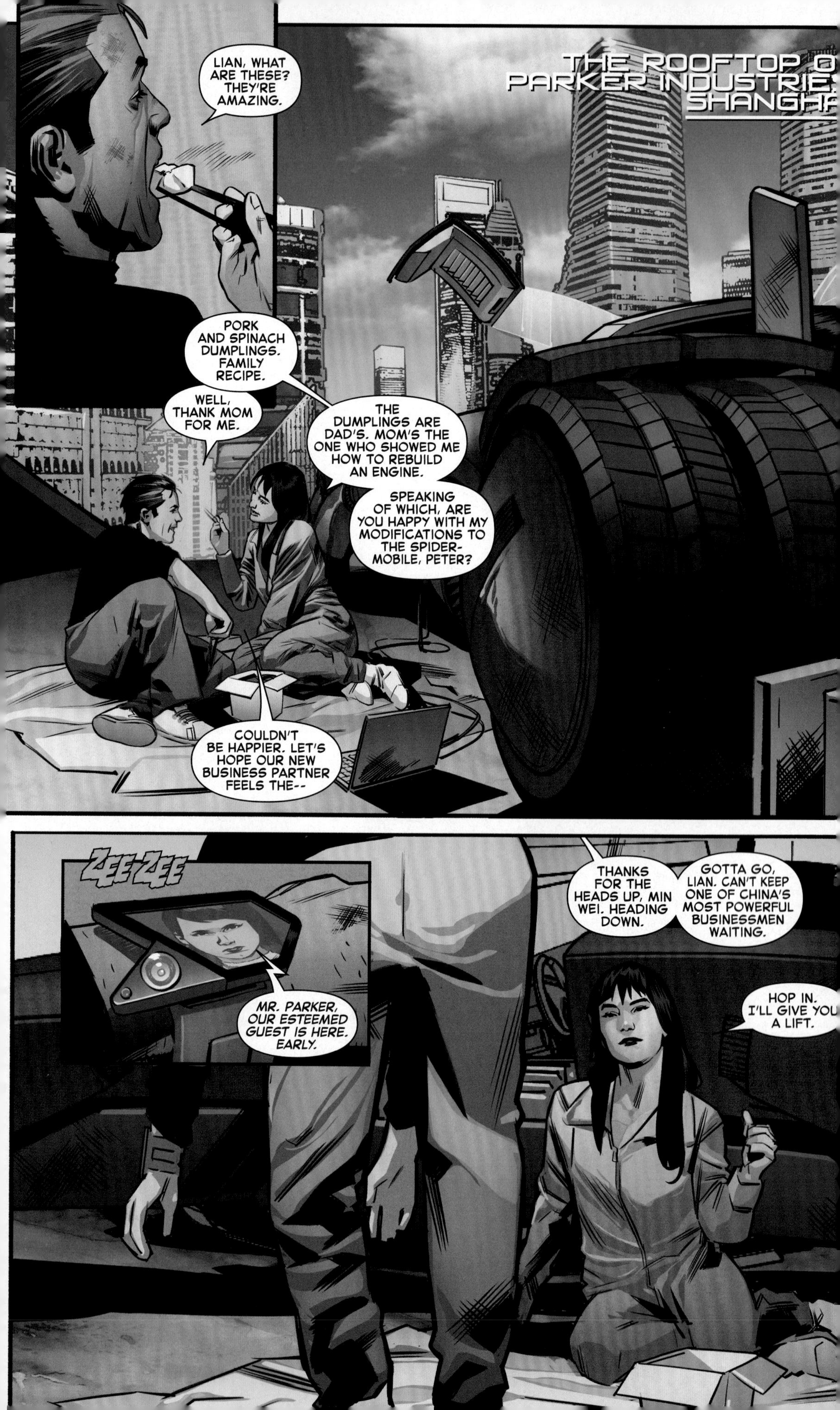
THE ROOFTOP O
PARKER INDUSTRIE
SHANGHA
LIAN, WHAT ARE THESE? THEY'RE AMAZING.
PORK AND SPINACH DUMPLINGS. FAMILY RECIPE.
WELL, THANK MOM FOR ME.
THE DUMPLINGS ARE DAD'S. MOM'S THE ONE WHO SHOWED ME HOW TO REBUILD AN ENGINE.
SPEAKING OF WHICH, ARE YOU HAPPY WITH MY MODIFICATIONS TO THE SPIDER-MOBILE, PETER?
COULDN'T BE HAPPIER. LET'S HOPE OUR NEW BUSINESS PARTNER FEELS THE--
ZEE ZEE
MR. PARKER, OUR ESTEEMED GUEST IS HERE. EARLY.
THANKS FOR THE HEADS UP, MIN WEI. HEADING DOWN.
GOTTA GO, LIAN. CAN'T KEEP ONE OF CHINA'S MOST POWERFUL BUSINESSMEN WAITING.
HOP IN. I'LL GIVE YOU A LIFT.

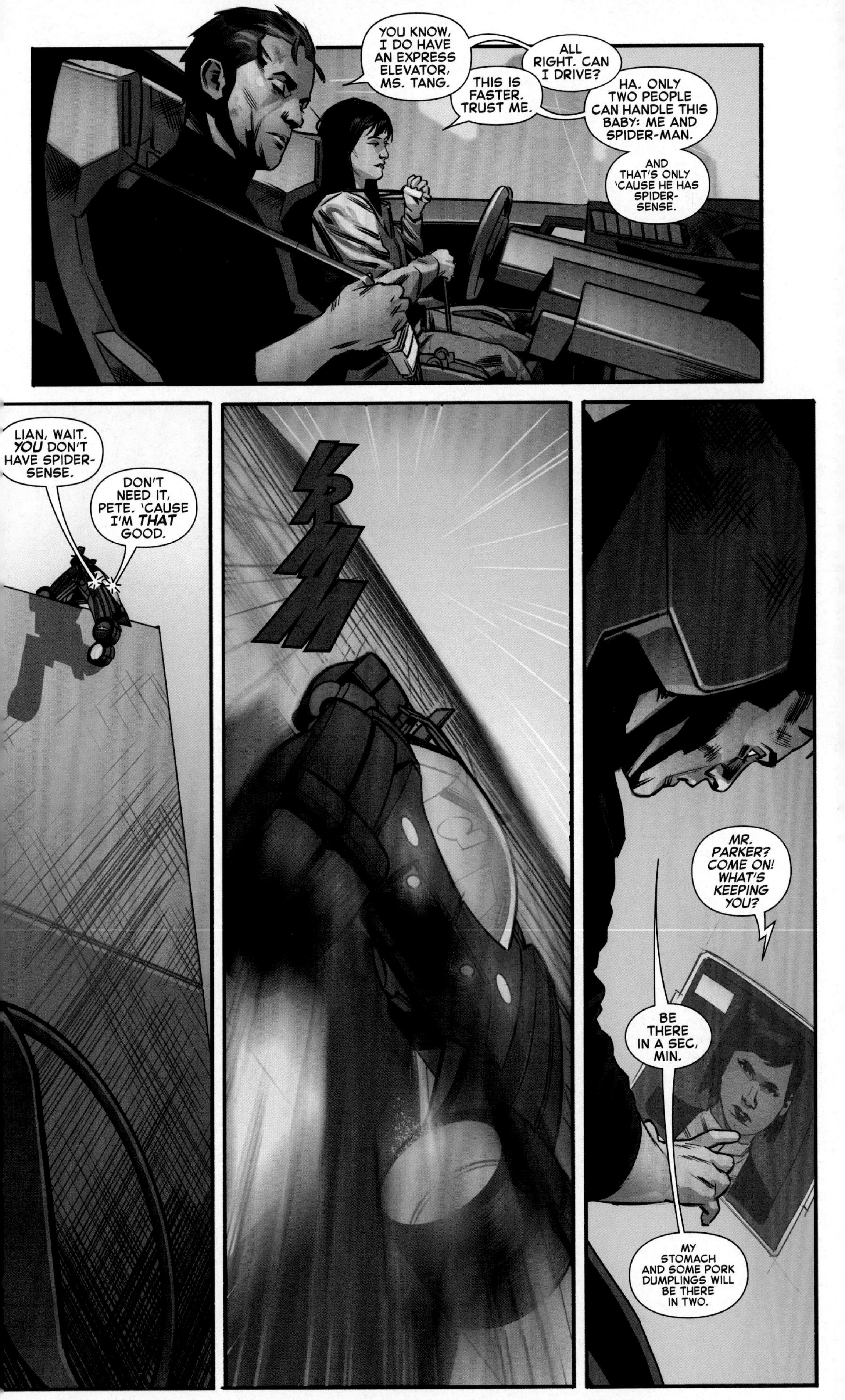

YOU KNOW, I DO HAVE AN EXPRESS ELEVATOR, MS. TANG.
ALL RIGHT. CAN I DRIVE?
THIS IS FASTER. TRUST ME.
HA. ONLY TWO PEOPLE CAN HANDLE THIS BABY: ME AND SPIDER-MAN.
AND THAT'S ONLY 'CAUSE HE HAS SPIDER-SENSE.
LIAN, WAIT. YOU DON'T HAVE SPIDER-SENSE.
DON'T NEED IT, PETE. 'CAUSE I'M THAT GOOD.
VRMMM
MR. PARKER? COME ON! WHAT'S KEEPING YOU?
BE THERE IN A SEC, MIN.
MY STOMACH AND SOME PORK DUMPLINGS WILL BE THERE IN TWO.

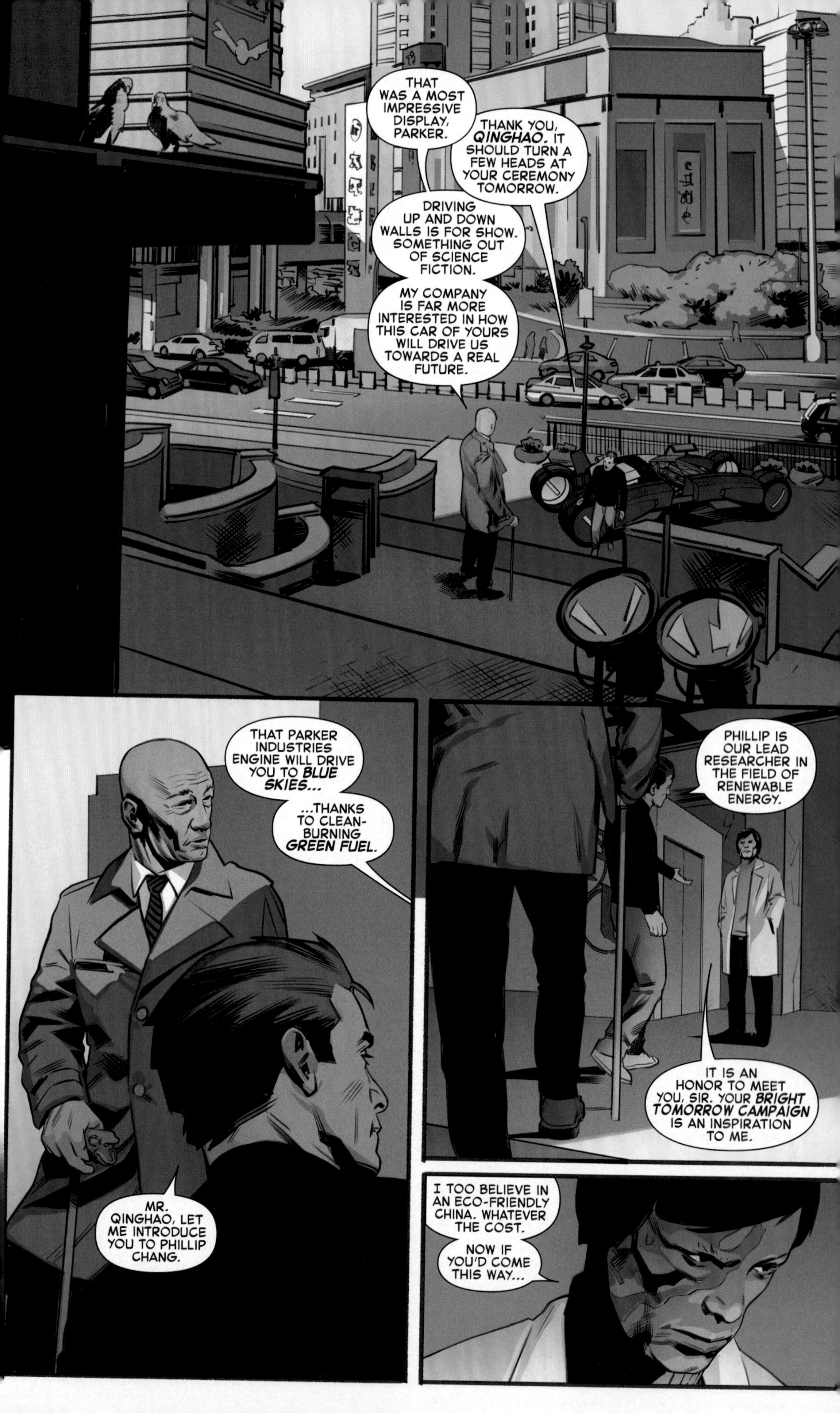
THAT WAS A MOST IMPRESSIVE DISPLAY, PARKER.
THANK YOU, QINGHAO. IT SHOULD TURN A FEW HEADS AT YOUR CEREMONY TOMORROW.
DRIVING UP AND DOWN WALLS IS FOR SHOW. SOMETHING OUT OF SCIENCE FICTION.
MY COMPANY IS FAR MORE INTERESTED IN HOW THIS CAR OF YOURS WILL DRIVE US TOWARDS A REAL FUTURE.
THAT PARKER INDUSTRIES ENGINE WILL DRIVE YOU TO BLUE SKIES...
...THANKS TO CLEAN-BURNING GREEN FUEL.
MR. QINGHAO, LET ME INTRODUCE YOU TO PHILLIP CHANG.
PHILLIP IS OUR LEAD RESEARCHER IN THE FIELD OF RENEWABLE ENERGY.
IT IS AN HONOR TO MEET YOU, SIR. YOUR BRIGHT TOMORROW CAMPAIGN IS AN INSPIRATION TO ME.
I TOO BELIEVE IN AN ECO-FRIENDLY CHINA. WHATEVER THE COST.
NOW IF YOU'D COME THIS WAY...

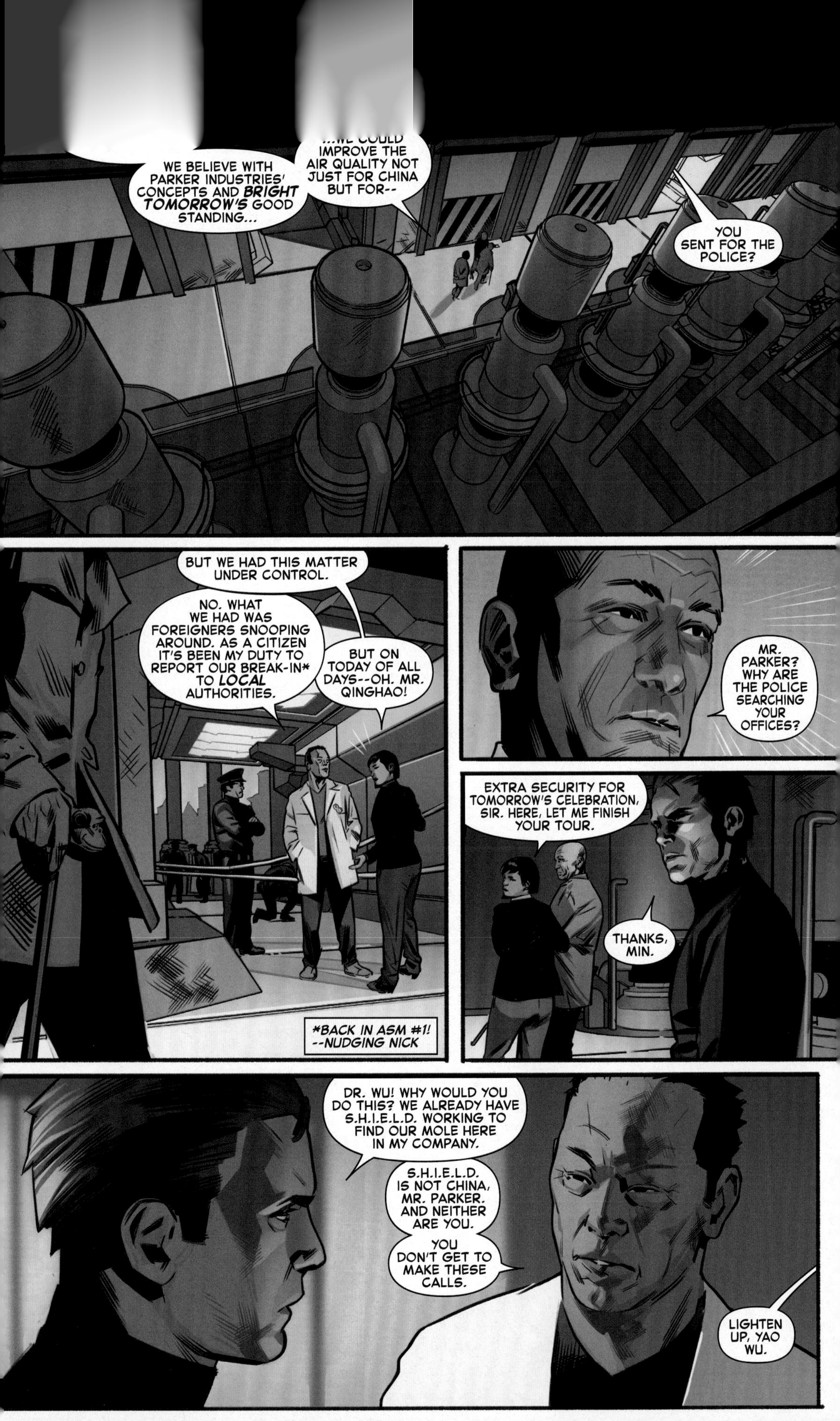
WE BELIEVE WITH PARKER INDUSTRIES' CONCEPTS AND **BRIGHT TOMORROW'S** GOOD STANDING...
IMPROVE THE AIR QUALITY NOT JUST FOR CHINA BUT FOR--
YOU SENT FOR THE POLICE?
BUT WE HAD THIS MATTER UNDER CONTROL.
NO. WHAT WE HAD WAS FOREIGNERS SNOOPING AROUND. AS A CITIZEN IT'S BEEN MY DUTY TO REPORT OUR BREAK-IN* TO **LOCAL** AUTHORITIES.
BUT ON TODAY OF ALL DAYS--OH. MR. QINGHAO!
*BACK IN ASM #1! --NUDGING NICK
MR. PARKER? WHY ARE THE POLICE SEARCHING YOUR OFFICES?
EXTRA SECURITY FOR TOMORROW'S CELEBRATION, SIR. HERE, LET ME FINISH YOUR TOUR.
THANKS, MIN.
DR. WU! WHY WOULD YOU DO THIS? WE ALREADY HAVE S.H.I.E.L.D. WORKING TO FIND OUR MOLE HERE IN MY COMPANY.
S.H.I.E.L.D. IS NOT CHINA, MR. PARKER. AND NEITHER ARE YOU.
YOU DON'T GET TO MAKE THESE CALLS.
LIGHTEN UP, YAO WU.

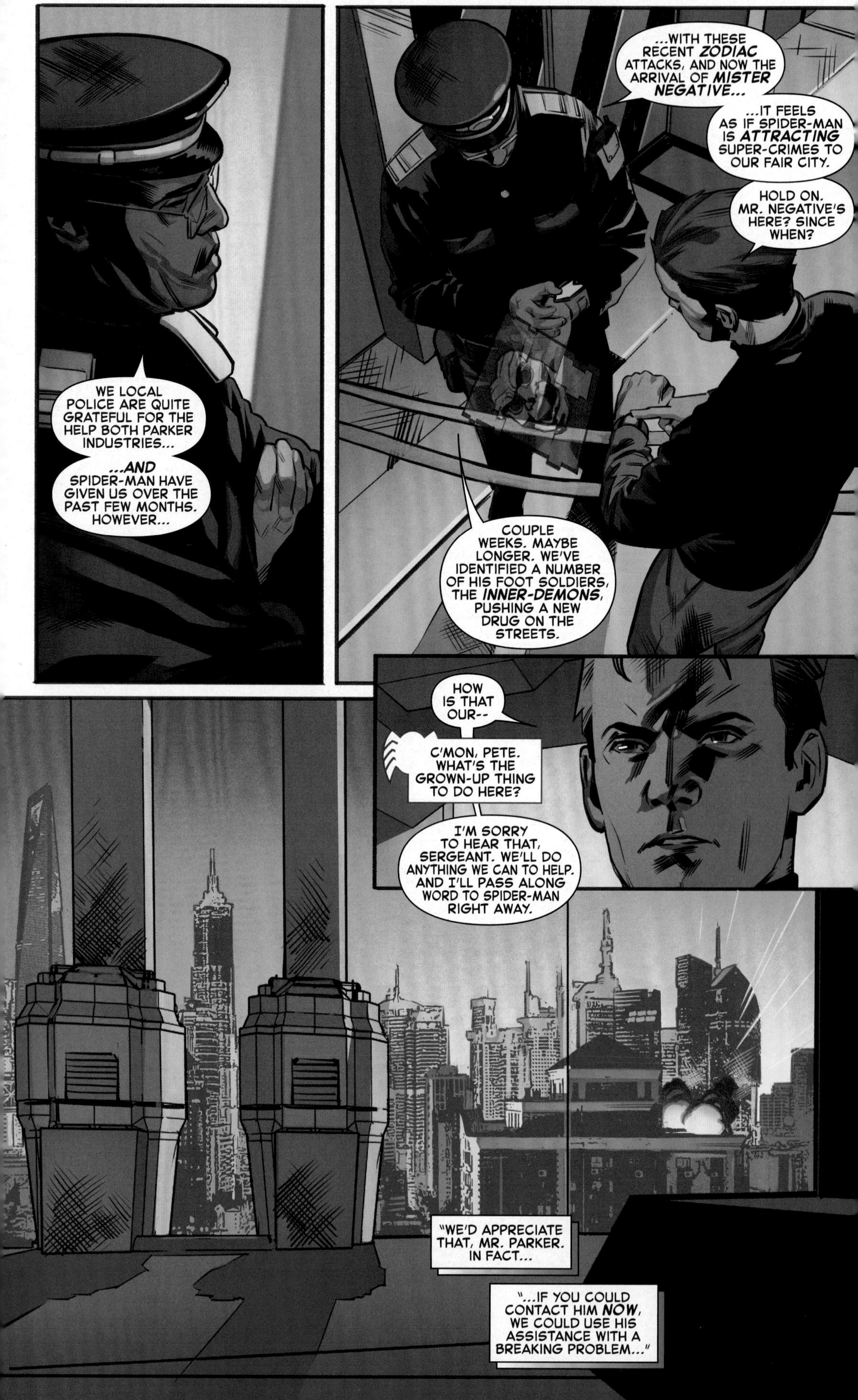
WE LOCAL POLICE ARE QUITE GRATEFUL FOR THE HELP BOTH PARKER INDUSTRIES...
...AND SPIDER-MAN HAVE GIVEN US OVER THE PAST FEW MONTHS. HOWEVER...
...WITH THESE RECENT ZODIAC ATTACKS, AND NOW THE ARRIVAL OF MISTER NEGATIVE...
...IT FEELS AS IF SPIDER-MAN IS ATTRACTING SUPER-CRIMES TO OUR FAIR CITY.
HOLD ON. MR. NEGATIVE'S HERE? SINCE WHEN?
COUPLE WEEKS. MAYBE LONGER. WE'VE IDENTIFIED A NUMBER OF HIS FOOT SOLDIERS, THE INNER-DEMONS, PUSHING A NEW DRUG ON THE STREETS.
HOW IS THAT OUR--
C'MON, PETE. WHAT'S THE GROWN-UP THING TO DO HERE?
I'M SORRY TO HEAR THAT, SERGEANT. WE'LL DO ANYTHING WE CAN TO HELP. AND I'LL PASS ALONG WORD TO SPIDER-MAN RIGHT AWAY.
"WE'D APPRECIATE THAT, MR. PARKER. IN FACT...
"...IF YOU COULD CONTACT HIM NOW, WE COULD USE HIS ASSISTANCE WITH A BREAKING PROBLEM..."

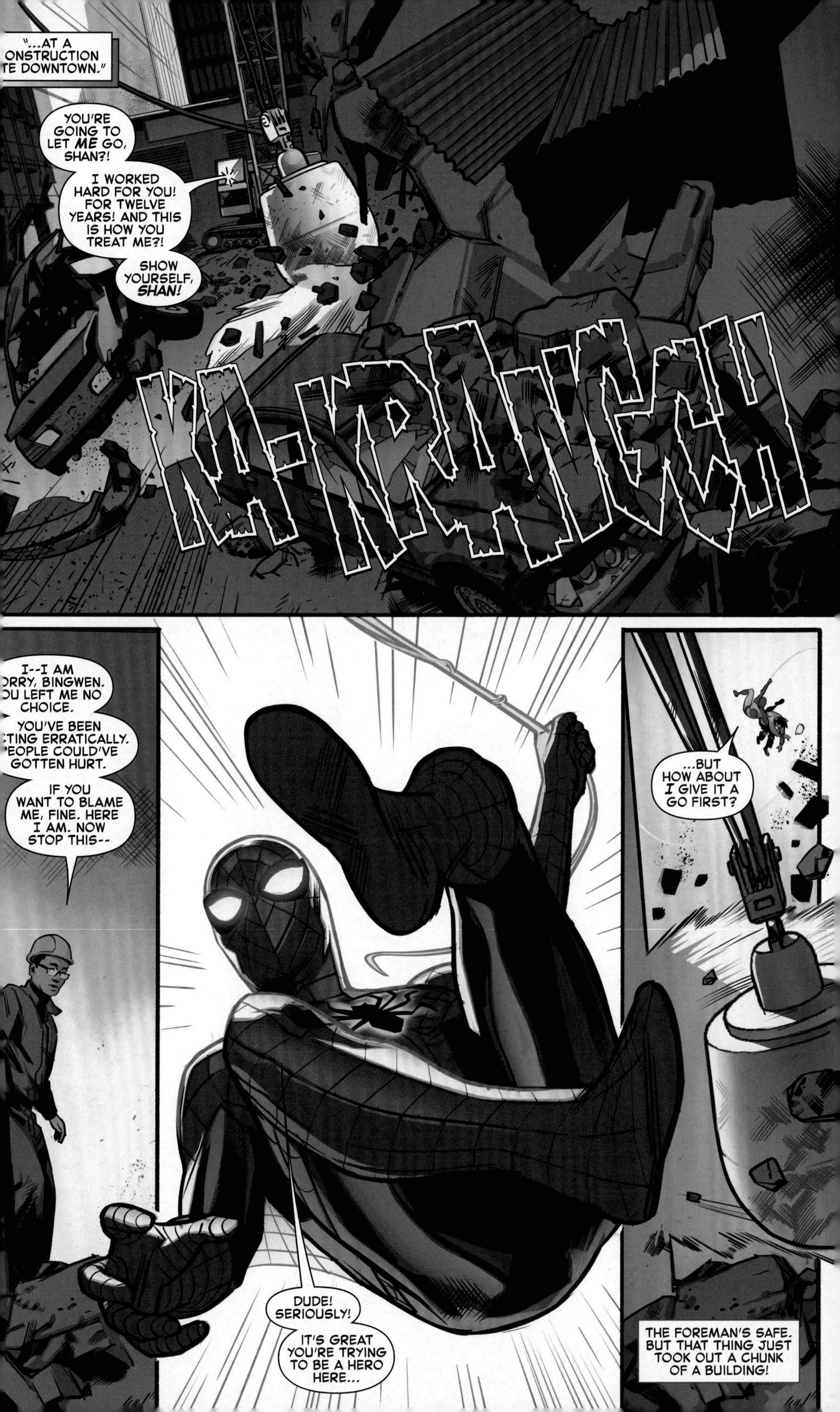
"...AT A
ONSTRUCTION
TE DOWNTOWN."
YOU'RE GOING TO LET ME GO, SHAN?!
I WORKED HARD FOR YOU! FOR TWELVE YEARS! AND THIS IS HOW YOU TREAT ME?!
SHOW YOURSELF, SHAN!
KA-KRUNCH
I--I AM ORRY, BINGWEN. OU LEFT ME NO CHOICE.
YOU'VE BEEN TING ERRATICALLY. EOPLE COULD'VE GOTTEN HURT.
IF YOU WANT TO BLAME ME, FINE. HERE I AM. NOW STOP THIS--
DUDE! SERIOUSLY!
IT'S GREAT YOU'RE TRYING TO BE A HERO HERE...
...BUT HOW ABOUT I GIVE IT A GO FIRST?
THE FOREMAN'S SAFE. BUT THAT THING JUST TOOK OUT A CHUNK OF A BUILDING!

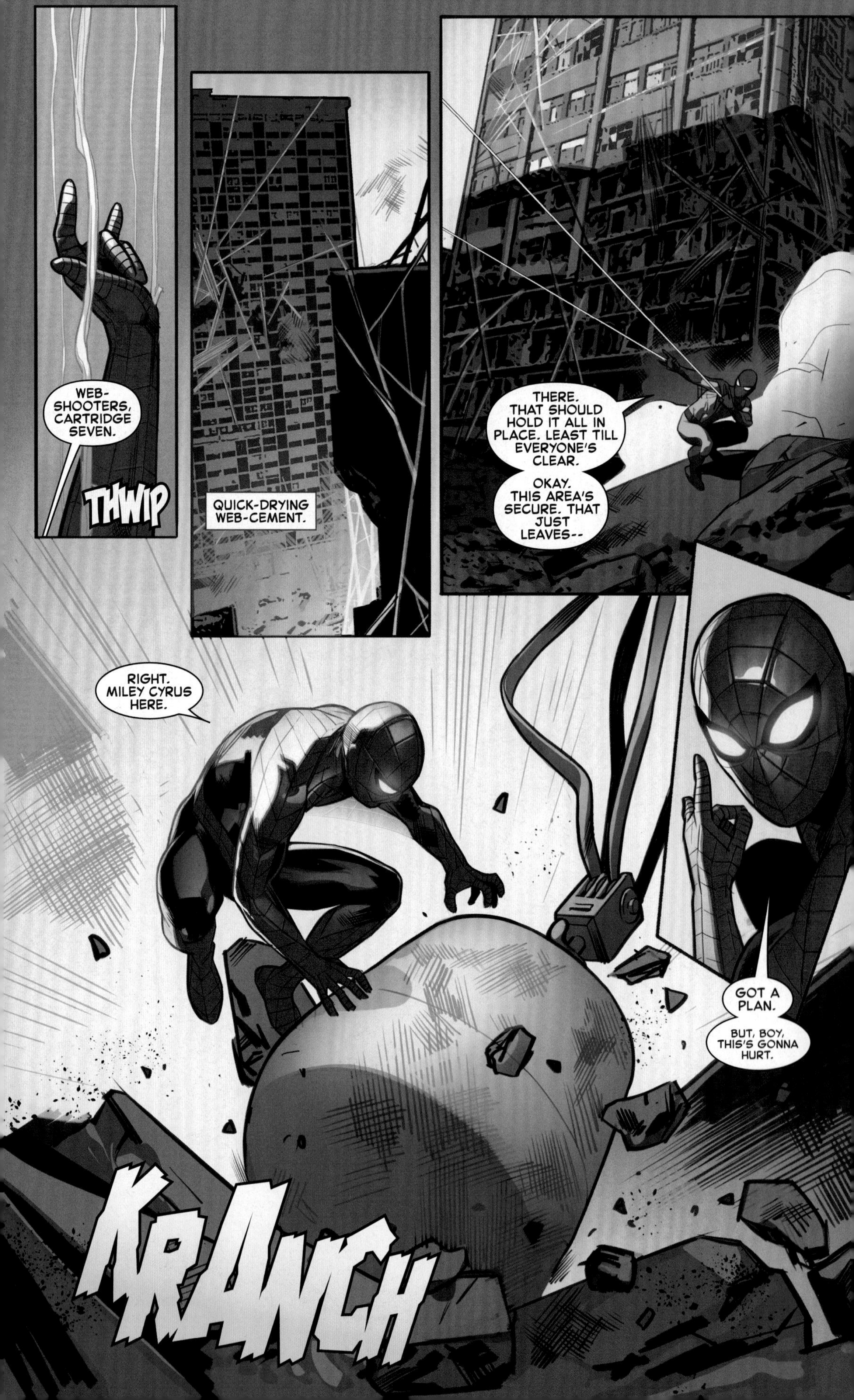
WEB-SHOOTERS, CARTRIDGE SEVEN.
THWIP
QUICK-DRYING WEB-CEMENT.
THERE. THAT SHOULD HOLD IT ALL IN PLACE. LEAST TILL EVERYONE'S CLEAR.
OKAY. THIS AREA'S SECURE. THAT JUST LEAVES--
RIGHT. MILEY CYRUS HERE.
GOT A PLAN.
BUT, BOY, THIS'S GONNA HURT.
KRANCH

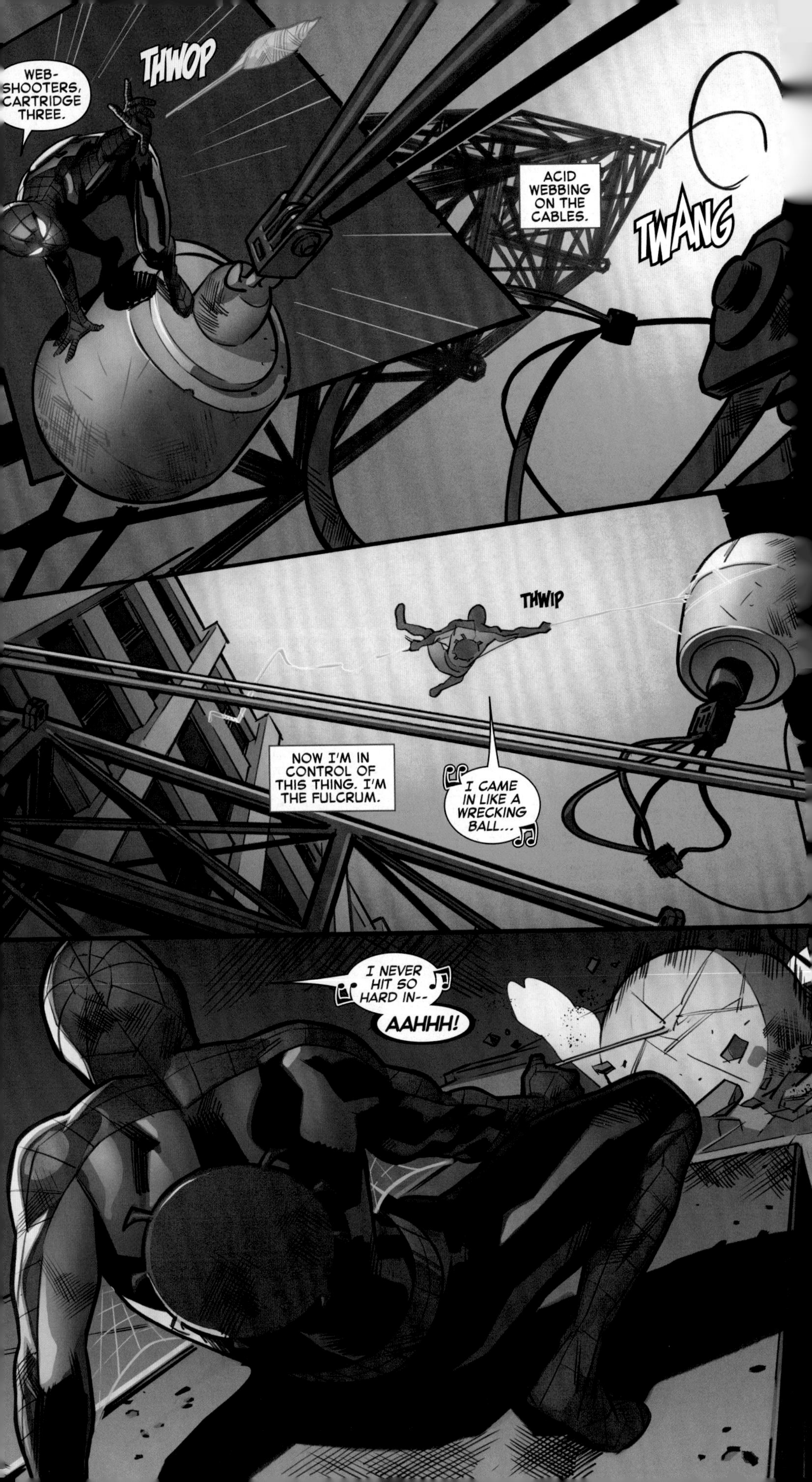
WEB-SHOOTERS, CARTRIDGE THREE.
THWOP
ACID WEBBING ON THE CABLES.
TWANG
THWIP
NOW I'M IN CONTROL OF THIS THING. I'M THE FULCRUM.
I CAME IN LIKE A WRECKING BALL...
I NEVER HIT SO HARD IN--
AAHHH!

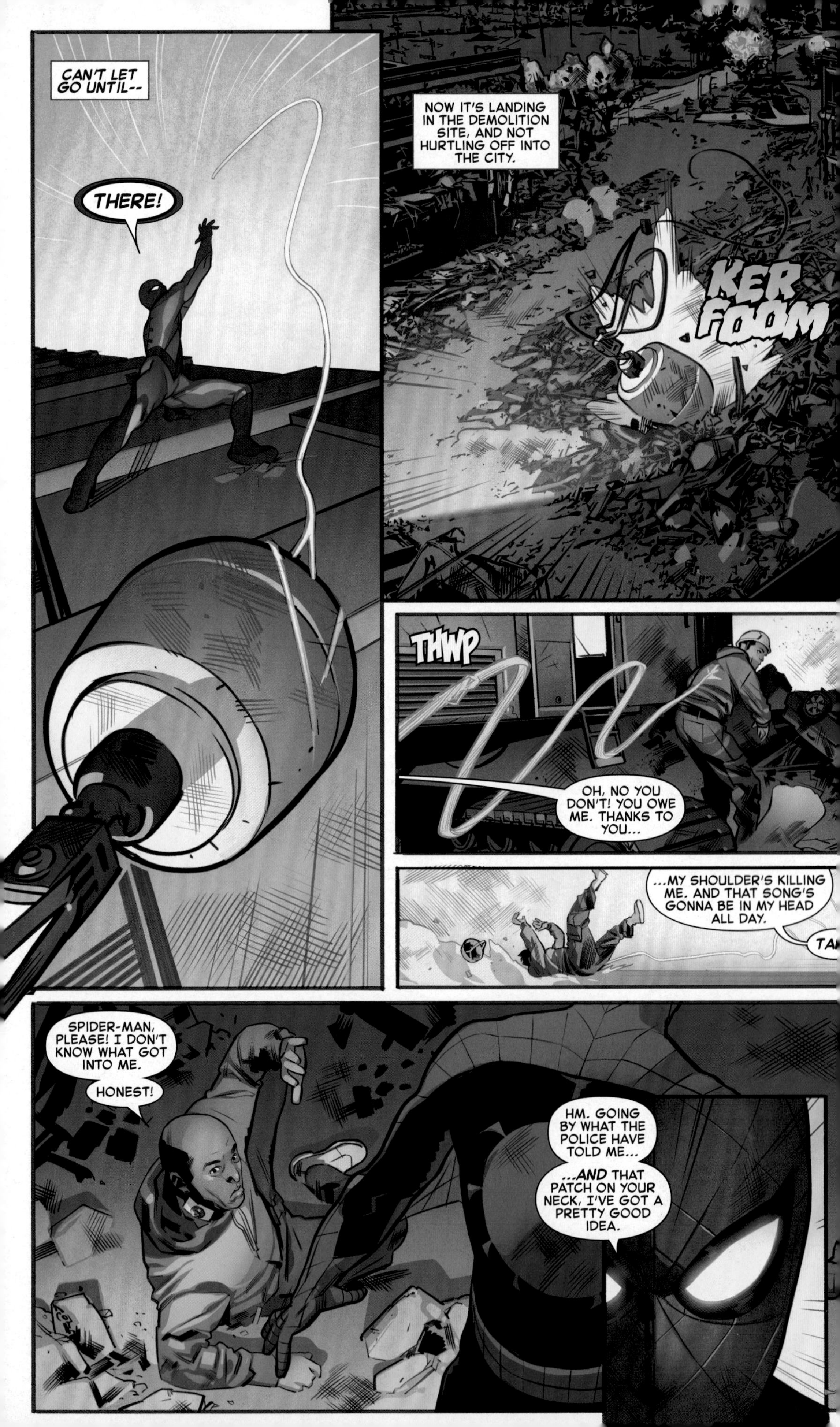

CAN'T LET GO UNTIL--
THERE!
NOW IT'S LANDING IN THE DEMOLITION SITE, AND NOT HURTLING OFF INTO THE CITY.
KER FOOM
THWP
OH, NO YOU DON'T! YOU OWE ME. THANKS TO YOU...
...MY SHOULDER'S KILLING ME. AND THAT SONG'S GONNA BE IN MY HEAD ALL DAY.
SPIDER-MAN, PLEASE! I DON'T KNOW WHAT GOT INTO ME.
HONEST!
HM. GOING BY WHAT THE POLICE HAVE TOLD ME...
...AND THAT PATCH ON YOUR NECK, I'VE GOT A PRETTY GOOD IDEA.

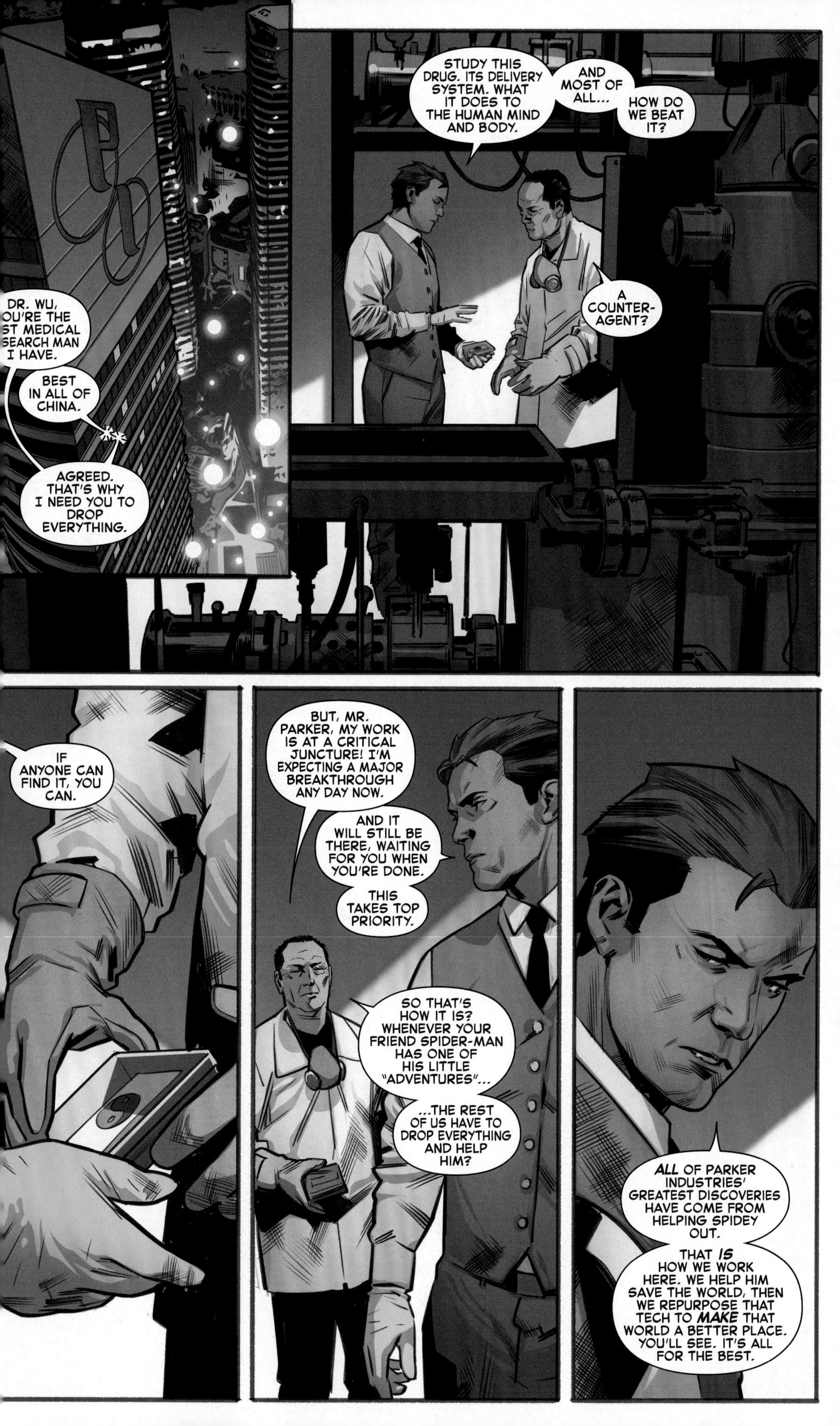

DR. WU, OU'RE THE ST MEDICAL SEARCH MAN I HAVE.
BEST IN ALL OF CHINA.
AGREED. THAT'S WHY I NEED YOU TO DROP EVERYTHING.
STUDY THIS DRUG. ITS DELIVERY SYSTEM. WHAT IT DOES TO THE HUMAN MIND AND BODY.
AND MOST OF ALL...
HOW DO WE BEAT IT?
A COUNTER-AGENT?
IF ANYONE CAN FIND IT, YOU CAN.
BUT, MR. PARKER, MY WORK IS AT A CRITICAL JUNCTURE! I'M EXPECTING A MAJOR BREAKTHROUGH ANY DAY NOW.
AND IT WILL STILL BE THERE, WAITING FOR YOU WHEN YOU'RE DONE.
THIS TAKES TOP PRIORITY.
SO THAT'S HOW IT IS? WHENEVER YOUR FRIEND SPIDER-MAN HAS ONE OF HIS LITTLE "ADVENTURES"...
...THE REST OF US HAVE TO DROP EVERYTHING AND HELP HIM?
ALL OF PARKER INDUSTRIES' GREATEST DISCOVERIES HAVE COME FROM HELPING SPIDEY OUT.
THAT *IS* HOW WE WORK HERE. WE HELP HIM SAVE THE WORLD, THEN WE REPURPOSE THAT TECH TO *MAKE* THAT WORLD A BETTER PLACE. YOU'LL SEE. IT'S ALL FOR THE BEST.

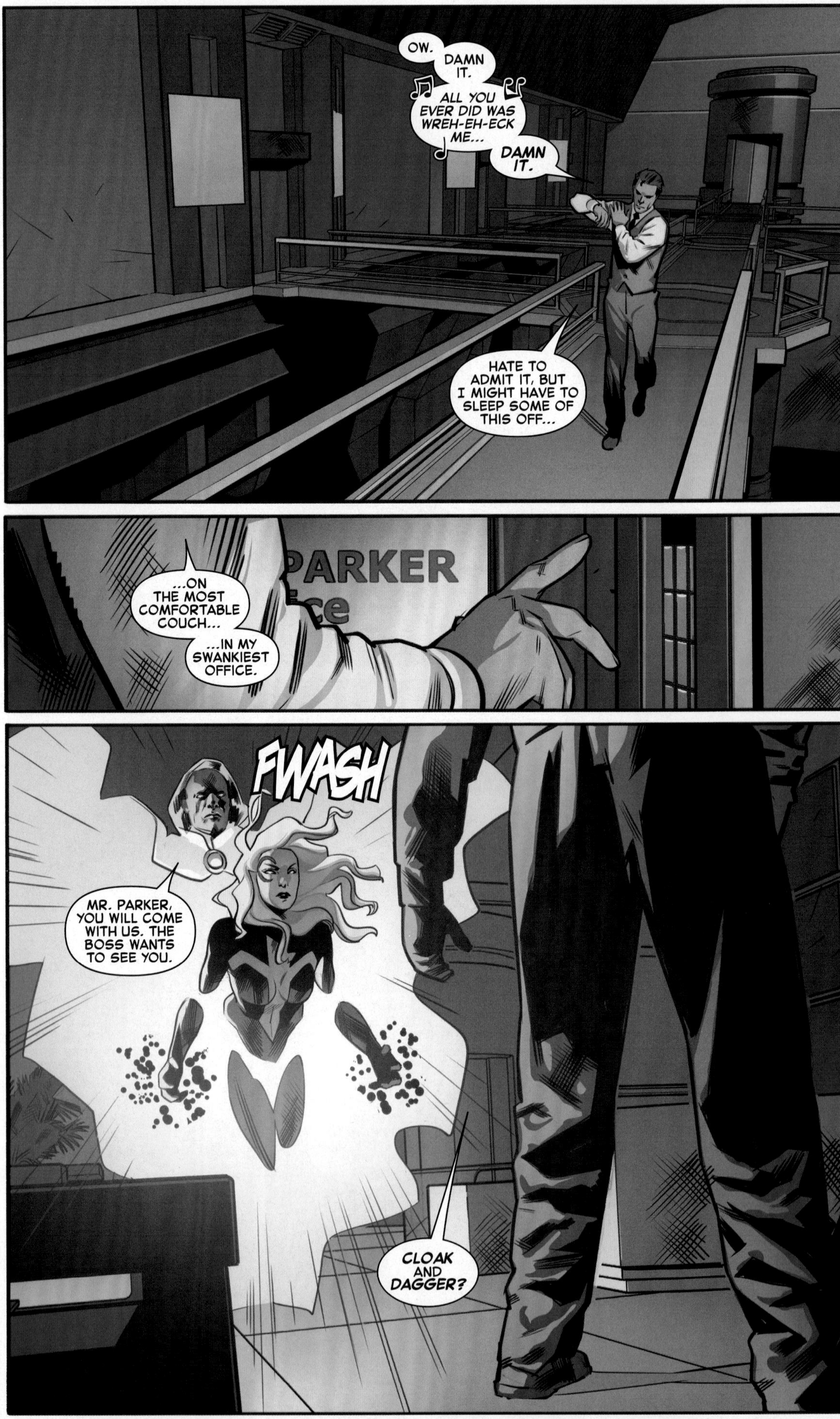
OW.
DAMN IT.
ALL YOU EVER DID WAS WREH-EH-ECK ME...
DAMN IT.
HATE TO ADMIT IT, BUT I MIGHT HAVE TO SLEEP SOME OF THIS OFF...
...ON THE MOST COMFORTABLE COUCH...
...IN MY SWANKIEST OFFICE.
PARKER
FWASH
MR. PARKER, YOU WILL COME WITH US. THE BOSS WANTS TO SEE YOU.
CLOAK AND DAGGER?

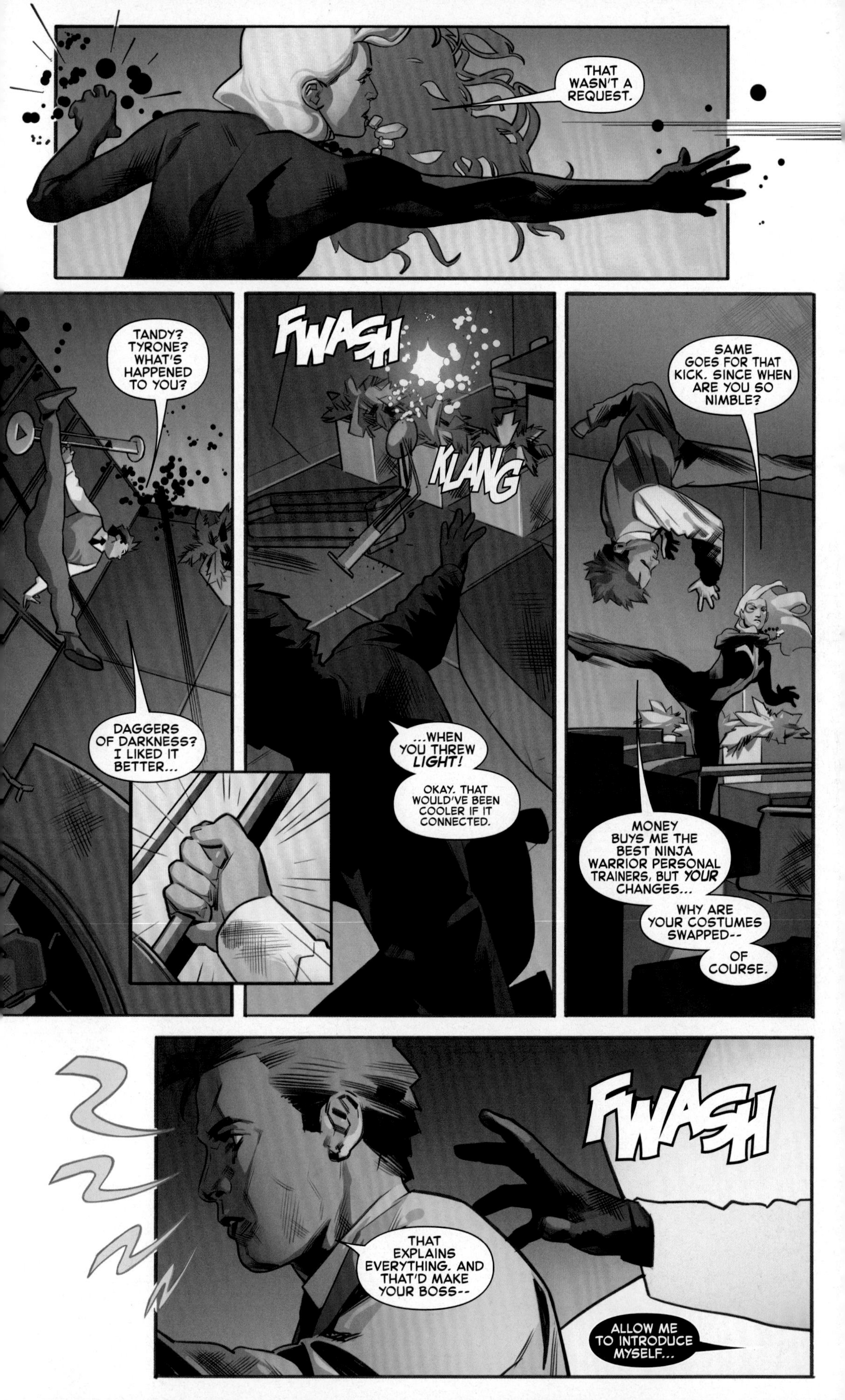
THAT WASN'T A REQUEST.
TANDY? TYRONE? WHAT'S HAPPENED TO YOU?
DAGGERS OF DARKNESS? I LIKED IT BETTER...
FWASH
KLANG
...WHEN YOU THREW LIGHT!
OKAY. THAT WOULD'VE BEEN COOLER IF IT CONNECTED.
SAME GOES FOR THAT KICK. SINCE WHEN ARE YOU SO NIMBLE?
MONEY BUYS ME THE BEST NINJA WARRIOR PERSONAL TRAINERS, BUT YOUR CHANGES...
WHY ARE YOUR COSTUMES SWAPPED--
OF COURSE.
FWASH
THAT EXPLAINS EVERYTHING. AND THAT'D MAKE YOUR BOSS--
ALLOW ME TO INTRODUCE MYSELF...

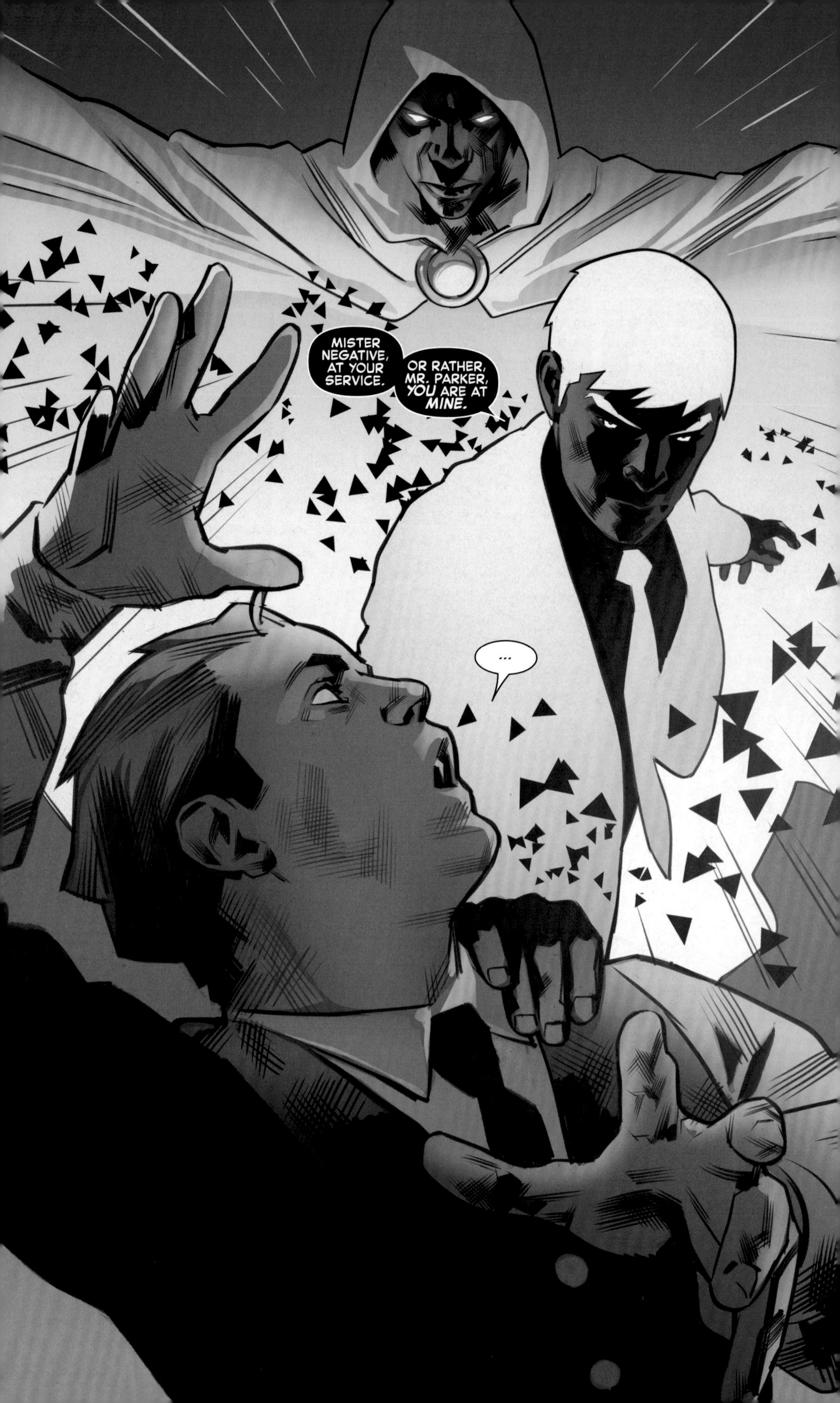
MISTER NEGATIVE, AT YOUR SERVICE.
OR RATHER, MR. PARKER, YOU ARE AT MINE.
...

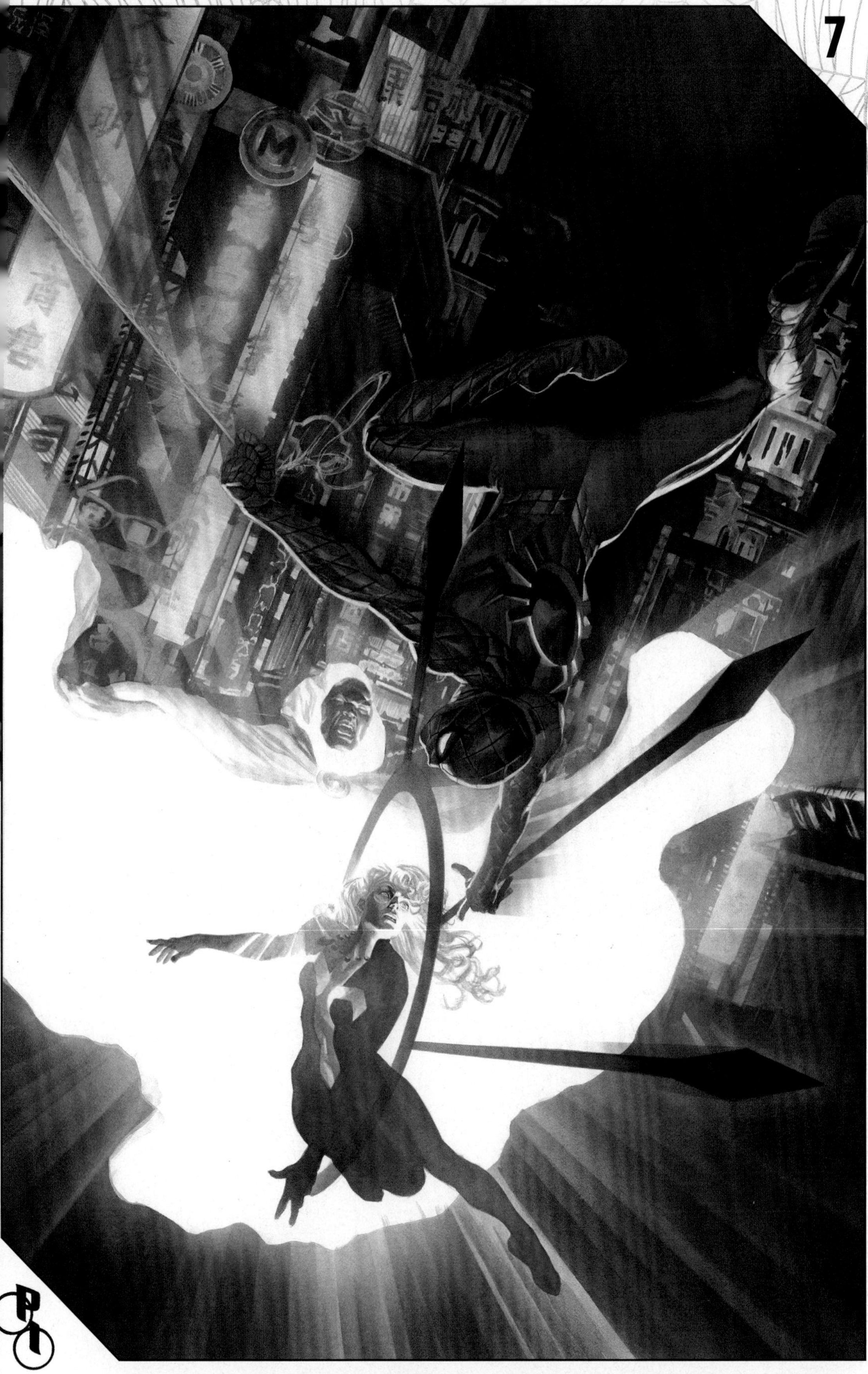

THE DARK KINGDOM - PART 2: "OPPOSING FORCES"

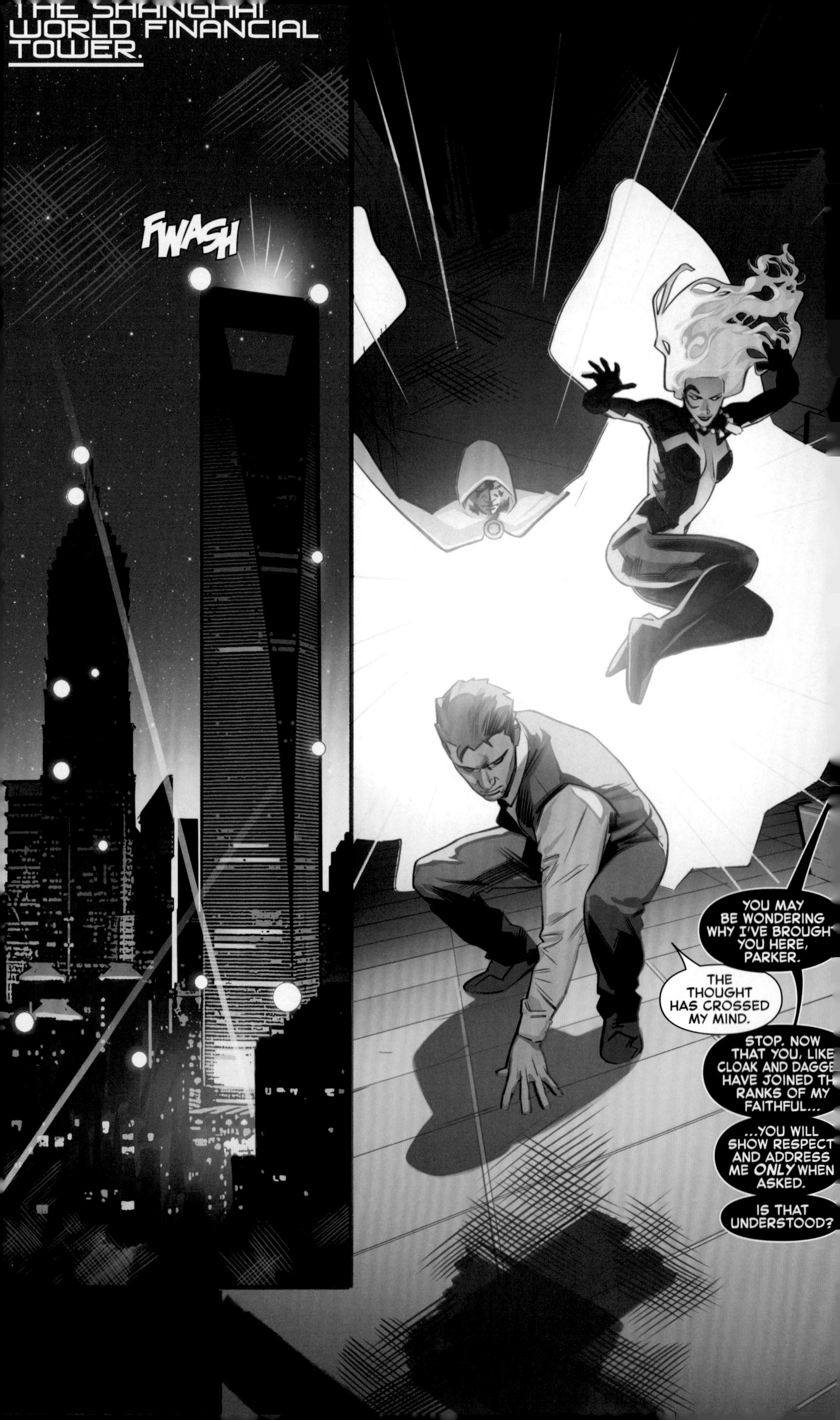
THE SHANGHAI WORLD FINANCIAL TOWER.
FWASH
YOU MAY BE WONDERING WHY I'VE BROUGHT YOU HERE, PARKER.
THE THOUGHT HAS CROSSED MY MIND.
STOP. NOW THAT YOU, LIKE CLOAK AND DAGGE HAVE JOINED TH RANKS OF MY FAITHFUL...
...YOU WILL SHOW RESPECT AND ADDRESS ME *ONLY* WHEN ASKED.
IS THAT UNDERSTOOD?

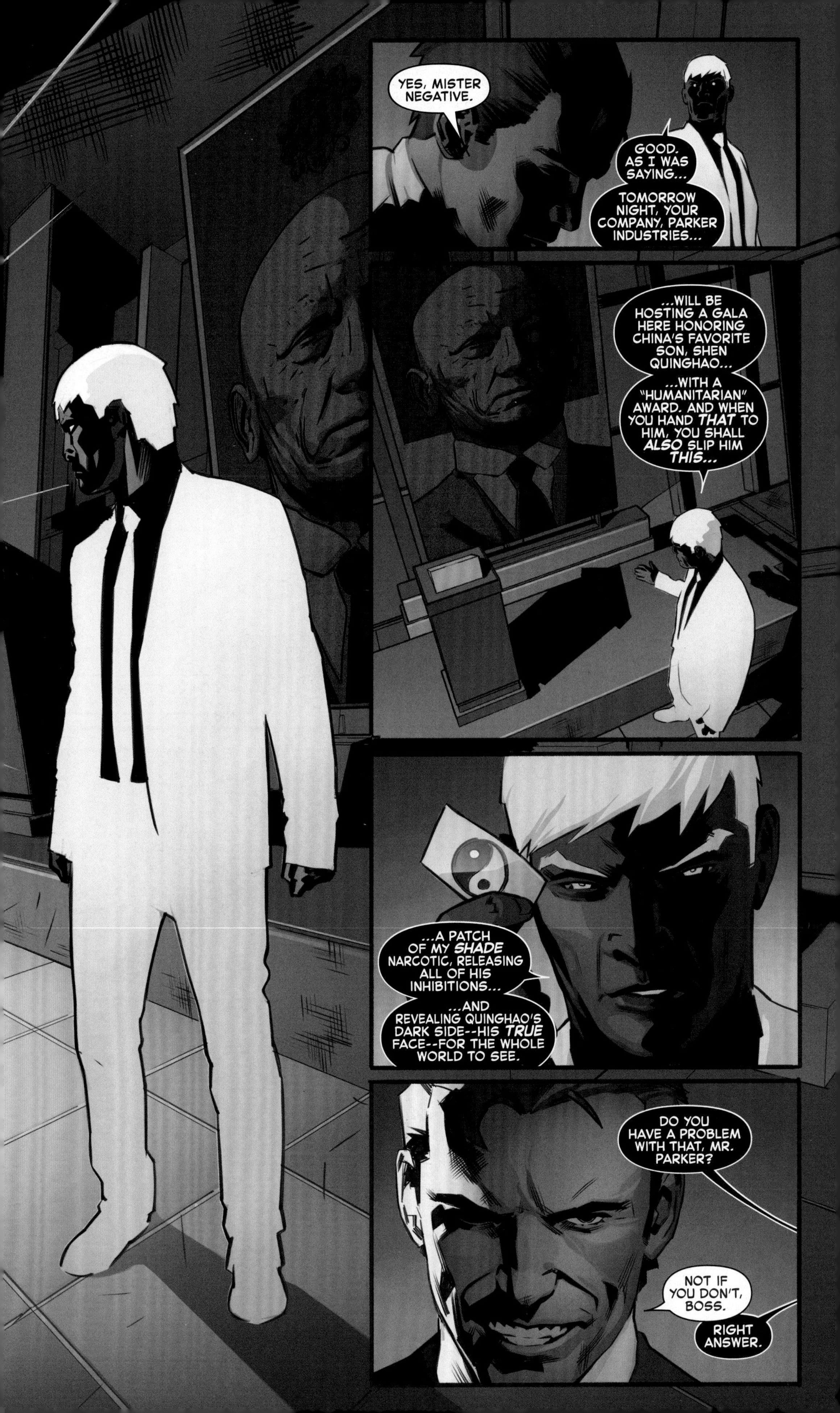
YES, MISTER NEGATIVE.
GOOD. AS I WAS SAYING...
TOMORROW NIGHT, YOUR COMPANY, PARKER INDUSTRIES...
...WILL BE HOSTING A GALA HERE HONORING CHINA'S FAVORITE SON, SHEN QUINGHAO...
...WITH A "HUMANITARIAN" AWARD. AND WHEN YOU HAND THAT TO HIM, YOU SHALL ALSO SLIP HIM THIS...
...A PATCH OF MY SHADE NARCOTIC, RELEASING ALL OF HIS INHIBITIONS...
...AND REVEALING QUINGHAO'S DARK SIDE--HIS TRUE FACE--FOR THE WHOLE WORLD TO SEE.
DO YOU HAVE A PROBLEM WITH THAT, MR. PARKER?
NOT IF YOU DON'T, BOSS.
RIGHT ANSWER.

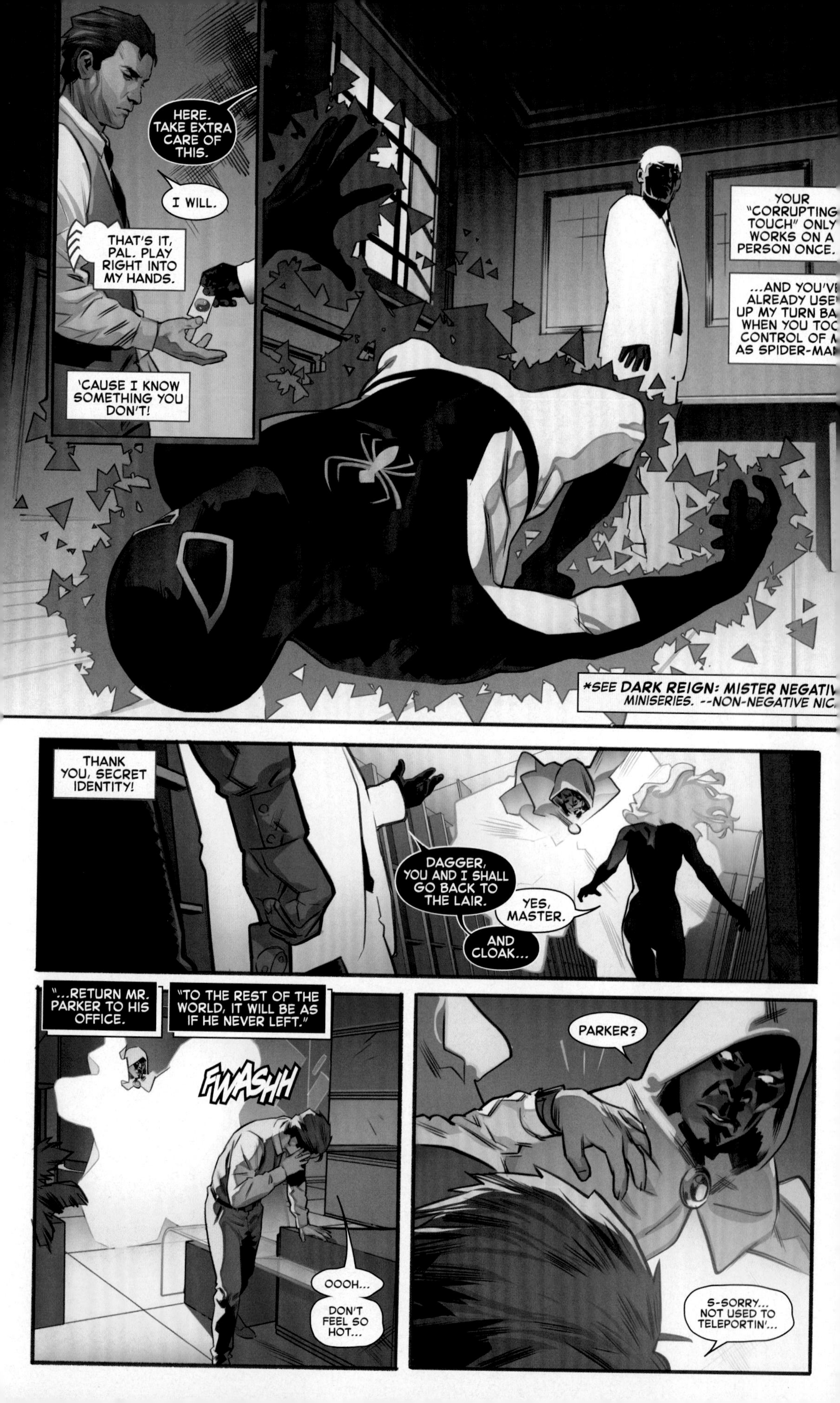
HERE. TAKE EXTRA CARE OF THIS.
I WILL.
THAT'S IT, PAL. PLAY RIGHT INTO MY HANDS.
'CAUSE I KNOW SOMETHING YOU DON'T!
YOUR "CORRUPTING TOUCH" ONLY WORKS ON A PERSON ONCE.
...AND YOU'VE ALREADY USED UP MY TURN BA WHEN YOU TOC CONTROL OF M AS SPIDER-MA
*SEE DARK REIGN: MISTER NEGATIV MINISERIES. --NON-NEGATIVE NIC
THANK YOU, SECRET IDENTITY!
DAGGER, YOU AND I SHALL GO BACK TO THE LAIR.
YES, MASTER.
AND CLOAK...
"...RETURN MR. PARKER TO HIS OFFICE.
"TO THE REST OF THE WORLD, IT WILL BE AS IF HE NEVER LEFT."
FWASHH
OOOH...
DON'T FEEL SO HOT...
PARKER?
S-SORRY... NOT USED TO TELEPORTIN'...

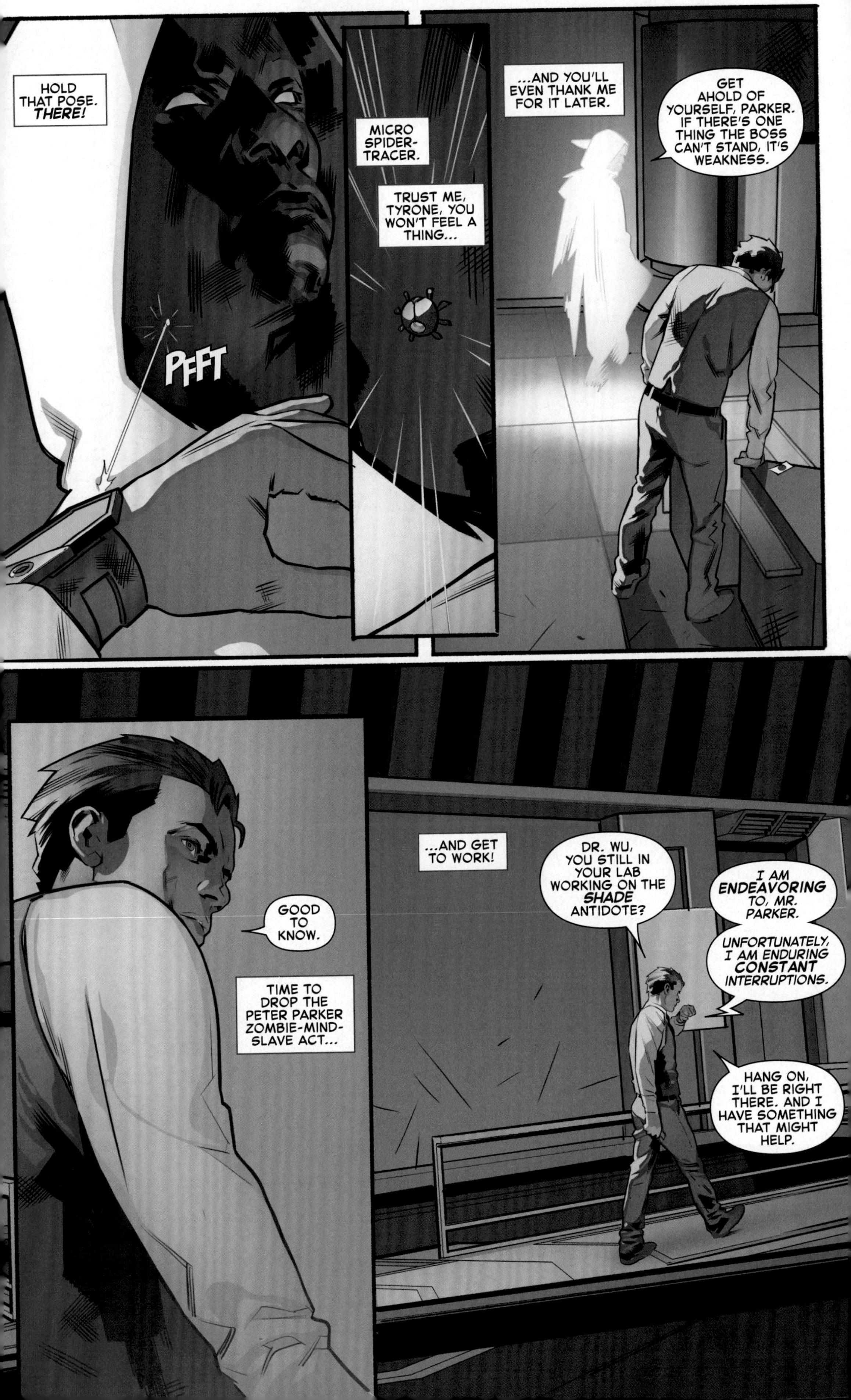

HOLD THAT POSE. *THERE!*
PFFT
MICRO SPIDER-TRACER.
TRUST ME, TYRONE, YOU WON'T FEEL A THING...
...AND YOU'LL EVEN THANK ME FOR IT LATER.
GET AHOLD OF YOURSELF, PARKER. IF THERE'S ONE THING THE BOSS CAN'T STAND, IT'S WEAKNESS.
GOOD TO KNOW.
TIME TO DROP THE PETER PARKER ZOMBIE-MIND-SLAVE ACT...
...AND GET TO WORK!
DR. WU, YOU STILL IN YOUR LAB WORKING ON THE *SHADE* ANTIDOTE?
I AM *ENDEAVORING* TO, MR. PARKER.
UNFORTUNATELY, I AM ENDURING *CONSTANT* INTERRUPTIONS.
HANG ON, I'LL BE RIGHT THERE. AND I HAVE SOMETHING THAT MIGHT HELP.

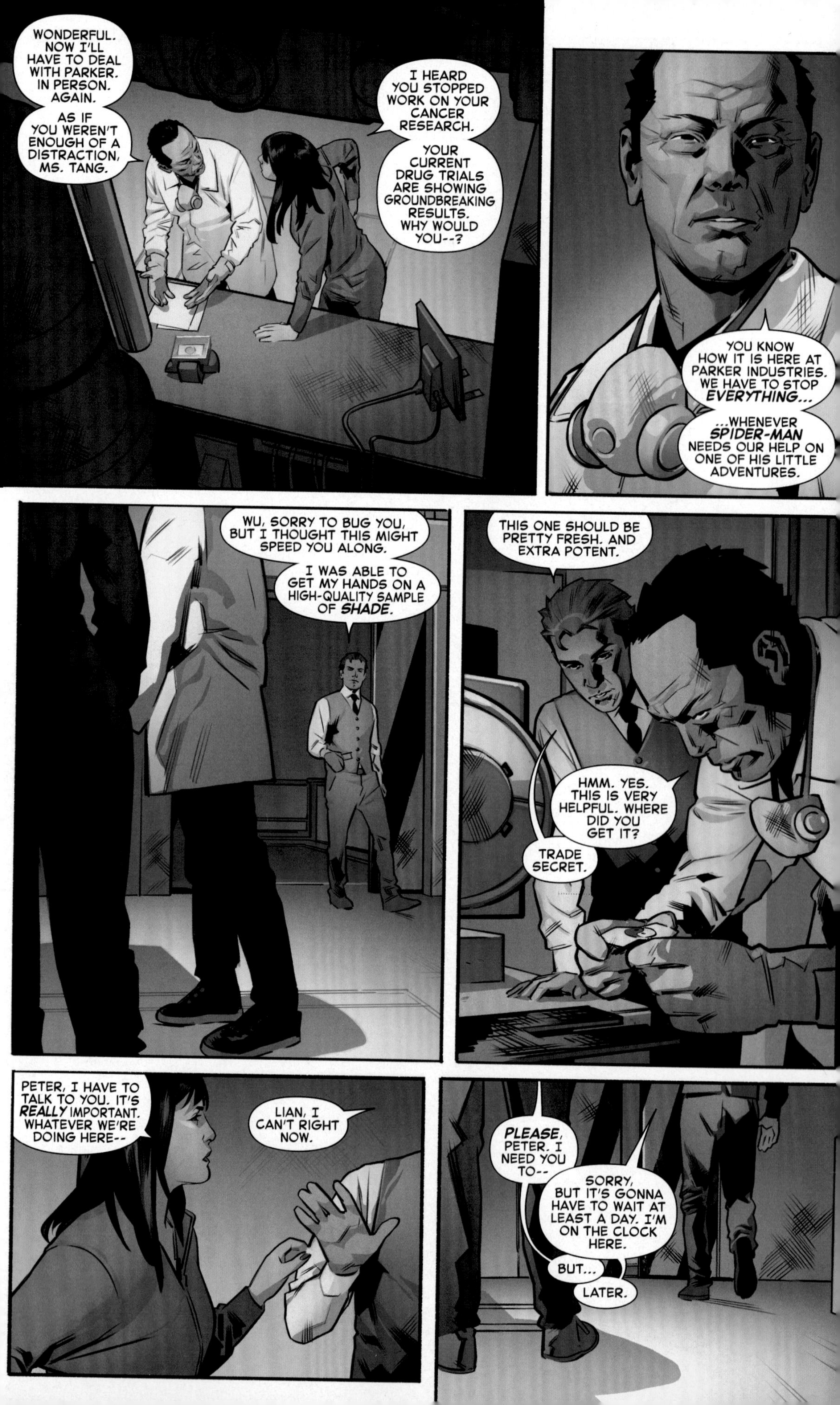
WONDERFUL. NOW I'LL HAVE TO DEAL WITH PARKER. IN PERSON. AGAIN.
AS IF YOU WEREN'T ENOUGH OF A DISTRACTION, MS. TANG.
I HEARD YOU STOPPED WORK ON YOUR CANCER RESEARCH.
YOUR CURRENT DRUG TRIALS ARE SHOWING GROUNDBREAKING RESULTS. WHY WOULD YOU--?
YOU KNOW HOW IT IS HERE AT PARKER INDUSTRIES. WE HAVE TO STOP EVERYTHING...
...WHENEVER SPIDER-MAN NEEDS OUR HELP ON ONE OF HIS LITTLE ADVENTURES.
WU, SORRY TO BUG YOU, BUT I THOUGHT THIS MIGHT SPEED YOU ALONG.
I WAS ABLE TO GET MY HANDS ON A HIGH-QUALITY SAMPLE OF SHADE.
THIS ONE SHOULD BE PRETTY FRESH. AND EXTRA POTENT.
HMM. YES. THIS IS VERY HELPFUL. WHERE DID YOU GET IT?
TRADE SECRET.
PETER, I HAVE TO TALK TO YOU. IT'S REALLY IMPORTANT. WHATEVER WE'RE DOING HERE--
LIAN, I CAN'T RIGHT NOW.
PLEASE, PETER. I NEED YOU TO--
SORRY, BUT IT'S GONNA HAVE TO WAIT AT LEAST A DAY. I'M ON THE CLOCK HERE.
BUT...
LATER.

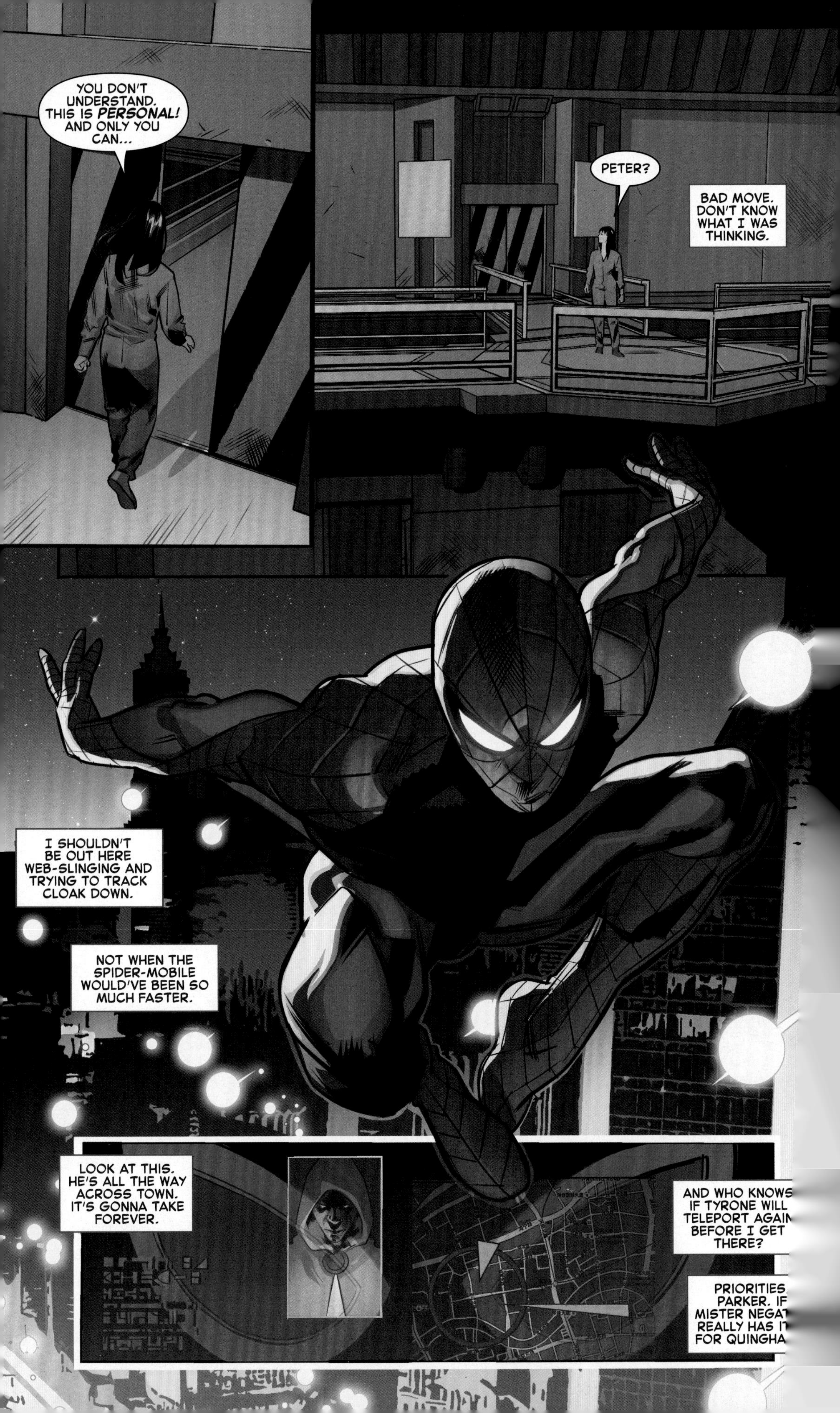
YOU DON'T UNDERSTAND. THIS IS PERSONAL! AND ONLY YOU CAN...
PETER?
BAD MOVE. DON'T KNOW WHAT I WAS THINKING.
I SHOULDN'T BE OUT HERE WEB-SLINGING AND TRYING TO TRACK CLOAK DOWN.
NOT WHEN THE SPIDER-MOBILE WOULD'VE BEEN SO MUCH FASTER.
LOOK AT THIS. HE'S ALL THE WAY ACROSS TOWN. IT'S GONNA TAKE FOREVER.
AND WHO KNOWS IF TYRONE WILL TELEPORT AGAIN BEFORE I GET THERE?
PRIORITIES, PARKER. IF MISTER NEGAT REALLY HAS IT FOR QUINGHA

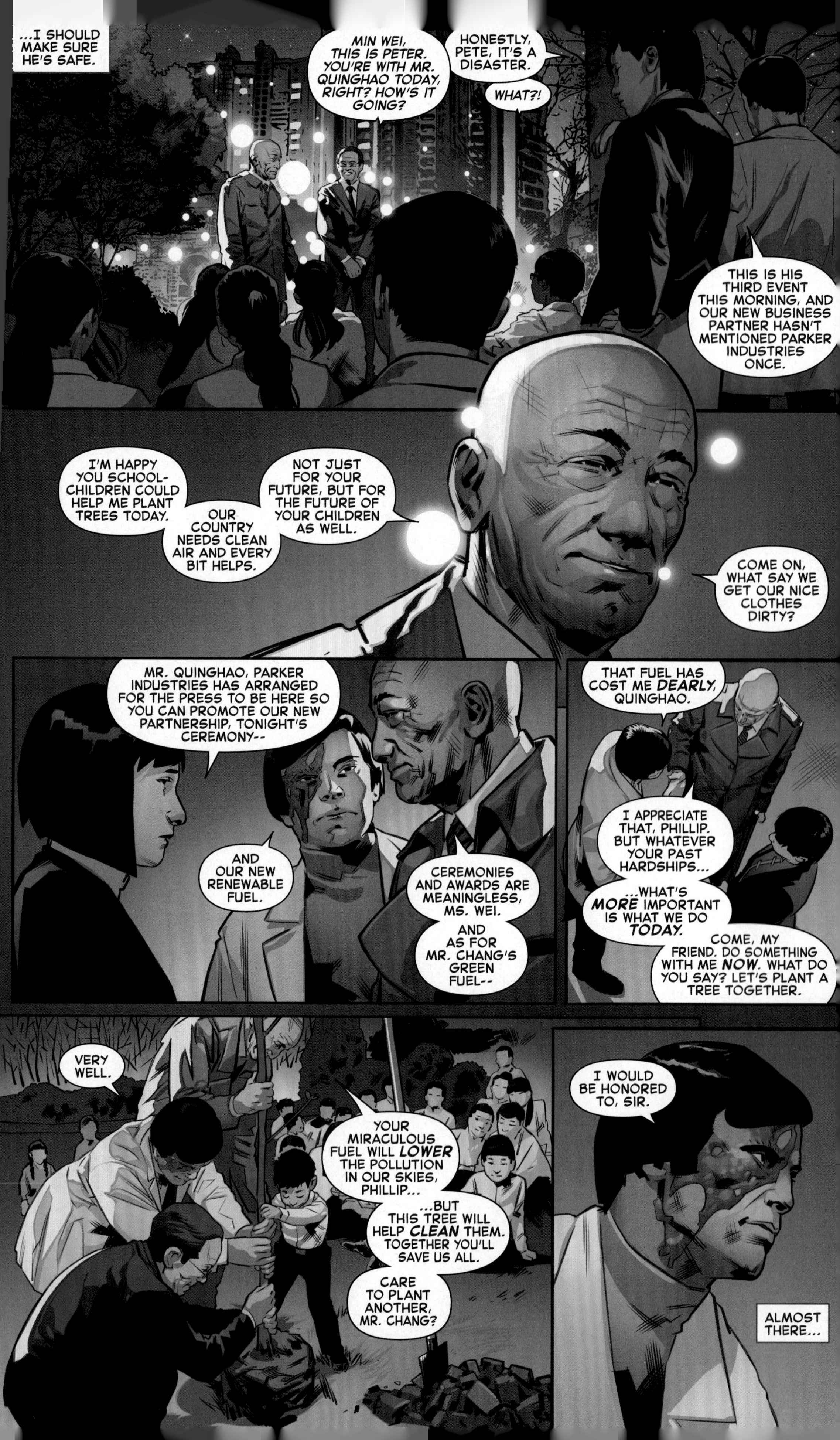
...I SHOULD MAKE SURE HE'S SAFE.
MIN WEI, THIS IS PETER. YOU'RE WITH MR. QUINGHAO TODAY, RIGHT? HOW'S IT GOING?
HONESTLY, PETE, IT'S A DISASTER.
WHAT?!
THIS IS HIS THIRD EVENT THIS MORNING, AND OUR NEW BUSINESS PARTNER HASN'T MENTIONED PARKER INDUSTRIES ONCE.
I'M HAPPY YOU SCHOOL-CHILDREN COULD HELP ME PLANT TREES TODAY.
OUR COUNTRY NEEDS CLEAN AIR AND EVERY BIT HELPS.
NOT JUST FOR YOUR FUTURE, BUT FOR THE FUTURE OF YOUR CHILDREN AS WELL.
COME ON, WHAT SAY WE GET OUR NICE CLOTHES DIRTY?
MR. QUINGHAO, PARKER INDUSTRIES HAS ARRANGED FOR THE PRESS TO BE HERE SO YOU CAN PROMOTE OUR NEW PARTNERSHIP, TONIGHT'S CEREMONY--
AND OUR NEW RENEWABLE FUEL.
CEREMONIES AND AWARDS ARE MEANINGLESS, MS. WEI.
AND AS FOR MR. CHANG'S GREEN FUEL--
THAT FUEL HAS COST ME DEARLY, QUINGHAO.
I APPRECIATE THAT, PHILLIP. BUT WHATEVER YOUR PAST HARDSHIPS...
...WHAT'S MORE IMPORTANT IS WHAT WE DO TODAY.
COME, MY FRIEND. DO SOMETHING WITH ME NOW. WHAT DO YOU SAY? LET'S PLANT A TREE TOGETHER.
VERY WELL.
YOUR MIRACULOUS FUEL WILL LOWER THE POLLUTION IN OUR SKIES, PHILLIP...
...BUT THIS TREE WILL HELP CLEAN THEM. TOGETHER YOU'LL SAVE US ALL.
CARE TO PLANT ANOTHER, MR. CHANG?
I WOULD BE HONORED TO, SIR.
ALMOST THERE...

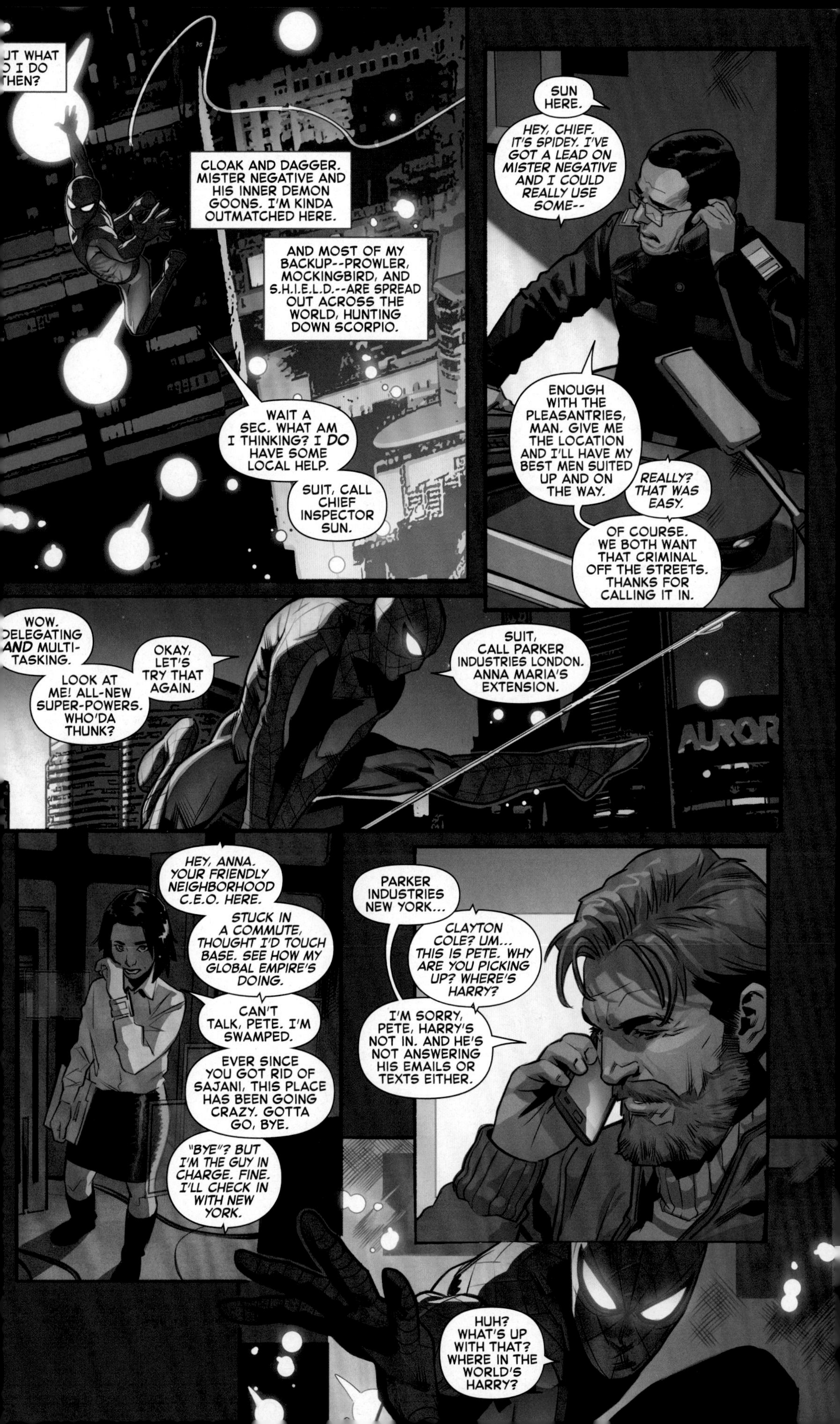
UT WHAT
D I DO
THEN?
CLOAK AND DAGGER. MISTER NEGATIVE AND HIS INNER DEMON GOONS. I'M KINDA OUTMATCHED HERE.
AND MOST OF MY BACKUP--PROWLER, MOCKINGBIRD, AND S.H.I.E.L.D.--ARE SPREAD OUT ACROSS THE WORLD, HUNTING DOWN SCORPIO.
WAIT A SEC. WHAT AM I THINKING? I DO HAVE SOME LOCAL HELP.
SUIT, CALL CHIEF INSPECTOR SUN.
SUN HERE.
HEY, CHIEF. IT'S SPIDEY. I'VE GOT A LEAD ON MISTER NEGATIVE AND I COULD REALLY USE SOME--
ENOUGH WITH THE PLEASANTRIES, MAN. GIVE ME THE LOCATION AND I'LL HAVE MY BEST MEN SUITED UP AND ON THE WAY.
REALLY? THAT WAS EASY.
OF COURSE. WE BOTH WANT THAT CRIMINAL OFF THE STREETS. THANKS FOR CALLING IT IN.
WOW. DELEGATING AND MULTI-TASKING.
LOOK AT ME! ALL-NEW SUPER-POWERS. WHO'DA THUNK?
OKAY, LET'S TRY THAT AGAIN.
SUIT, CALL PARKER INDUSTRIES LONDON. ANNA MARIA'S EXTENSION.
AUROR
HEY, ANNA. YOUR FRIENDLY NEIGHBORHOOD C.E.O. HERE.
STUCK IN A COMMUTE, THOUGHT I'D TOUCH BASE. SEE HOW MY GLOBAL EMPIRE'S DOING.
CAN'T TALK, PETE. I'M SWAMPED.
EVER SINCE YOU GOT RID OF SAJANI, THIS PLACE HAS BEEN GOING CRAZY. GOTTA GO, BYE.
"BYE"? BUT I'M THE GUY IN CHARGE. FINE. I'LL CHECK IN WITH NEW YORK.
PARKER INDUSTRIES NEW YORK...
CLAYTON COLE? UM... THIS IS PETE. WHY ARE YOU PICKING UP? WHERE'S HARRY?
I'M SORRY, PETE, HARRY'S NOT IN. AND HE'S NOT ANSWERING HIS EMAILS OR TEXTS EITHER.
HUH? WHAT'S UP WITH THAT? WHERE IN THE WORLD'S HARRY?

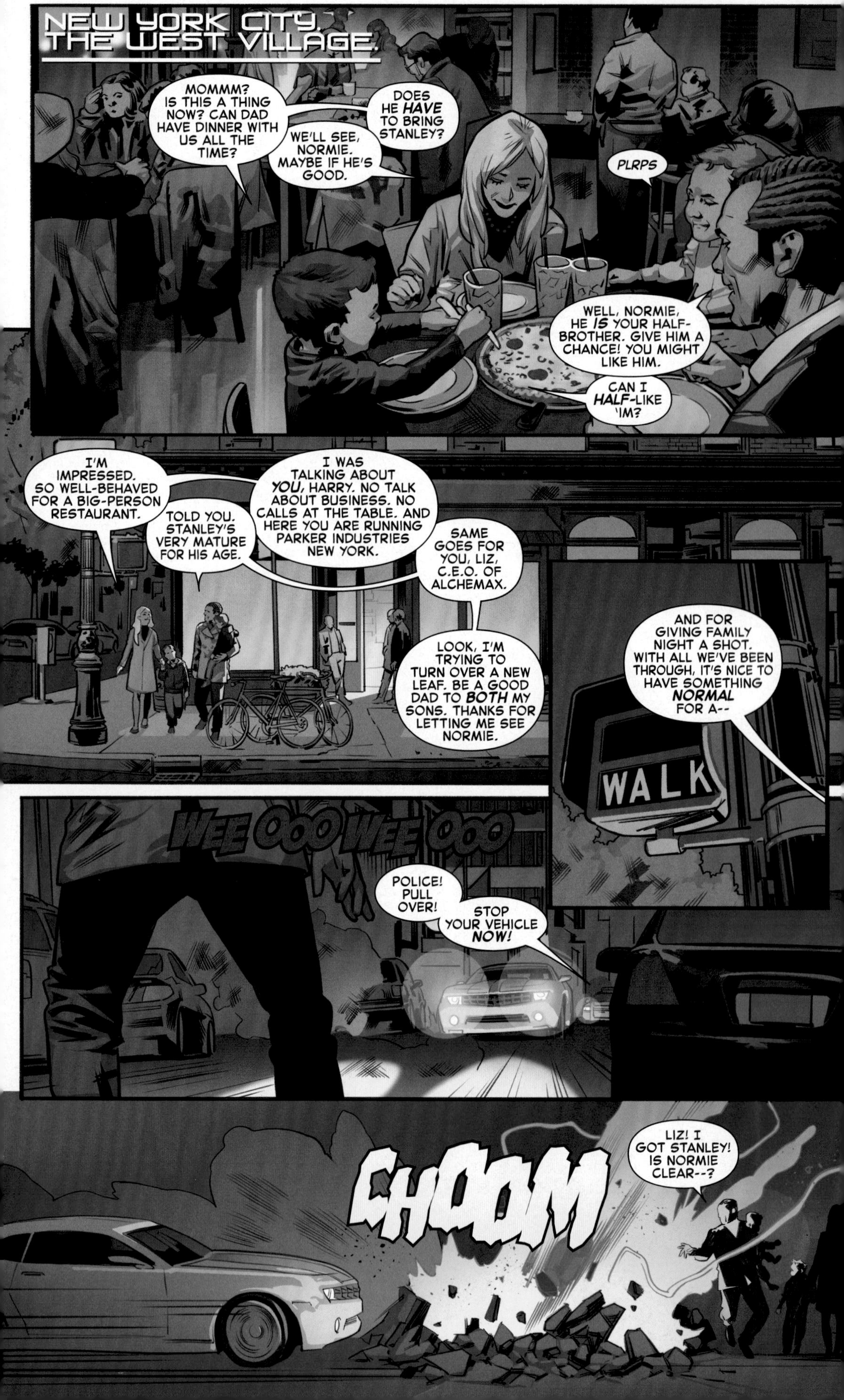
NEW YORK CITY. THE WEST VILLAGE.
MOMMM? IS THIS A THING NOW? CAN DAD HAVE DINNER WITH US ALL THE TIME?
DOES HE HAVE TO BRING STANLEY?
WE'LL SEE, NORMIE. MAYBE IF HE'S GOOD.
PLRPS
WELL, NORMIE, HE IS YOUR HALF-BROTHER. GIVE HIM A CHANCE! YOU MIGHT LIKE HIM.
CAN I HALF-LIKE 'IM?
I'M IMPRESSED. SO WELL-BEHAVED FOR A BIG-PERSON RESTAURANT.
TOLD YOU. STANLEY'S VERY MATURE FOR HIS AGE.
I WAS TALKING ABOUT YOU, HARRY. NO TALK ABOUT BUSINESS. NO CALLS AT THE TABLE. AND HERE YOU ARE RUNNING PARKER INDUSTRIES NEW YORK.
SAME GOES FOR YOU, LIZ, C.E.O. OF ALCHEMAX.
LOOK, I'M TRYING TO TURN OVER A NEW LEAF. BE A GOOD DAD TO BOTH MY SONS. THANKS FOR LETTING ME SEE NORMIE.
AND FOR GIVING FAMILY NIGHT A SHOT. WITH ALL WE'VE BEEN THROUGH, IT'S NICE TO HAVE SOMETHING NORMAL FOR A--
WALK
WEE OOO WEE OOO
POLICE! PULL OVER!
STOP YOUR VEHICLE NOW!
CHOOM
LIZ! I GOT STANLEY! IS NORMIE CLEAR--?

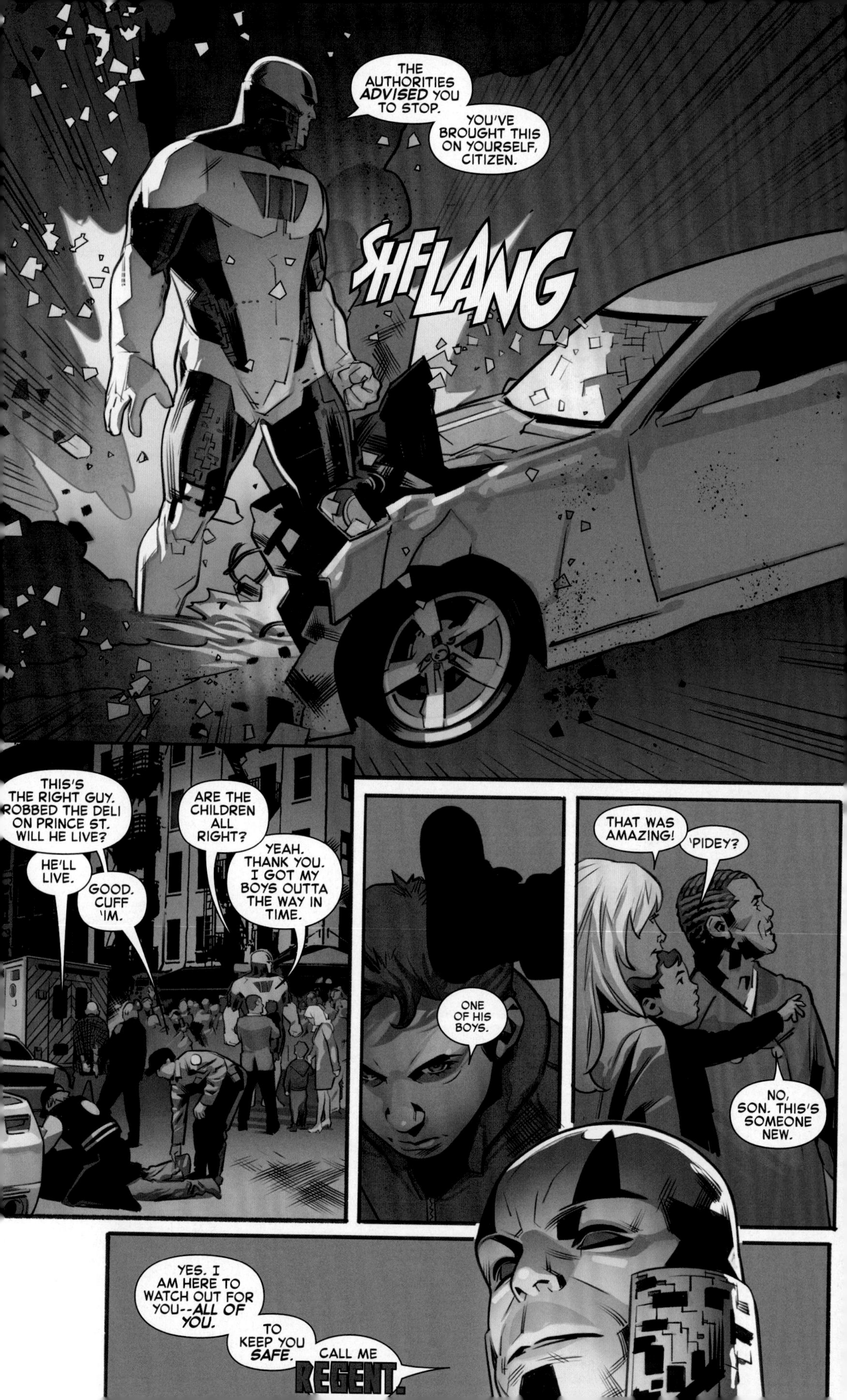
THE AUTHORITIES ADVISED YOU TO STOP.
YOU'VE BROUGHT THIS ON YOURSELF, CITIZEN.
SHFLANG
THIS'S THE RIGHT GUY. ROBBED THE DELI ON PRINCE ST. WILL HE LIVE?
HE'LL LIVE.
GOOD. CUFF 'IM.
ARE THE CHILDREN ALL RIGHT?
YEAH. THANK YOU. I GOT MY BOYS OUTTA THE WAY IN TIME.
ONE OF HIS BOYS.
THAT WAS AMAZING!
'PIDEY?
NO, SON. THIS'S SOMEONE NEW.
YES. I AM HERE TO WATCH OUT FOR YOU--ALL OF YOU.
TO KEEP YOU SAFE.
CALL ME
REGENT.

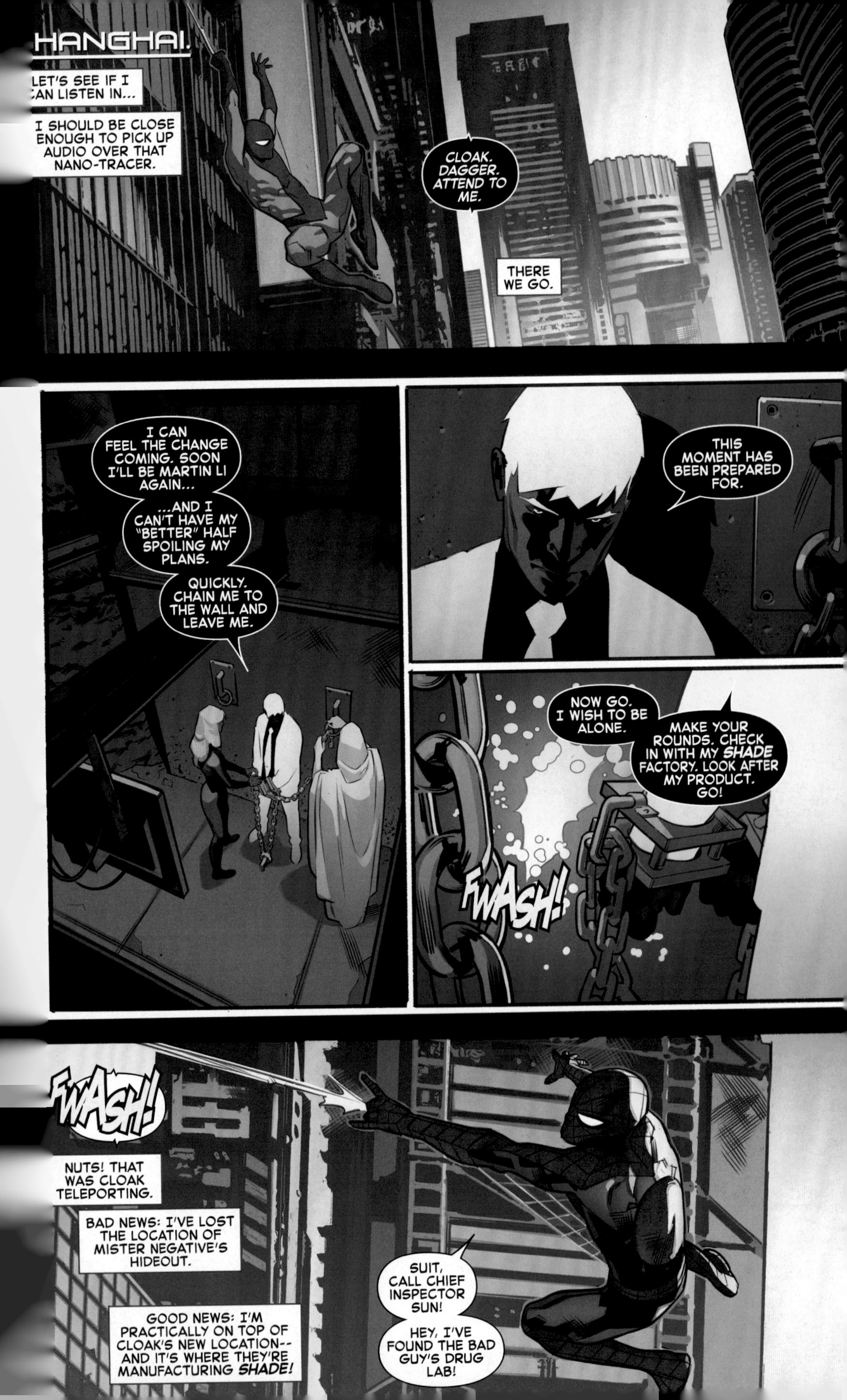
HANGHAI.
LET'S SEE IF I CAN LISTEN IN...
I SHOULD BE CLOSE ENOUGH TO PICK UP AUDIO OVER THAT NANO-TRACER.
CLOAK. DAGGER. ATTEND TO ME.
THERE WE GO.
I CAN FEEL THE CHANGE COMING. SOON I'LL BE MARTIN LI AGAIN...
...AND I CAN'T HAVE MY "BETTER" HALF SPOILING MY PLANS.
QUICKLY. CHAIN ME TO THE WALL AND LEAVE ME.
THIS MOMENT HAS BEEN PREPARED FOR.
NOW GO. I WISH TO BE ALONE.
MAKE YOUR ROUNDS. CHECK IN WITH MY SHADE FACTORY. LOOK AFTER MY PRODUCT. GO!
FWASH!
FWASH!
NUTS! THAT WAS CLOAK TELEPORTING.
BAD NEWS: I'VE LOST THE LOCATION OF MISTER NEGATIVE'S HIDEOUT.
GOOD NEWS: I'M PRACTICALLY ON TOP OF CLOAK'S NEW LOCATION--AND IT'S WHERE THEY'RE MANUFACTURING SHADE!
SUIT, CALL CHIEF INSPECTOR SUN!
HEY, I'VE FOUND THE BAD GUY'S DRUG LAB!

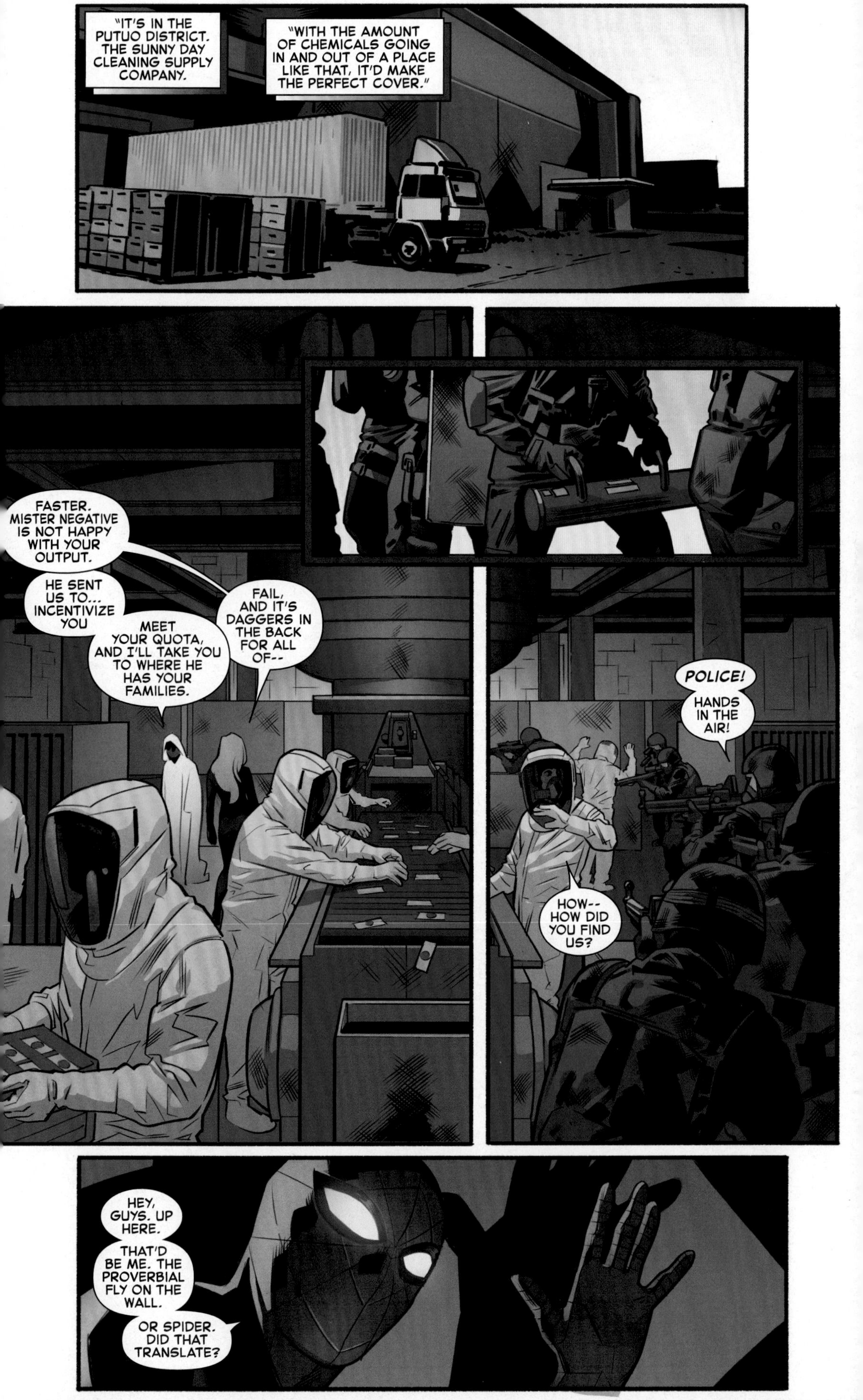
"IT'S IN THE PUTUO DISTRICT. THE SUNNY DAY CLEANING SUPPLY COMPANY.
"WITH THE AMOUNT OF CHEMICALS GOING IN AND OUT OF A PLACE LIKE THAT, IT'D MAKE THE PERFECT COVER."
FASTER. MISTER NEGATIVE IS NOT HAPPY WITH YOUR OUTPUT.
HE SENT US TO... INCENTIVIZE YOU
MEET YOUR QUOTA, AND I'LL TAKE YOU TO WHERE HE HAS YOUR FAMILIES.
FAIL, AND IT'S DAGGERS IN THE BACK FOR ALL OF--
POLICE!
HANDS IN THE AIR!
HOW-- HOW DID YOU FIND US?
HEY, GUYS. UP HERE.
THAT'D BE ME. THE PROVERBIAL FLY ON THE WALL.
OR SPIDER. DID THAT TRANSLATE?

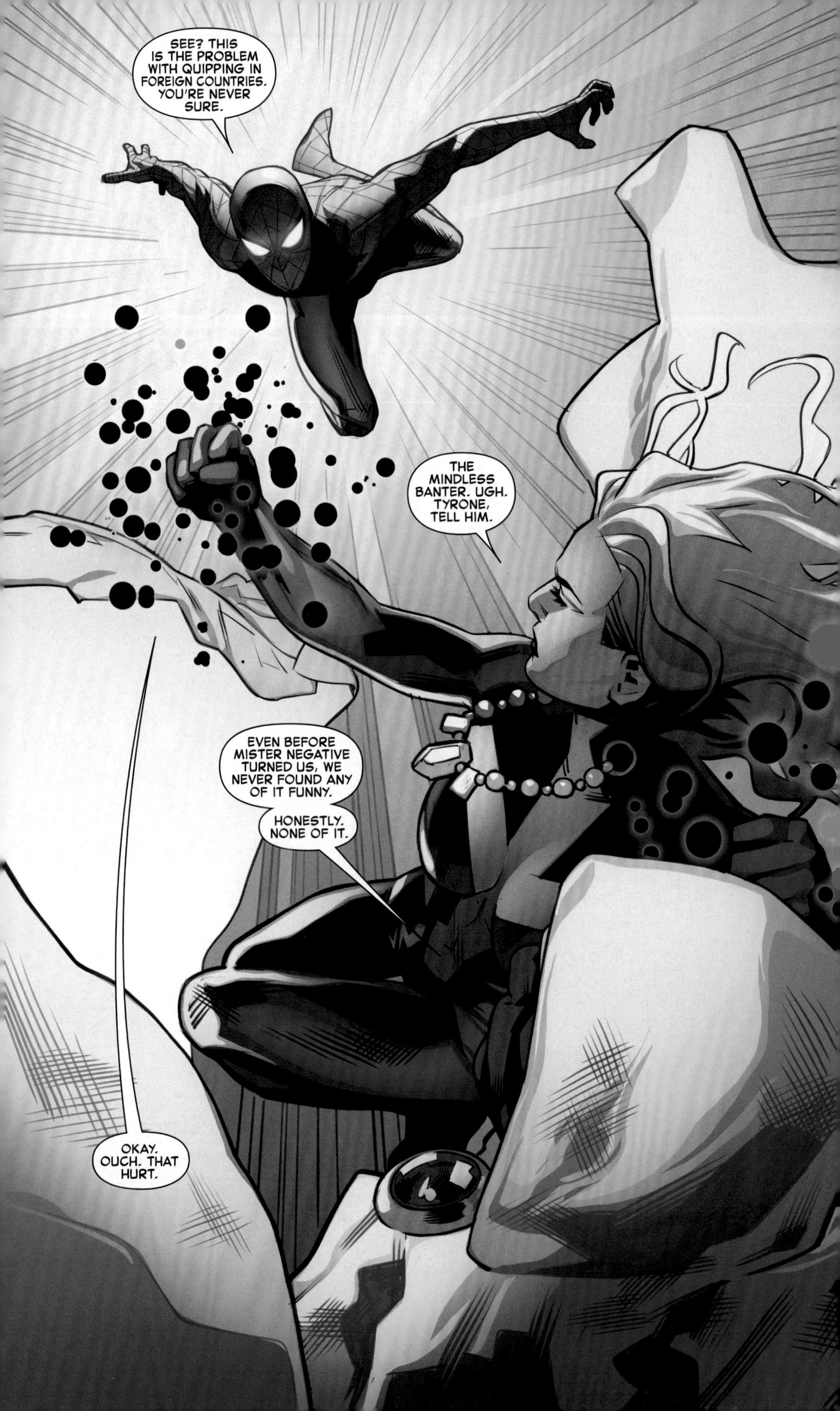
SEE? THIS IS THE PROBLEM WITH QUIPPING IN FOREIGN COUNTRIES. YOU'RE NEVER SURE.
THE MINDLESS BANTER. UGH. TYRONE, TELL HIM.
EVEN BEFORE MISTER NEGATIVE TURNED US, WE NEVER FOUND ANY OF IT FUNNY.
HONESTLY. NONE OF IT.
OKAY. OUCH. THAT HURT.

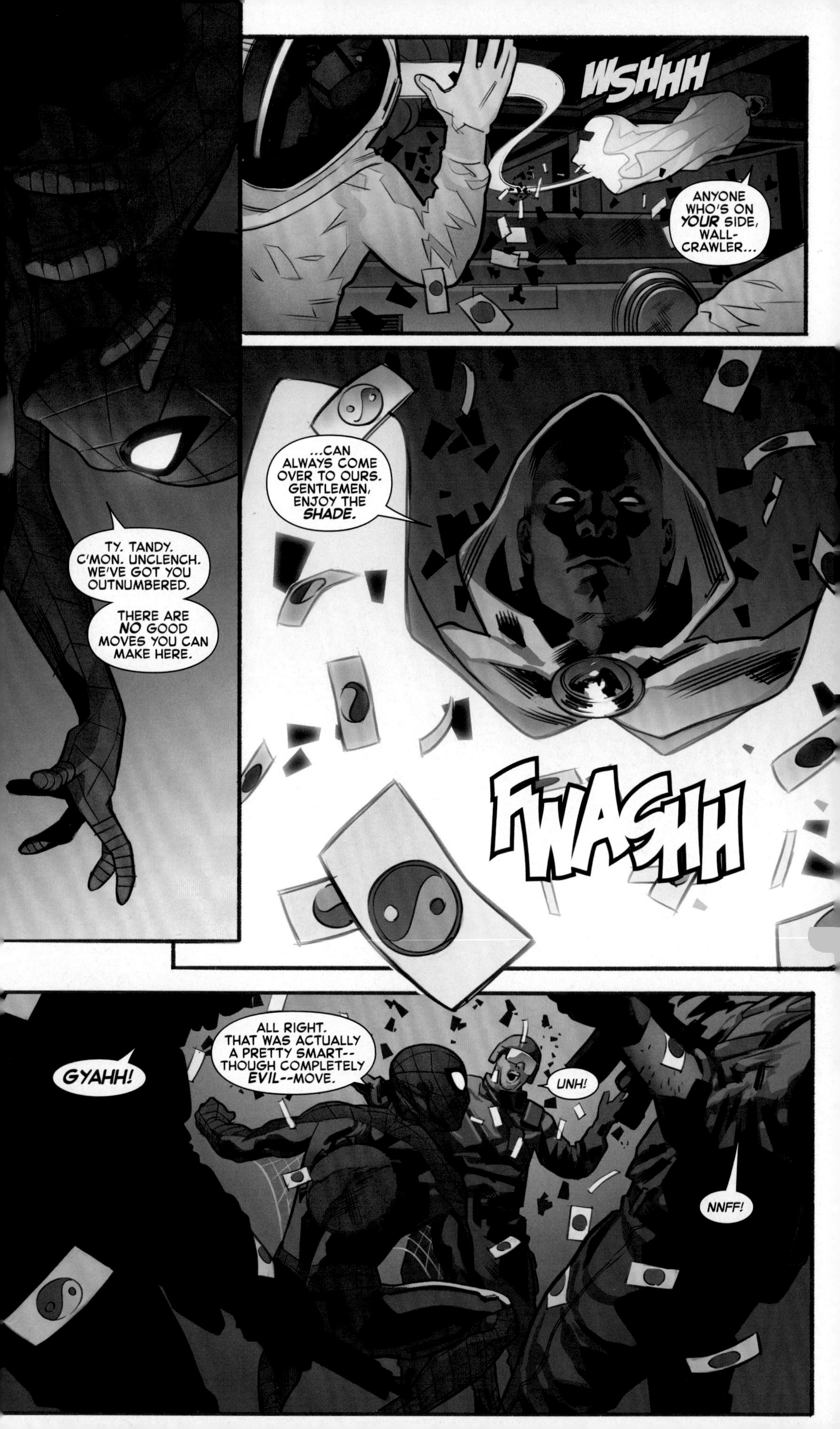
WSHHH
ANYONE WHO'S ON *YOUR* SIDE, WALL-CRAWLER...
TY. TANDY. C'MON. UNCLENCH. WE'VE GOT YOU OUTNUMBERED.
THERE ARE *NO* GOOD MOVES YOU CAN MAKE HERE.
...CAN ALWAYS COME OVER TO OURS. GENTLEMEN, ENJOY THE *SHADE.*
FWASHH
GYAHH!
ALL RIGHT. THAT WAS ACTUALLY A PRETTY SMART--THOUGH COMPLETELY *EVIL*--MOVE.
UNH!
NNFF!

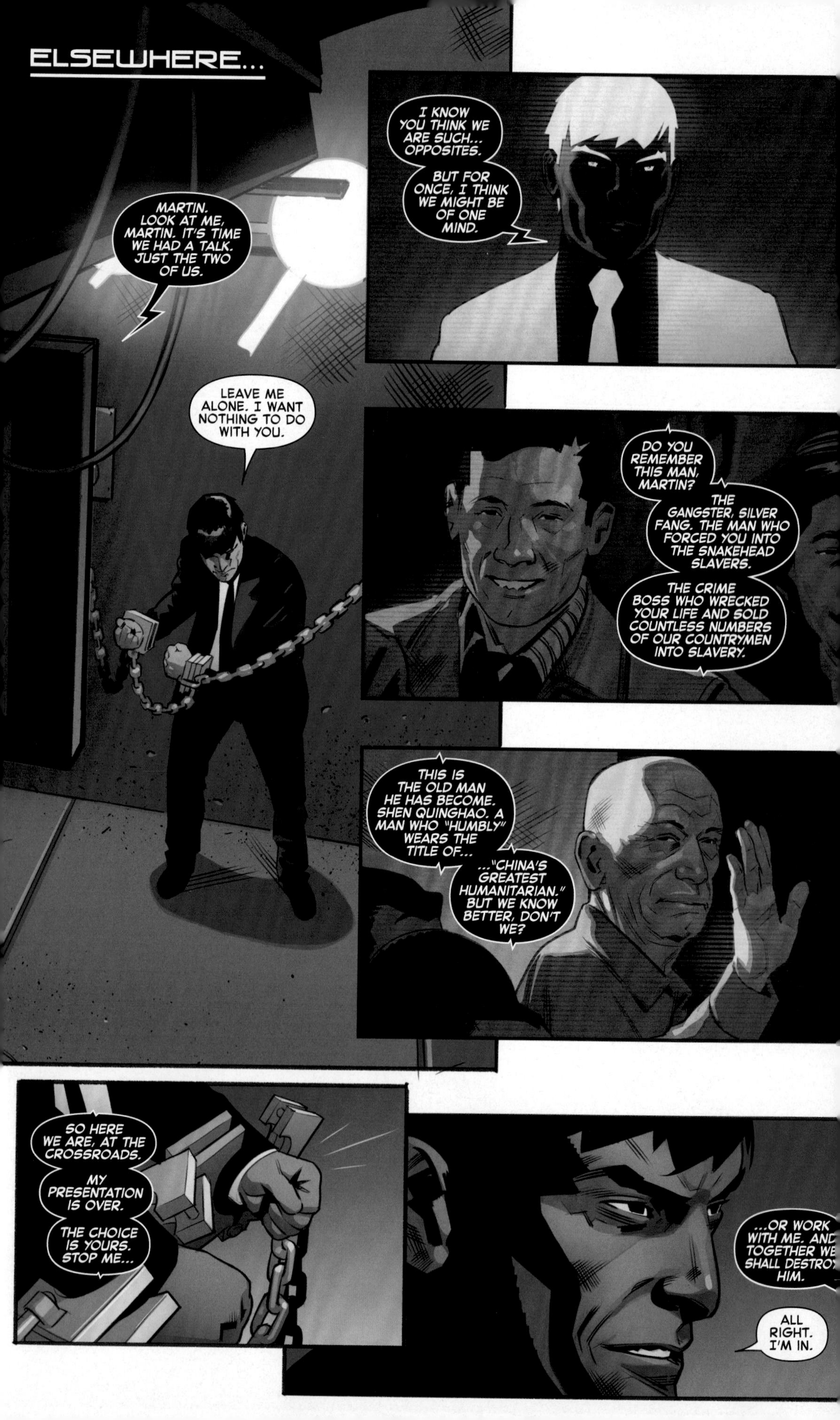
ELSEWHERE...
MARTIN. LOOK AT ME, MARTIN. IT'S TIME WE HAD A TALK. JUST THE TWO OF US.
I KNOW YOU THINK WE ARE SUCH... OPPOSITES.
BUT FOR ONCE, I THINK WE MIGHT BE OF ONE MIND.
LEAVE ME ALONE. I WANT NOTHING TO DO WITH YOU.
DO YOU REMEMBER THIS MAN, MARTIN?
THE GANGSTER, SILVER FANG. THE MAN WHO FORCED YOU INTO THE SNAKEHEAD SLAVERS.
THE CRIME BOSS WHO WRECKED YOUR LIFE AND SOLD COUNTLESS NUMBERS OF OUR COUNTRYMEN INTO SLAVERY.
THIS IS THE OLD MAN HE HAS BECOME. SHEN QUINGHAO. A MAN WHO "HUMBLY" WEARS THE TITLE OF...
..."CHINA'S GREATEST HUMANITARIAN." BUT WE KNOW BETTER, DON'T WE?
SO HERE WE ARE, AT THE CROSSROADS.
MY PRESENTATION IS OVER.
THE CHOICE IS YOURS. STOP ME...
...OR WORK WITH ME. AND TOGETHER WE SHALL DESTROY HIM.
ALL RIGHT. I'M IN.

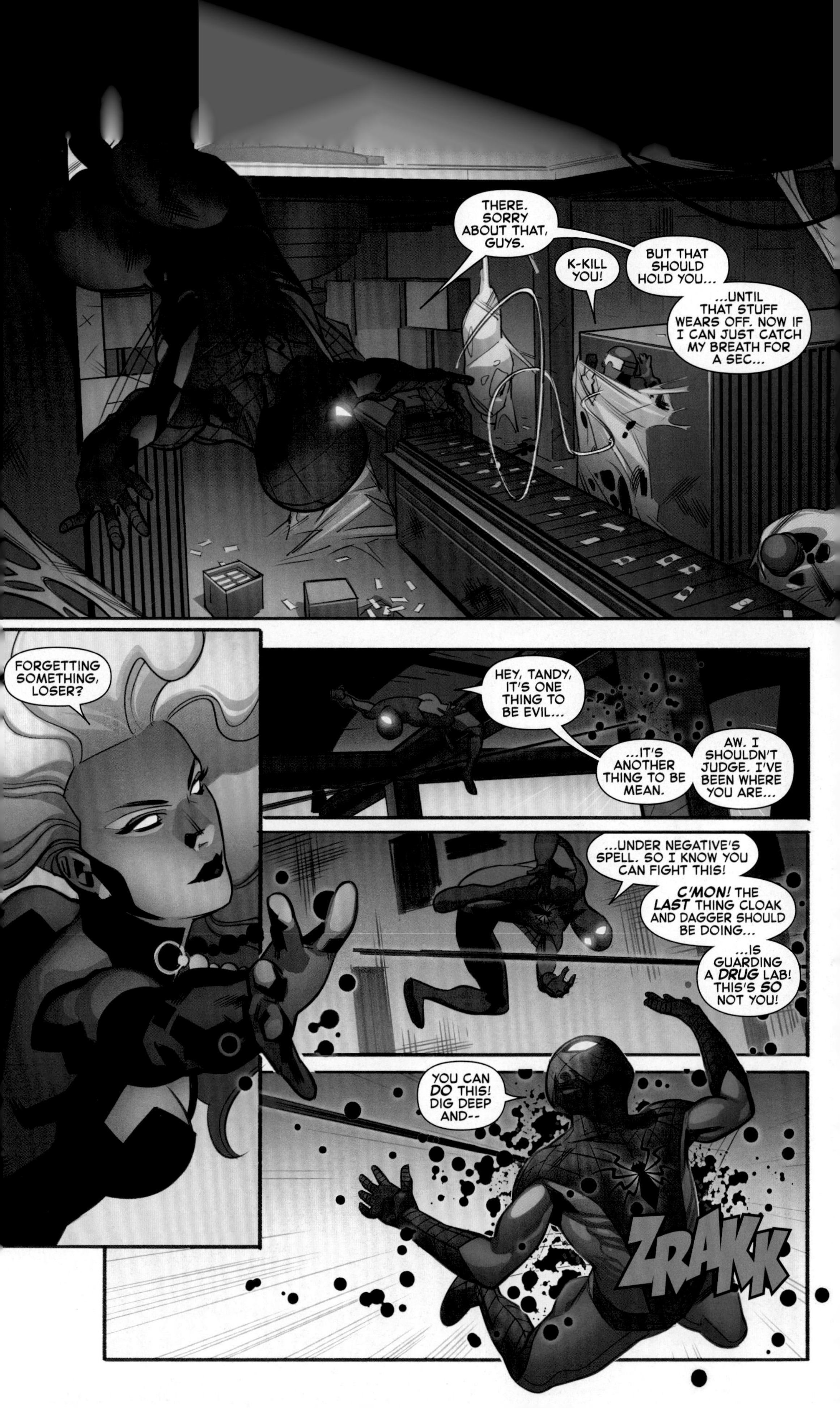
THERE. SORRY ABOUT THAT, GUYS.
K-KILL YOU!
BUT THAT SHOULD HOLD YOU...
...UNTIL THAT STUFF WEARS OFF. NOW IF I CAN JUST CATCH MY BREATH FOR A SEC...
FORGETTING SOMETHING, LOSER?
HEY, TANDY, IT'S ONE THING TO BE EVIL...
...IT'S ANOTHER THING TO BE MEAN.
AW. I SHOULDN'T JUDGE. I'VE BEEN WHERE YOU ARE...
...UNDER NEGATIVE'S SPELL. SO I KNOW YOU CAN FIGHT THIS!
C'MON! THE LAST THING CLOAK AND DAGGER SHOULD BE DOING...
...IS GUARDING A DRUG LAB! THIS'S SO NOT YOU!
YOU CAN DO THIS! DIG DEEP AND--
ZRAKK

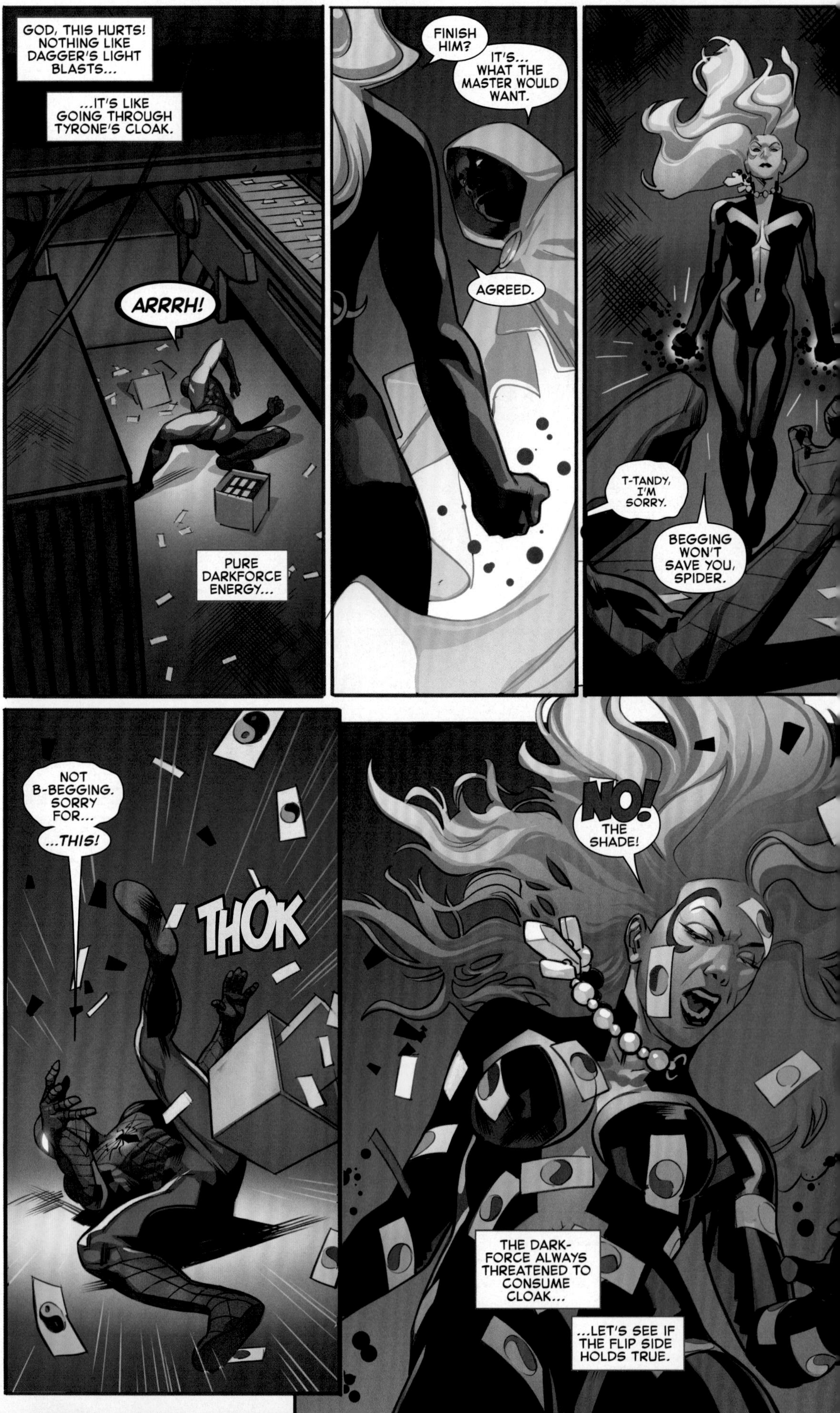
GOD, THIS HURTS! NOTHING LIKE DAGGER'S LIGHT BLASTS...
...IT'S LIKE GOING THROUGH TYRONE'S CLOAK.
ARRRH!
PURE DARKFORCE ENERGY...
FINISH HIM?
IT'S... WHAT THE MASTER WOULD WANT.
AGREED.
T-TANDY, I'M SORRY.
BEGGING WON'T SAVE YOU, SPIDER.
NOT B-BEGGING. SORRY FOR...
...THIS!
THOK
NO! THE SHADE!
THE DARK-FORCE ALWAYS THREATENED TO CONSUME CLOAK...
...LET'S SEE IF THE FLIP SIDE HOLDS TRUE.

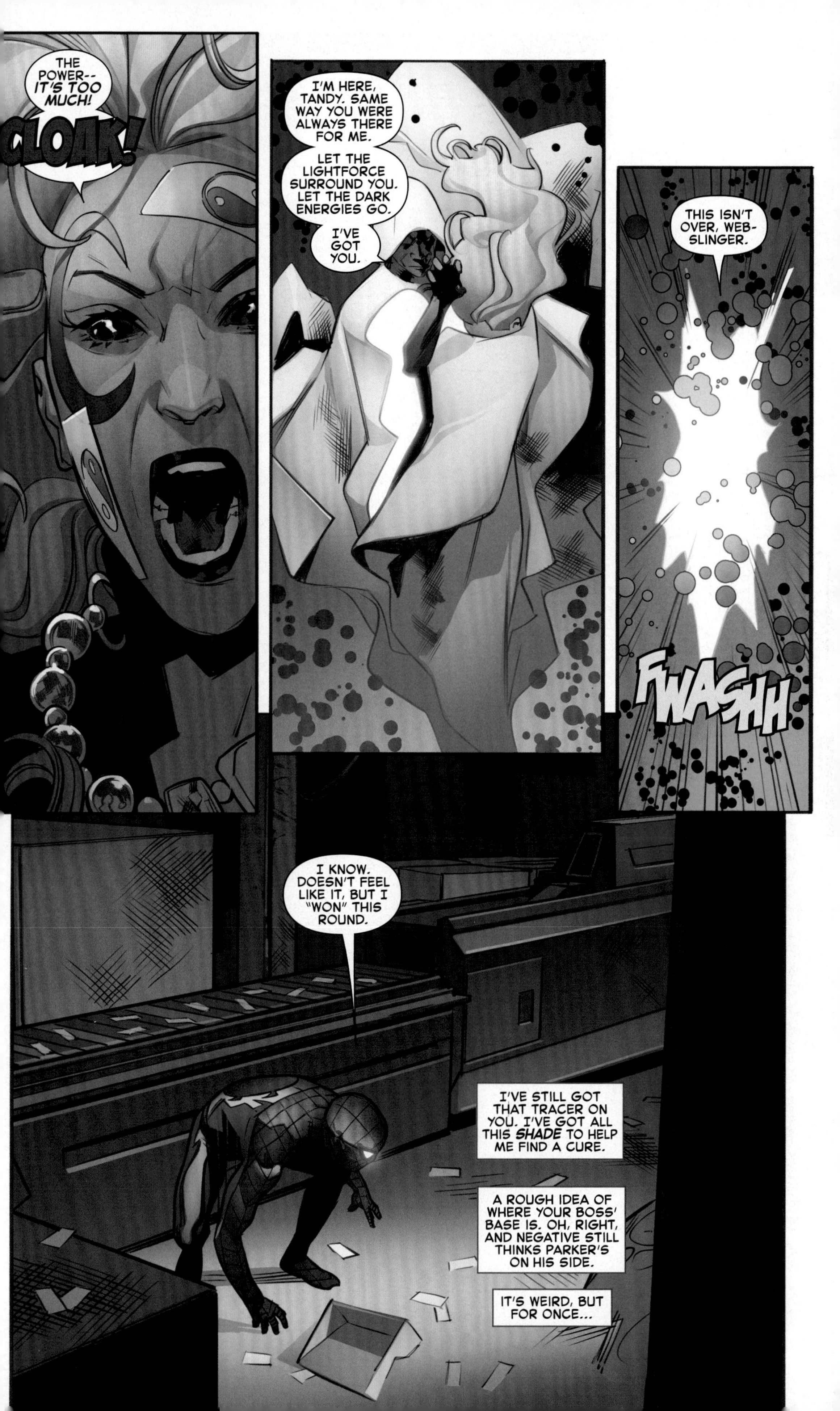

THE POWER-- IT'S TOO MUCH!
CLOAK!
I'M HERE, TANDY. SAME WAY YOU WERE ALWAYS THERE FOR ME.
LET THE LIGHTFORCE SURROUND YOU. LET THE DARK ENERGIES GO.
I'VE GOT YOU.
THIS ISN'T OVER, WEB-SLINGER.
FWASHH
I KNOW. DOESN'T FEEL LIKE IT, BUT I "WON" THIS ROUND.
I'VE STILL GOT THAT TRACER ON YOU. I'VE GOT ALL THIS SHADE TO HELP ME FIND A CURE.
A ROUGH IDEA OF WHERE YOUR BOSS' BASE IS. OH, RIGHT, AND NEGATIVE STILL THINKS PARKER'S ON HIS SIDE.
IT'S WEIRD, BUT FOR ONCE...

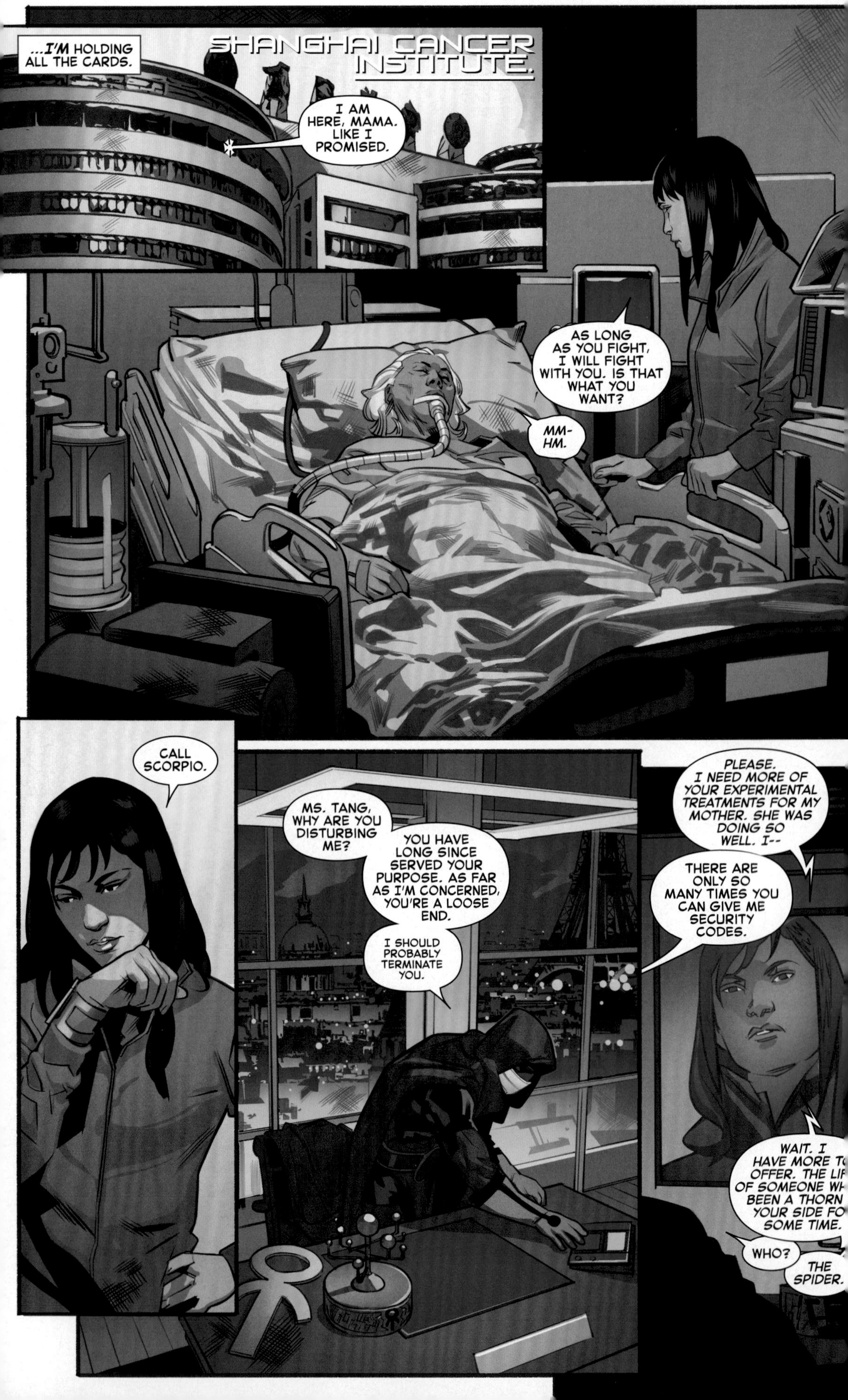

...I'M HOLDING ALL THE CARDS.
SHANGHAI CANCER INSTITUTE.
I AM HERE, MAMA. LIKE I PROMISED.
AS LONG AS YOU FIGHT, I WILL FIGHT WITH YOU. IS THAT WHAT YOU WANT?
MM-HM.
CALL SCORPIO.
MS. TANG, WHY ARE YOU DISTURBING ME?
YOU HAVE LONG SINCE SERVED YOUR PURPOSE. AS FAR AS I'M CONCERNED, YOU'RE A LOOSE END.
I SHOULD PROBABLY TERMINATE YOU.
PLEASE. I NEED MORE OF YOUR EXPERIMENTAL TREATMENTS FOR MY MOTHER. SHE WAS DOING SO WELL. I--
THERE ARE ONLY SO MANY TIMES YOU CAN GIVE ME SECURITY CODES.
WAIT. I HAVE MORE T OFFER. THE LIF OF SOMEONE WH BEEN A THORN YOUR SIDE FO SOME TIME.
WHO?
THE SPIDER.

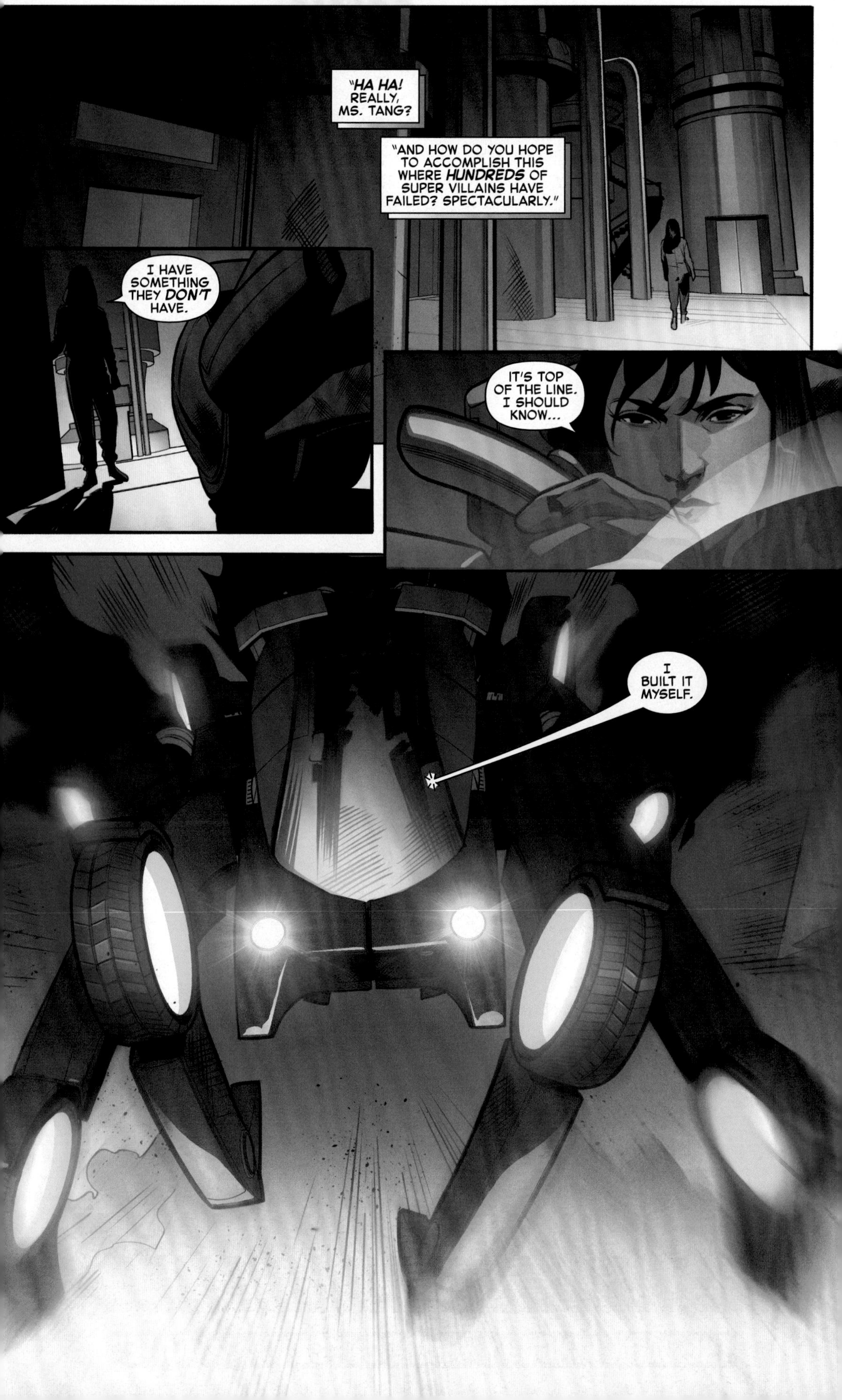
"HA HA! REALLY, MS. TANG?
"AND HOW DO YOU HOPE TO ACCOMPLISH THIS WHERE HUNDREDS OF SUPER VILLAINS HAVE FAILED? SPECTACULARLY."
I HAVE SOMETHING THEY DON'T HAVE.
IT'S TOP OF THE LINE. I SHOULD KNOW...
I BUILT IT MYSELF.

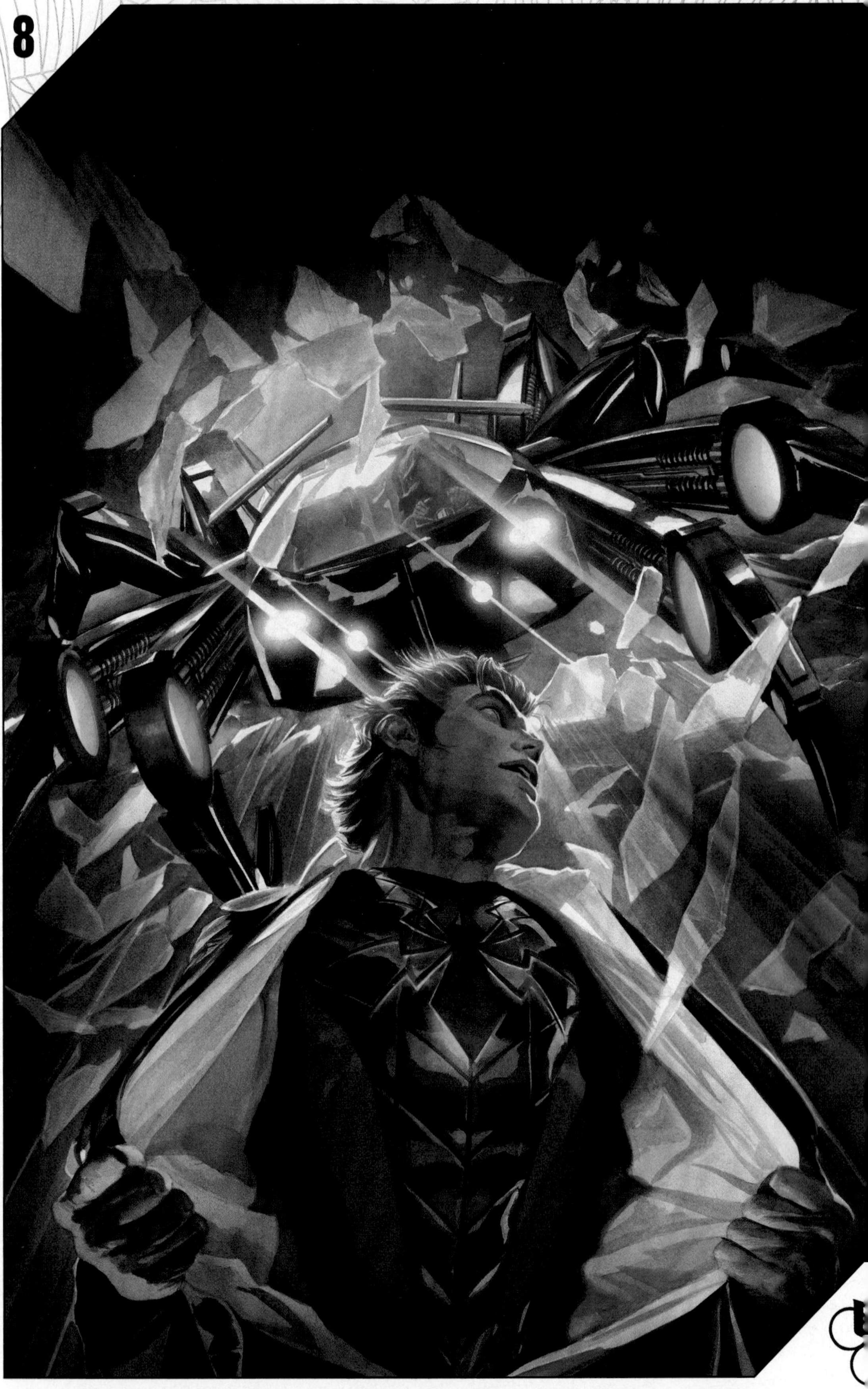

THE DARK KINGDOM - PART 3: "BLACK & WHITE"

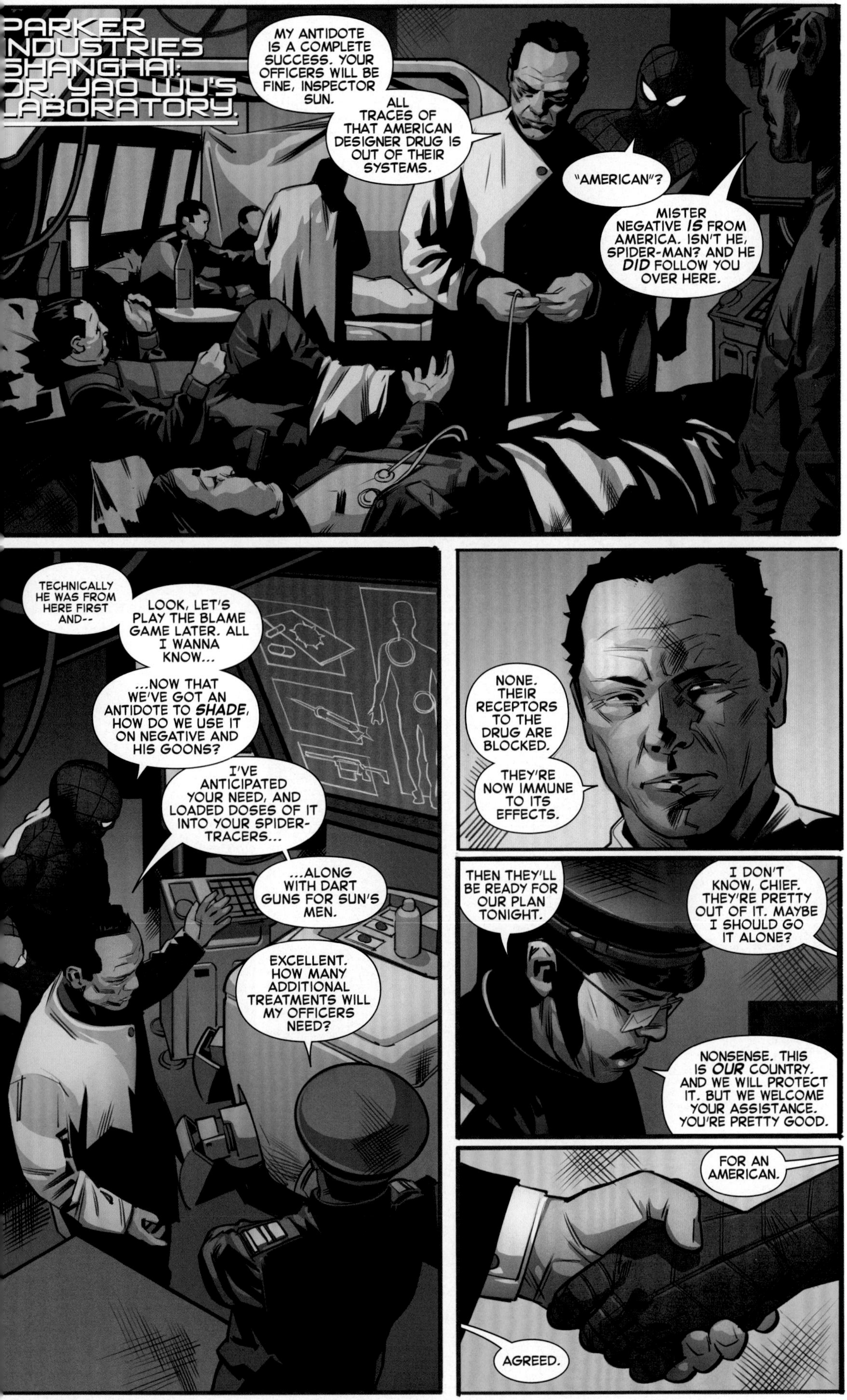
PARKER INDUSTRIES SHANGHAI: DR. YAO WU'S LABORATORY.
MY ANTIDOTE IS A COMPLETE SUCCESS. YOUR OFFICERS WILL BE FINE, INSPECTOR SUN.
ALL TRACES OF THAT AMERICAN DESIGNER DRUG IS OUT OF THEIR SYSTEMS.
"AMERICAN"?
MISTER NEGATIVE IS FROM AMERICA. ISN'T HE, SPIDER-MAN? AND HE DID FOLLOW YOU OVER HERE.
TECHNICALLY HE WAS FROM HERE FIRST AND--
LOOK, LET'S PLAY THE BLAME GAME LATER. ALL I WANNA KNOW...
...NOW THAT WE'VE GOT AN ANTIDOTE TO SHADE, HOW DO WE USE IT ON NEGATIVE AND HIS GOONS?
I'VE ANTICIPATED YOUR NEED, AND LOADED DOSES OF IT INTO YOUR SPIDER-TRACERS...
...ALONG WITH DART GUNS FOR SUN'S MEN.
EXCELLENT. HOW MANY ADDITIONAL TREATMENTS WILL MY OFFICERS NEED?
NONE. THEIR RECEPTORS TO THE DRUG ARE BLOCKED.
THEY'RE NOW IMMUNE TO ITS EFFECTS.
THEN THEY'LL BE READY FOR OUR PLAN TONIGHT.
I DON'T KNOW, CHIEF. THEY'RE PRETTY OUT OF IT. MAYBE I SHOULD GO IT ALONE?
NONSENSE. THIS IS OUR COUNTRY. AND WE WILL PROTECT IT. BUT WE WELCOME YOUR ASSISTANCE. YOU'RE PRETTY GOOD.
FOR AN AMERICAN.
AGREED.

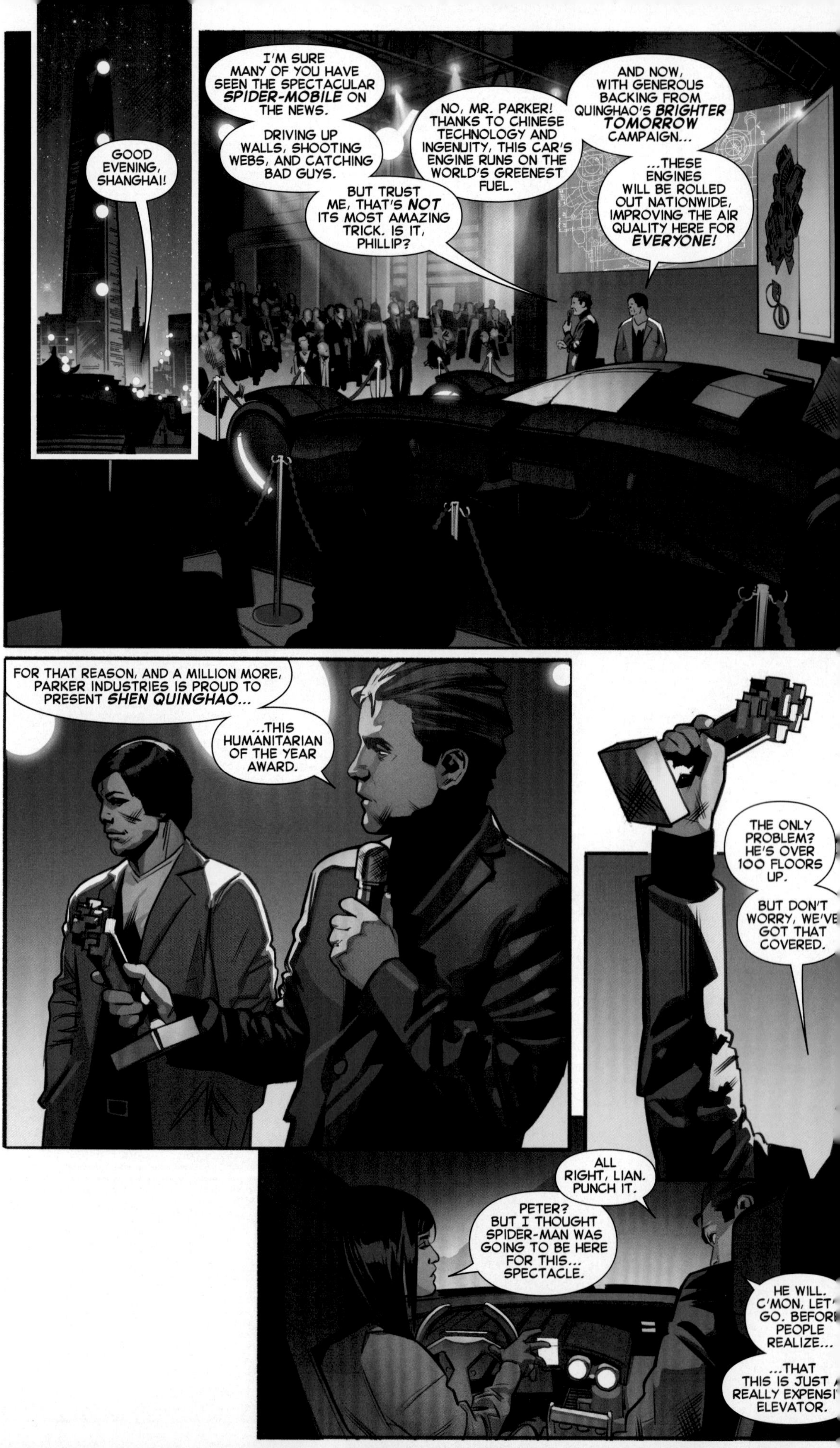
GOOD EVENING, SHANGHAI!
I'M SURE MANY OF YOU HAVE SEEN THE SPECTACULAR SPIDER-MOBILE ON THE NEWS.
DRIVING UP WALLS, SHOOTING WEBS, AND CATCHING BAD GUYS.
BUT TRUST ME, THAT'S NOT ITS MOST AMAZING TRICK. IS IT, PHILLIP?
NO, MR. PARKER! THANKS TO CHINESE TECHNOLOGY AND INGENUITY, THIS CAR'S ENGINE RUNS ON THE WORLD'S GREENEST FUEL.
AND NOW, WITH GENEROUS BACKING FROM QUINGHAO'S BRIGHTER TOMORROW CAMPAIGN...
...THESE ENGINES WILL BE ROLLED OUT NATIONWIDE, IMPROVING THE AIR QUALITY HERE FOR EVERYONE!
FOR THAT REASON, AND A MILLION MORE, PARKER INDUSTRIES IS PROUD TO PRESENT SHEN QUINGHAO...
...THIS HUMANITARIAN OF THE YEAR AWARD.
THE ONLY PROBLEM? HE'S OVER 100 FLOORS UP.
BUT DON'T WORRY, WE'VE GOT THAT COVERED.
ALL RIGHT, LIAN. PUNCH IT.
PETER? BUT I THOUGHT SPIDER-MAN WAS GOING TO BE HERE FOR THIS... SPECTACLE.
HE WILL. C'MON, LET GO. BEFOR PEOPLE REALIZE...
...THAT THIS IS JUST REALLY EXPENSI ELEVATOR.

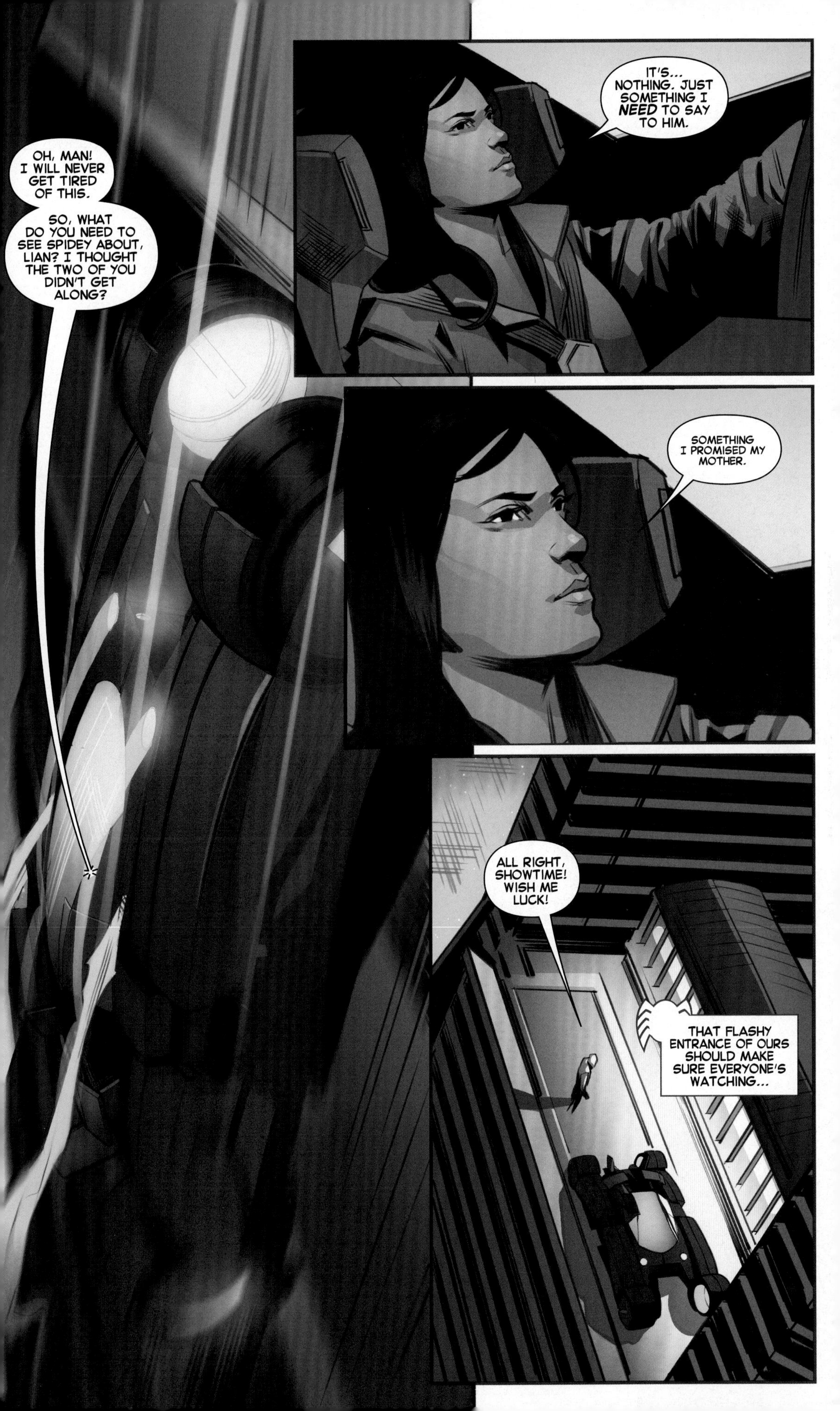

OH, MAN! I WILL NEVER GET TIRED OF THIS.
SO, WHAT DO YOU NEED TO SEE SPIDEY ABOUT, LIAN? I THOUGHT THE TWO OF YOU DIDN'T GET ALONG?
IT'S... NOTHING. JUST SOMETHING I NEED TO SAY TO HIM.
SOMETHING I PROMISED MY MOTHER.
ALL RIGHT, SHOWTIME! WISH ME LUCK!
THAT FLASHY ENTRANCE OF OURS SHOULD MAKE SURE EVERYONE'S WATCHING...

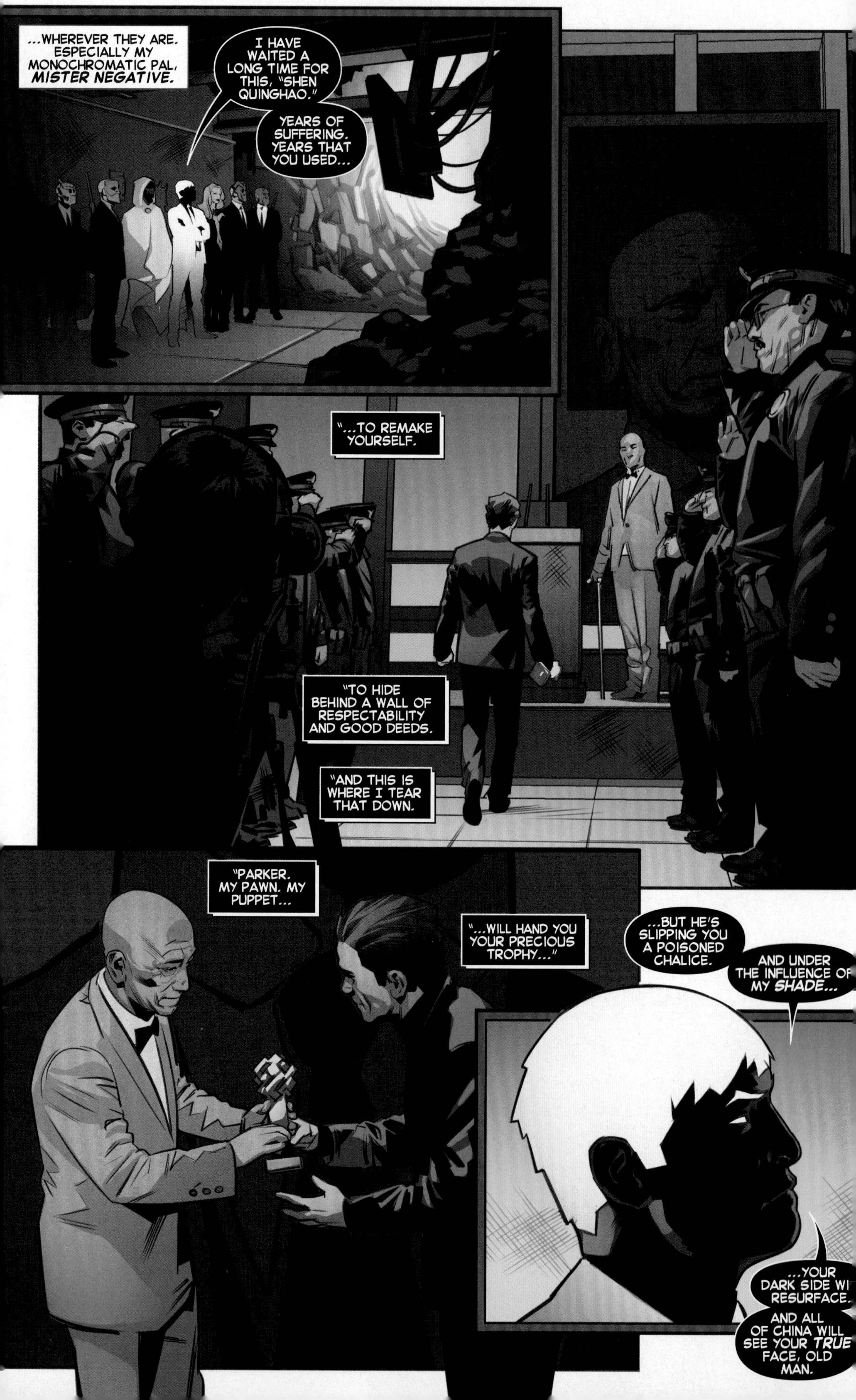
...WHEREVER THEY ARE. ESPECIALLY MY MONOCHROMATIC PAL, MISTER NEGATIVE.
I HAVE WAITED A LONG TIME FOR THIS, "SHEN QUINGHAO."
YEARS OF SUFFERING. YEARS THAT YOU USED...
"...TO REMAKE YOURSELF.
"TO HIDE BEHIND A WALL OF RESPECTABILITY AND GOOD DEEDS.
"AND THIS IS WHERE I TEAR THAT DOWN.
"PARKER. MY PAWN. MY PUPPET...
"...WILL HAND YOU YOUR PRECIOUS TROPHY..."
...BUT HE'S SLIPPING YOU A POISONED CHALICE.
AND UNDER THE INFLUENCE OF MY SHADE...
...YOUR DARK SIDE WI RESURFACE.
AND ALL OF CHINA WILL SEE YOUR TRUE FACE, OLD MAN.

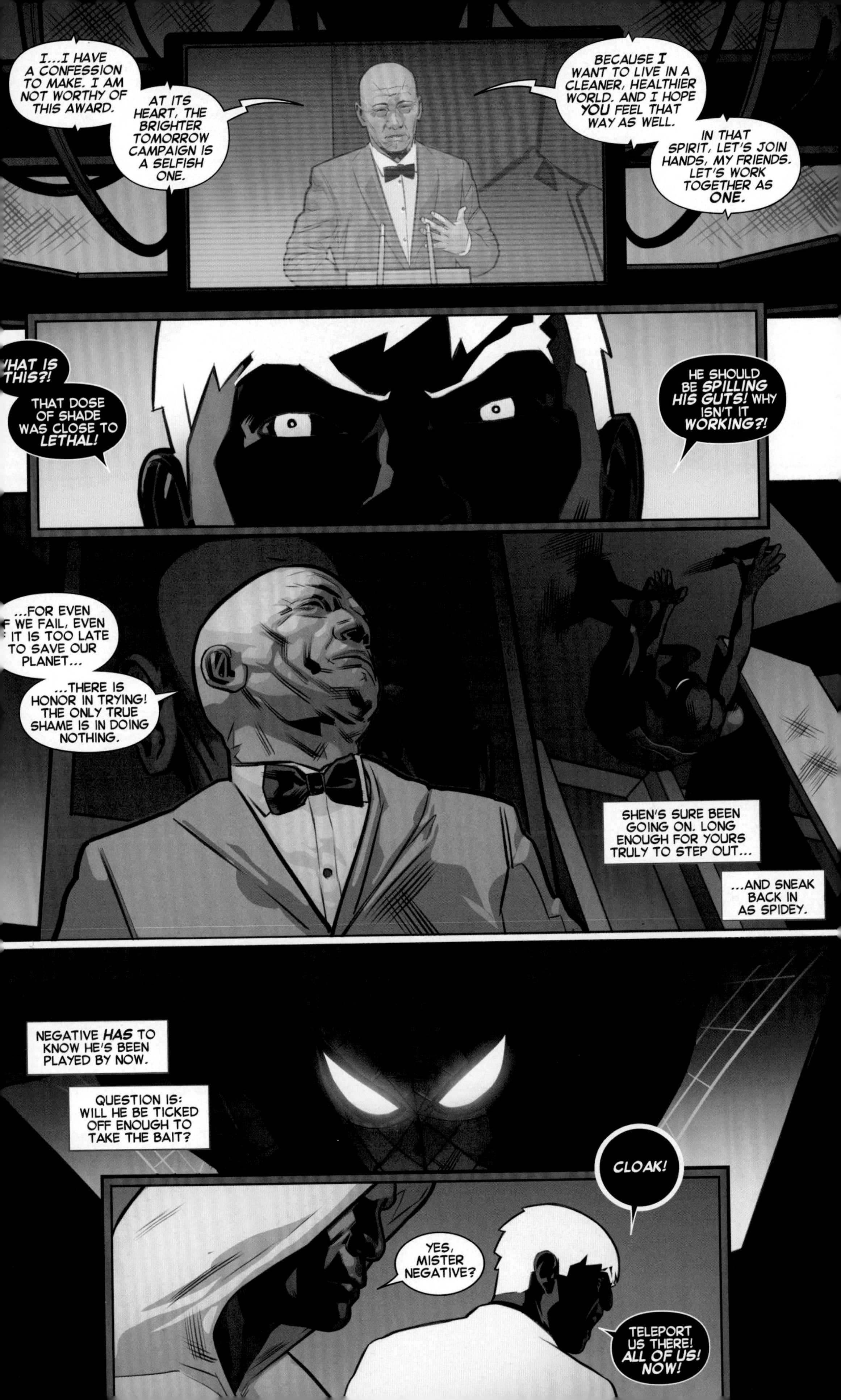

I...I HAVE A CONFESSION TO MAKE. I AM NOT WORTHY OF THIS AWARD.
AT ITS HEART, THE BRIGHTER TOMORROW CAMPAIGN IS A SELFISH ONE.
BECAUSE I WANT TO LIVE IN A CLEANER, HEALTHIER WORLD. AND I HOPE YOU FEEL THAT WAY AS WELL.
IN THAT SPIRIT, LET'S JOIN HANDS, MY FRIENDS. LET'S WORK TOGETHER AS ONE.
HAT IS THIS?!
THAT DOSE OF SHADE WAS CLOSE TO LETHAL!
HE SHOULD BE SPILLING HIS GUTS! WHY ISN'T IT WORKING?!
...FOR EVEN WE FAIL, EVEN IT IS TOO LATE TO SAVE OUR PLANET...
...THERE IS HONOR IN TRYING! THE ONLY TRUE SHAME IS IN DOING NOTHING.
SHEN'S SURE BEEN GOING ON. LONG ENOUGH FOR YOURS TRULY TO STEP OUT...
...AND SNEAK BACK IN AS SPIDEY.
NEGATIVE HAS TO KNOW HE'S BEEN PLAYED BY NOW.
QUESTION IS: WILL HE BE TICKED OFF ENOUGH TO TAKE THE BAIT?
CLOAK!
YES, MISTER NEGATIVE?
TELEPORT US THERE! ALL OF US! NOW!

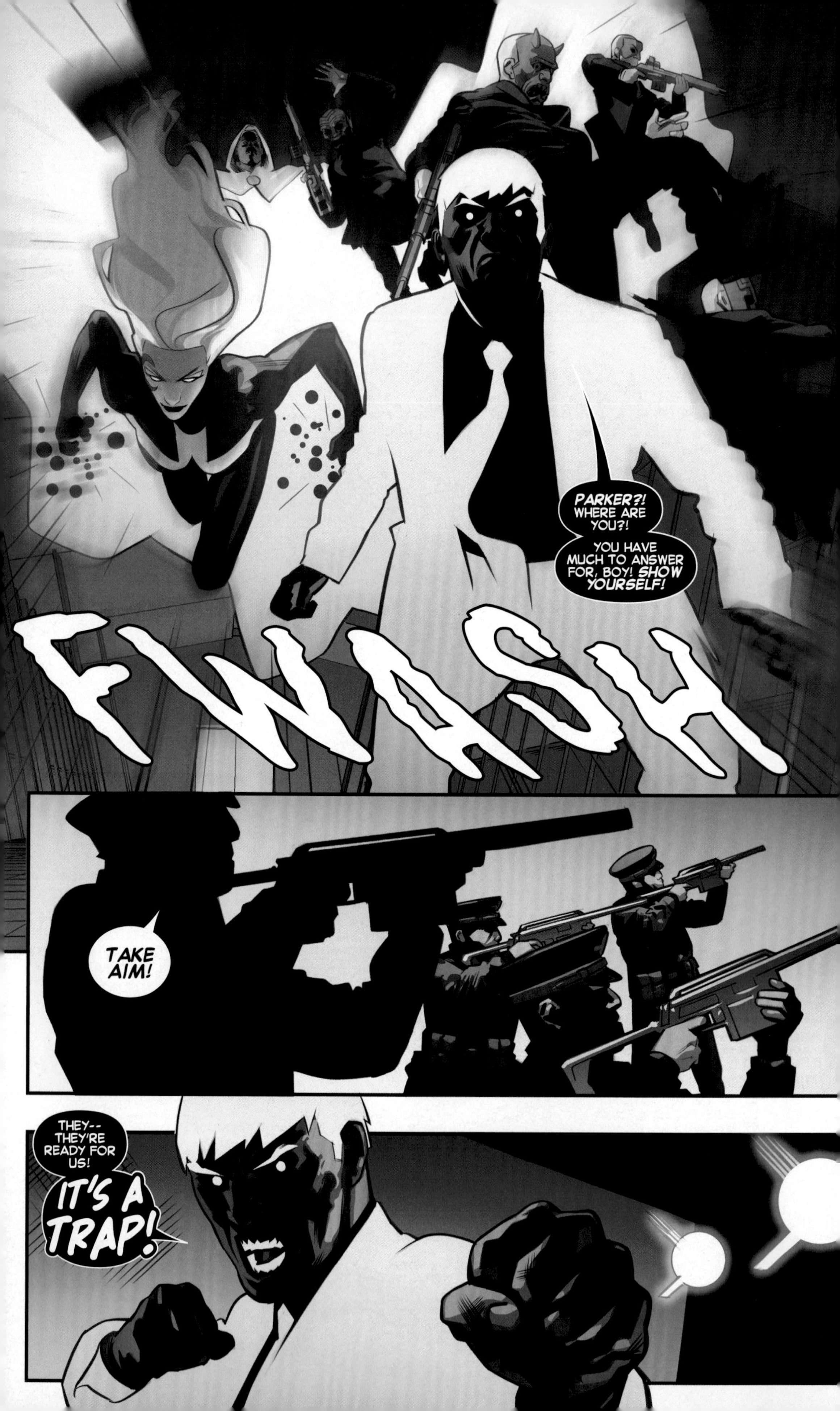

PARKER?! WHERE ARE YOU?!
YOU HAVE MUCH TO ANSWER FOR, BOY! SHOW YOURSELF!
FWASH
TAKE AIM!
THEY-- THEY'RE READY FOR US!
IT'S A TRAP!

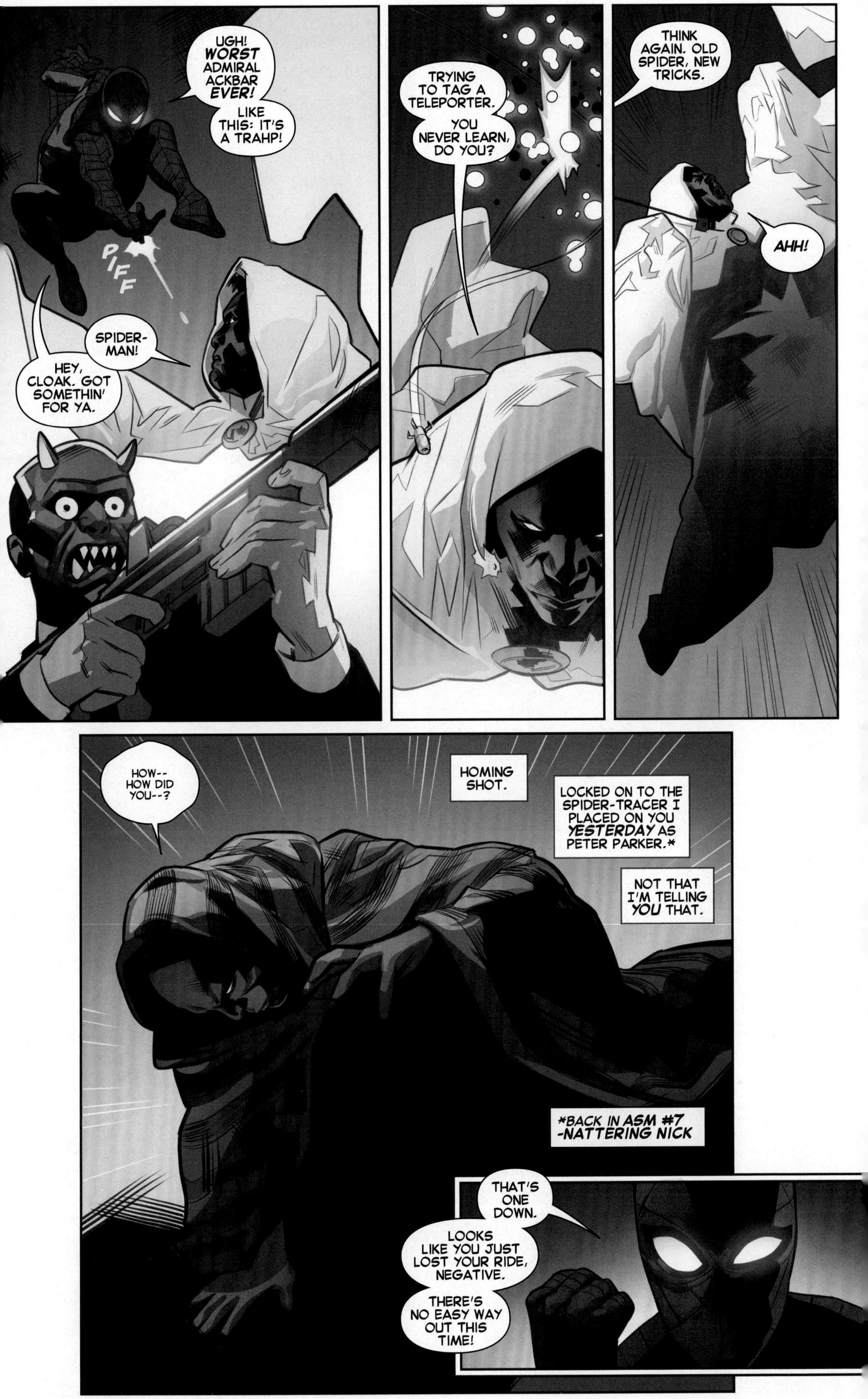
UGH! WORST ADMIRAL ACKBAR EVER!
LIKE THIS: IT'S A TRAHP!
PIFF
SPIDER-MAN!
HEY, CLOAK. GOT SOMETHIN' FOR YA.
TRYING TO TAG A TELEPORTER.
YOU NEVER LEARN, DO YOU?
THINK AGAIN. OLD SPIDER, NEW TRICKS.
AHH!
HOW-- HOW DID YOU--?
HOMING SHOT.
LOCKED ON TO THE SPIDER-TRACER I PLACED ON YOU YESTERDAY AS PETER PARKER.*
NOT THAT I'M TELLING YOU THAT.
*BACK IN ASM #7 -NATTERING NICK
THAT'S ONE DOWN.
LOOKS LIKE YOU JUST LOST YOUR RIDE, NEGATIVE.
THERE'S NO EASY WAY OUT THIS TIME!

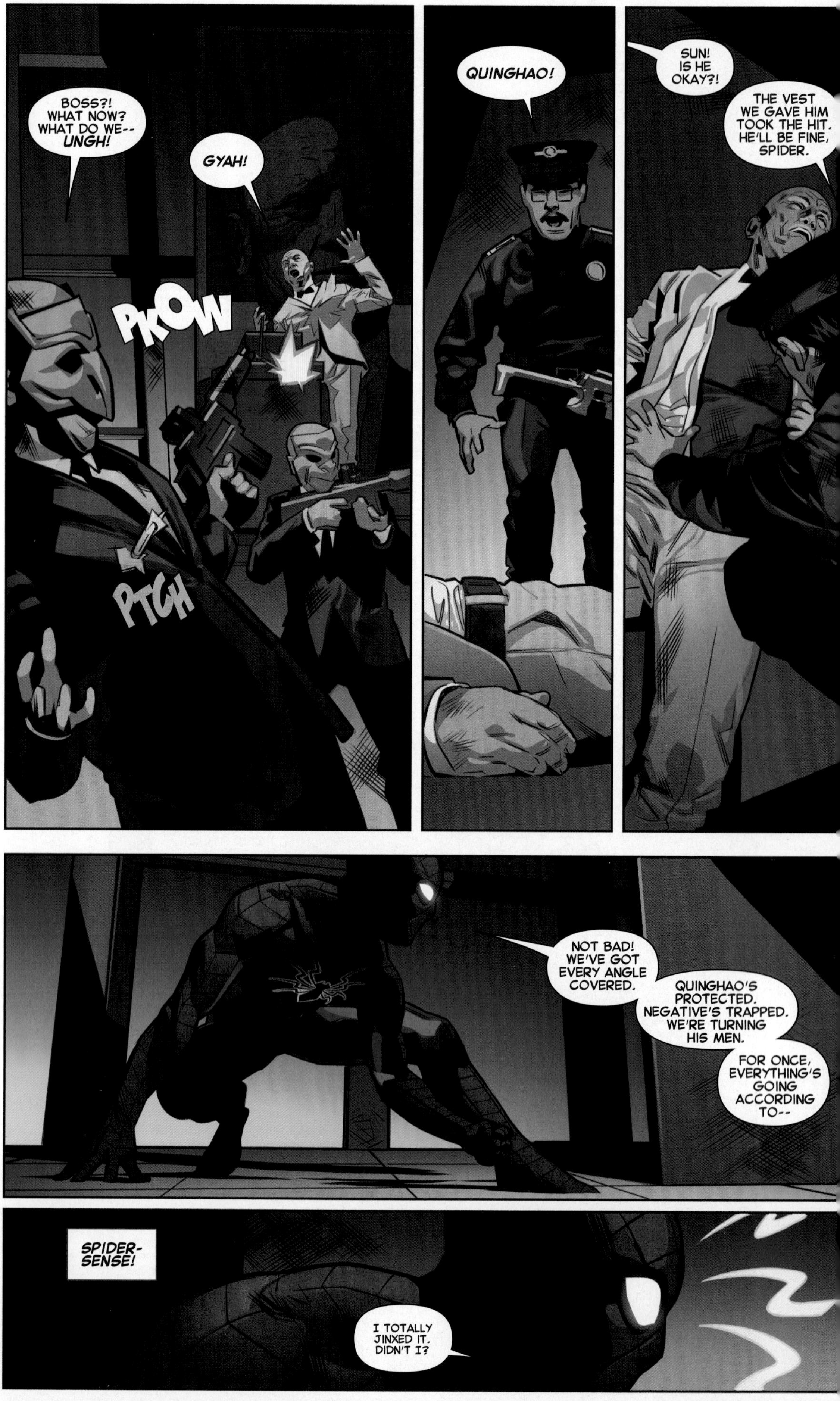
BOSS?! WHAT NOW? WHAT DO WE-- UNGH!
GYAH!
PKOW
PTCH
QUINGHAO!
SUN! IS HE OKAY?!
THE VEST WE GAVE HIM TOOK THE HIT. HE'LL BE FINE, SPIDER.
NOT BAD! WE'VE GOT EVERY ANGLE COVERED.
QUINGHAO'S PROTECTED. NEGATIVE'S TRAPPED. WE'RE TURNING HIS MEN.
FOR ONCE, EVERYTHING'S GOING ACCORDING TO--
SPIDER-SENSE!
I TOTALLY JINXED IT. DIDN'T I?

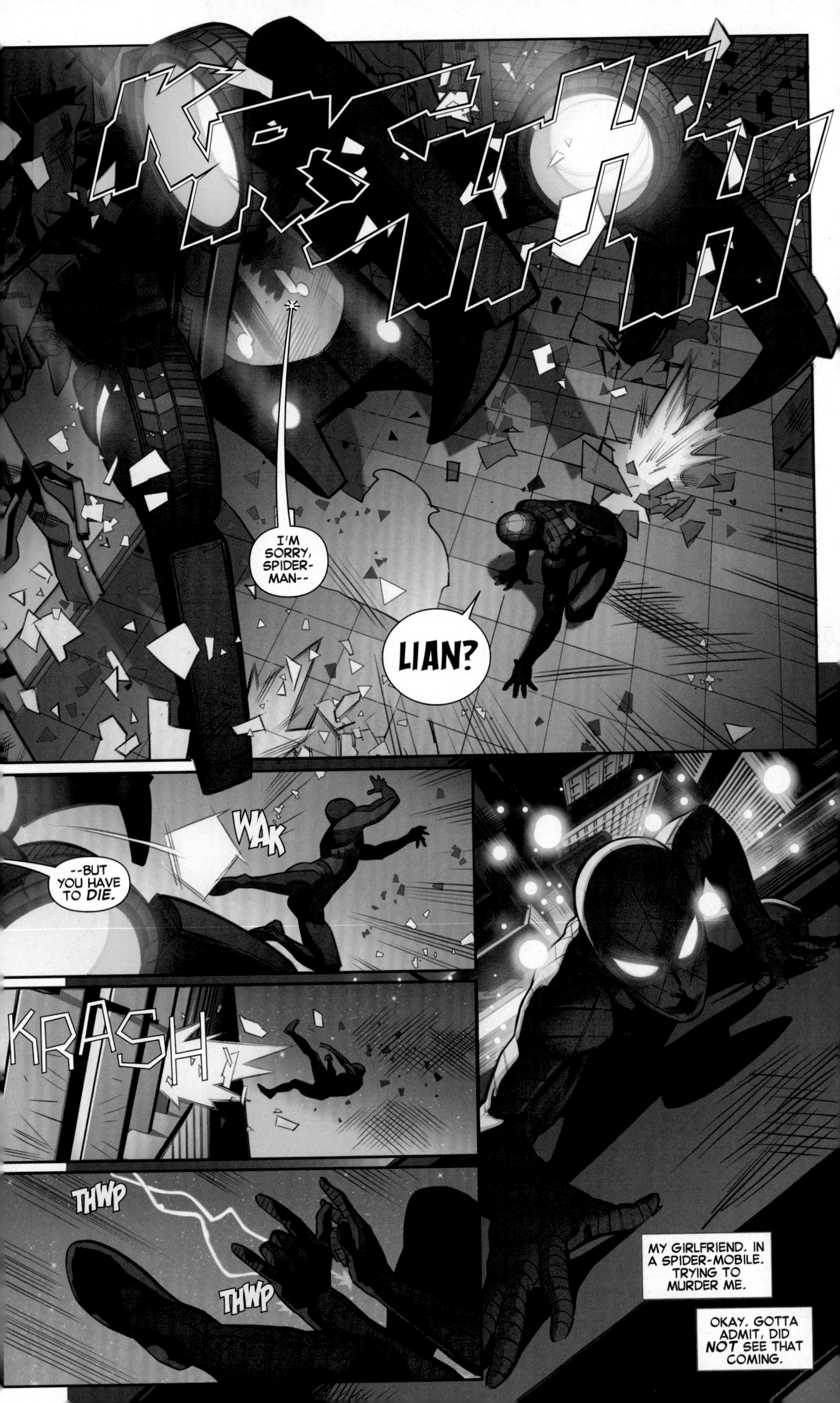
KRRSSHHH
I'M SORRY, SPIDER-MAN--
LIAN?
WAK
--BUT YOU HAVE TO DIE.
KRASH
THWP
THWP
MY GIRLFRIEND. IN A SPIDER-MOBILE. TRYING TO MURDER ME.
OKAY. GOTTA ADMIT, DID NOT SEE THAT COMING.

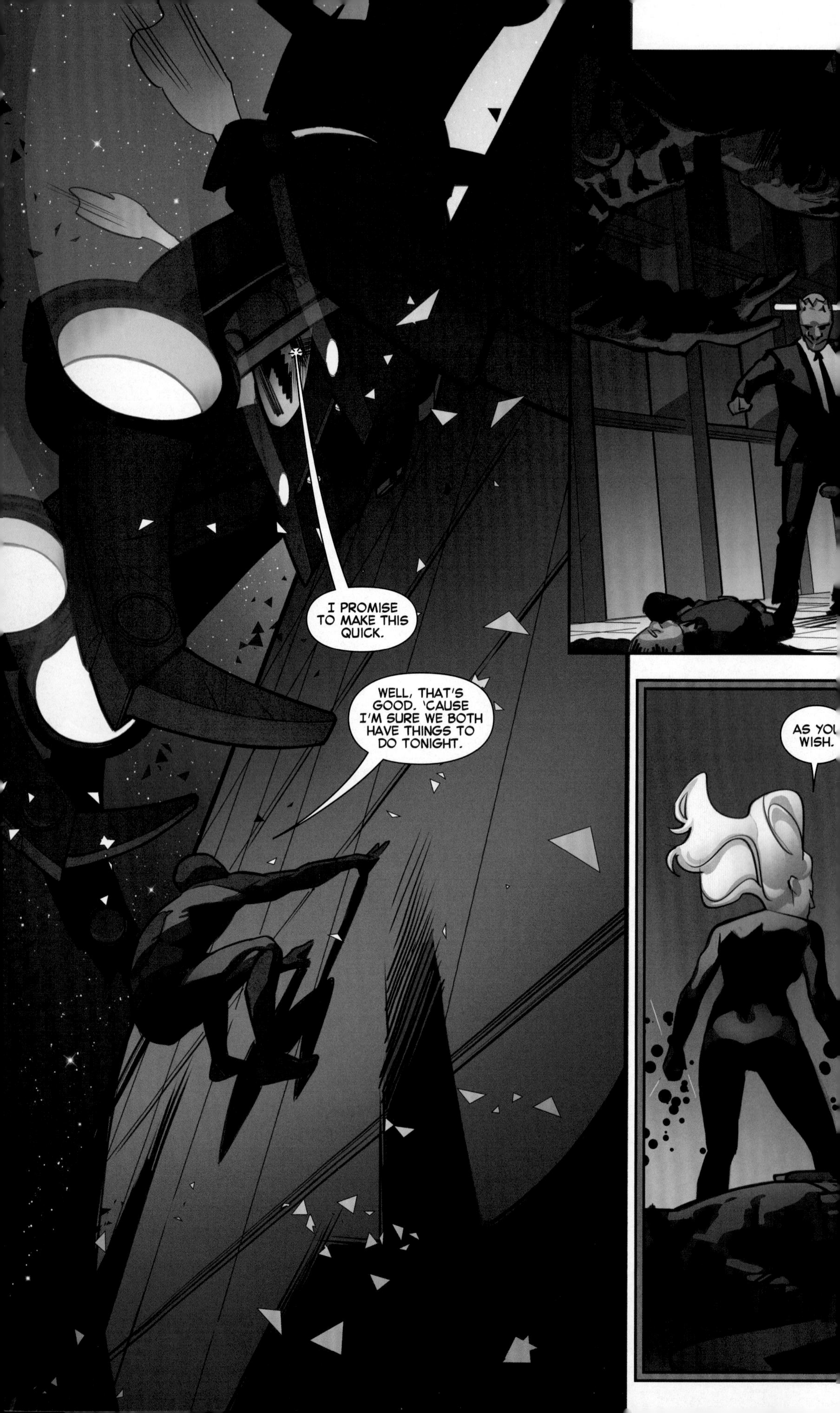

I PROMISE TO MAKE THIS QUICK.
WELL, THAT'S GOOD. 'CAUSE I'M SURE WE BOTH HAVE THINGS TO DO TONIGHT.
AS YOU WISH.

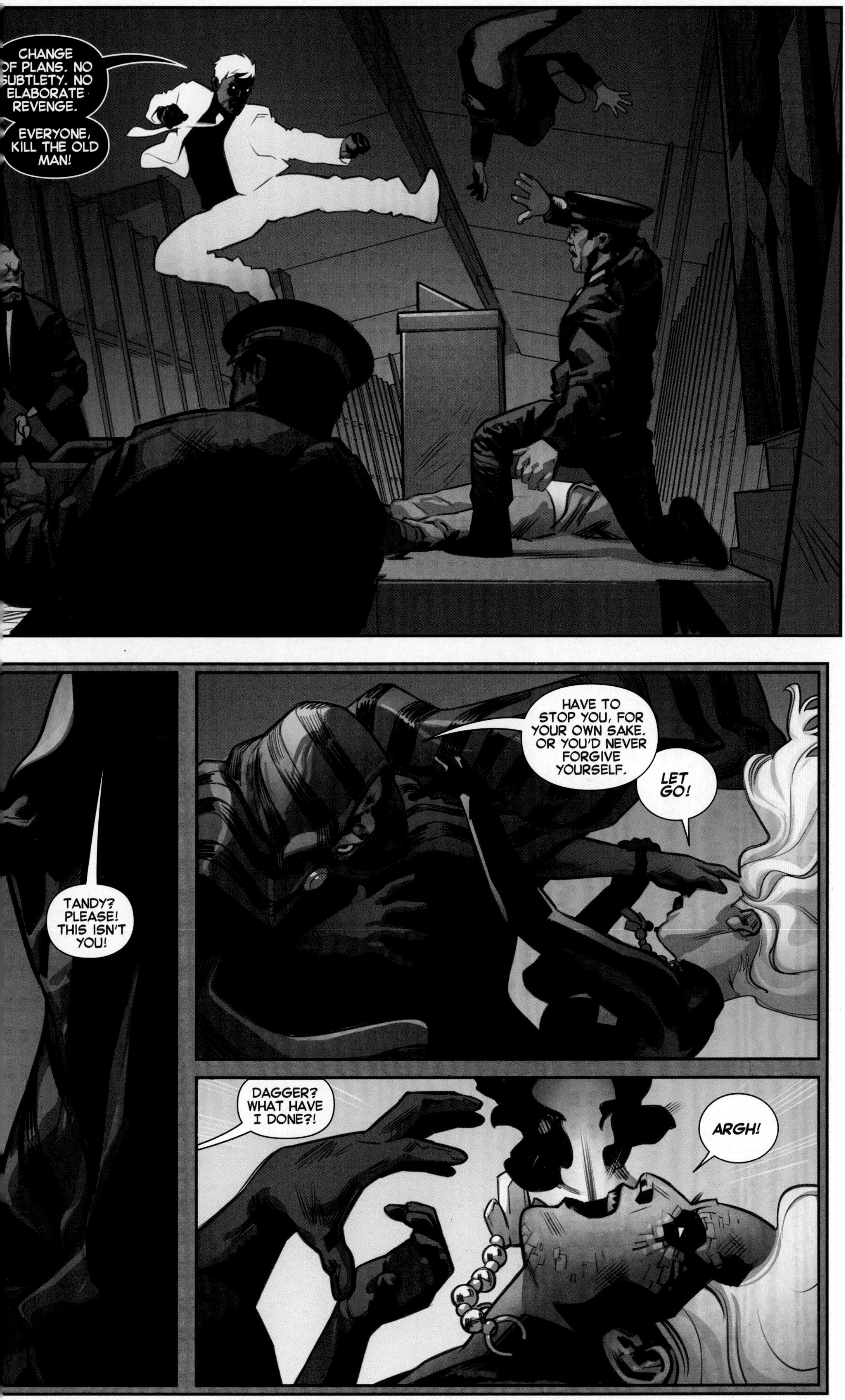
CHANGE OF PLANS. NO SUBTLETY. NO ELABORATE REVENGE.
EVERYONE, KILL THE OLD MAN!
TANDY? PLEASE! THIS ISN'T YOU!
HAVE TO STOP YOU, FOR YOUR OWN SAKE. OR YOU'D NEVER FORGIVE YOURSELF.
LET GO!
DAGGER? WHAT HAVE I DONE?!
ARGH!

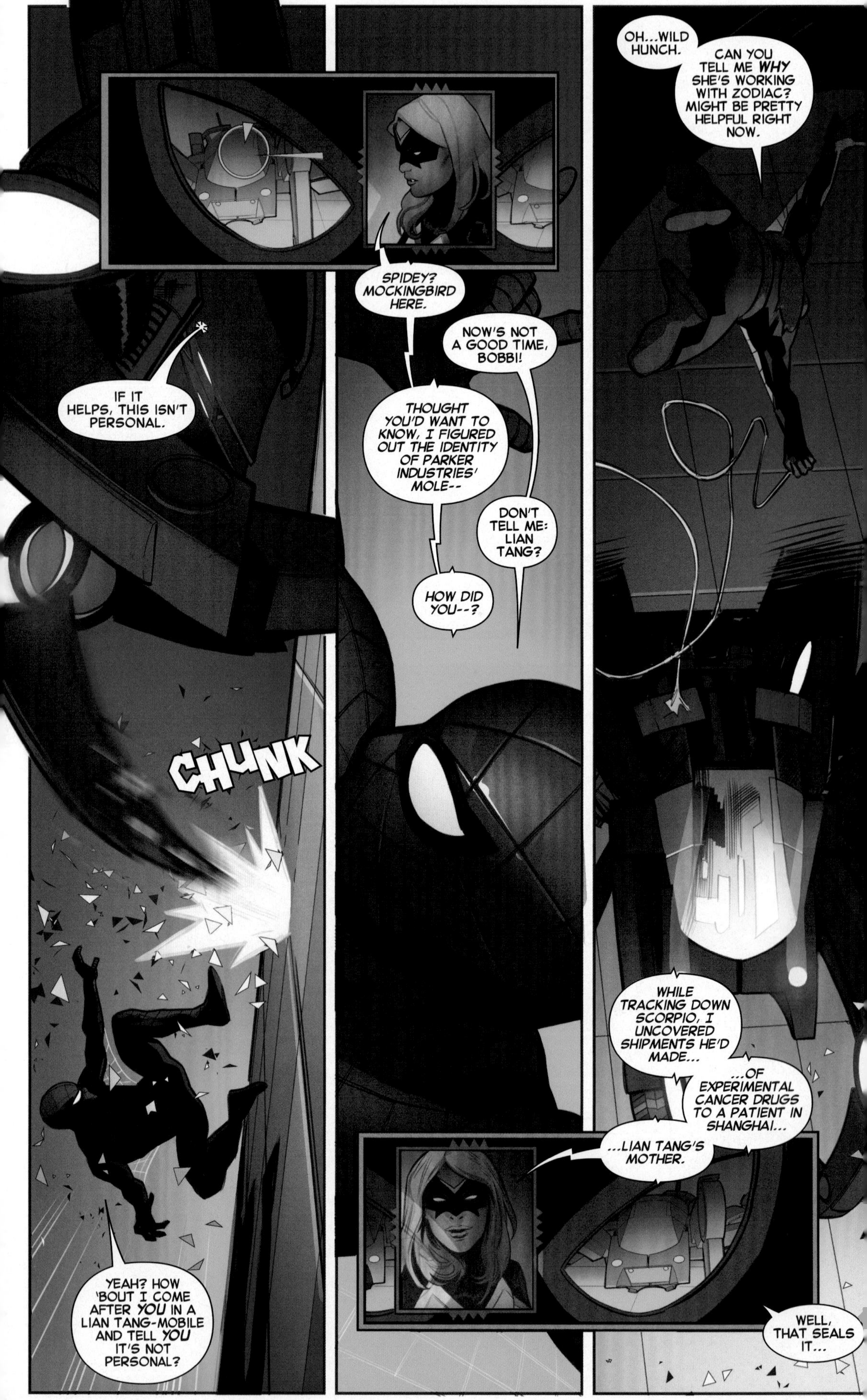
IF IT HELPS, THIS ISN'T PERSONAL.
CHUNK
YEAH? HOW 'BOUT I COME AFTER YOU IN A LIAN TANG-MOBILE AND TELL YOU IT'S NOT PERSONAL?
SPIDEY? MOCKINGBIRD HERE.
NOW'S NOT A GOOD TIME, BOBBI!
THOUGHT YOU'D WANT TO KNOW, I FIGURED OUT THE IDENTITY OF PARKER INDUSTRIES' MOLE--
DON'T TELL ME: LIAN TANG?
HOW DID YOU--?
OH...WILD HUNCH.
CAN YOU TELL ME WHY SHE'S WORKING WITH ZODIAC? MIGHT BE PRETTY HELPFUL RIGHT NOW.
WHILE TRACKING DOWN SCORPIO, I UNCOVERED SHIPMENTS HE'D MADE...
...OF EXPERIMENTAL CANCER DRUGS TO A PATIENT IN SHANGHAI...
...LIAN TANG'S MOTHER.
WELL, THAT SEALS IT...

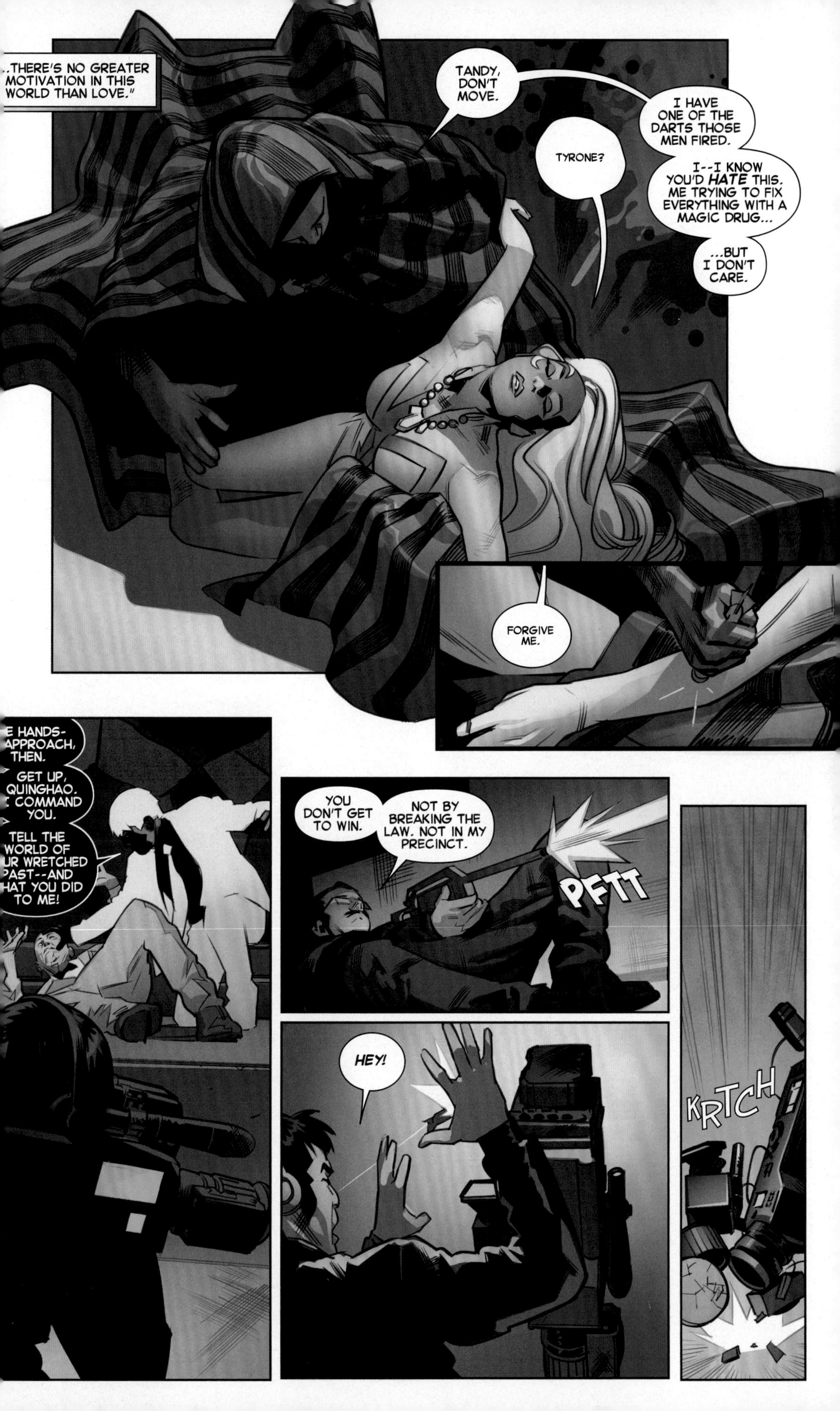
..THERE'S NO GREATER MOTIVATION IN THIS WORLD THAN LOVE."
TANDY, DON'T MOVE.
TYRONE?
I HAVE ONE OF THE DARTS THOSE MEN FIRED.
I--I KNOW YOU'D HATE THIS. ME TRYING TO FIX EVERYTHING WITH A MAGIC DRUG...
...BUT I DON'T CARE.
FORGIVE ME.
E HANDS- APPROACH, THEN.
GET UP, QUINGHAO. COMMAND YOU.
TELL THE WORLD OF UR WRETCHED PAST--AND HAT YOU DID TO ME!
YOU DON'T GET TO WIN.
NOT BY BREAKING THE LAW. NOT IN MY PRECINCT.
PFTT
HEY!
KRTCH

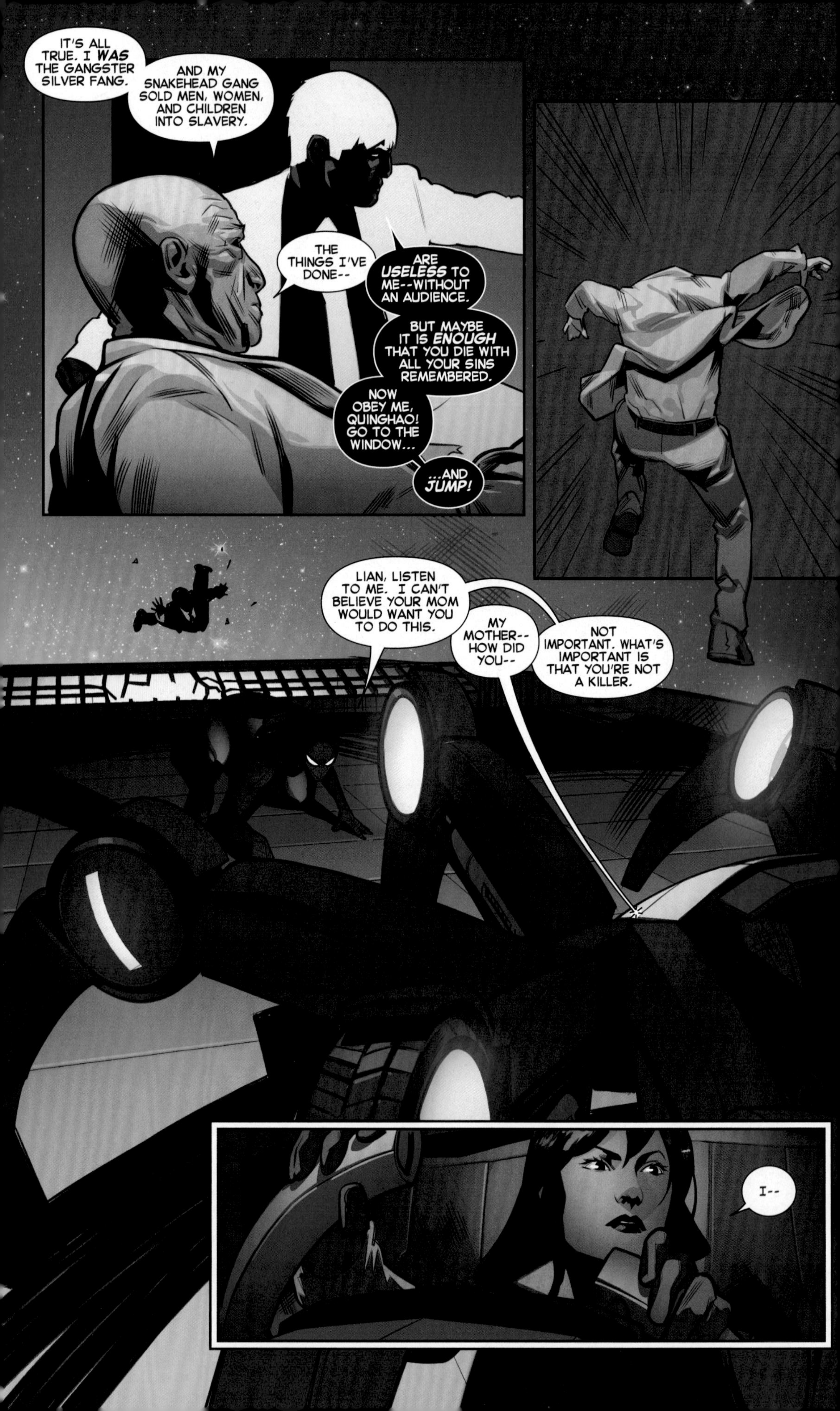
IT'S ALL TRUE. I WAS THE GANGSTER SILVER FANG.
AND MY SNAKEHEAD GANG SOLD MEN, WOMEN, AND CHILDREN INTO SLAVERY.
THE THINGS I'VE DONE--
ARE USELESS TO ME--WITHOUT AN AUDIENCE.
BUT MAYBE IT IS ENOUGH THAT YOU DIE WITH ALL YOUR SINS REMEMBERED.
NOW OBEY ME, QUINGHAO! GO TO THE WINDOW...
...AND JUMP!
LIAN, LISTEN TO ME. I CAN'T BELIEVE YOUR MOM WOULD WANT YOU TO DO THIS.
MY MOTHER--HOW DID YOU--
NOT IMPORTANT. WHAT'S IMPORTANT IS THAT YOU'RE NOT A KILLER.
I--

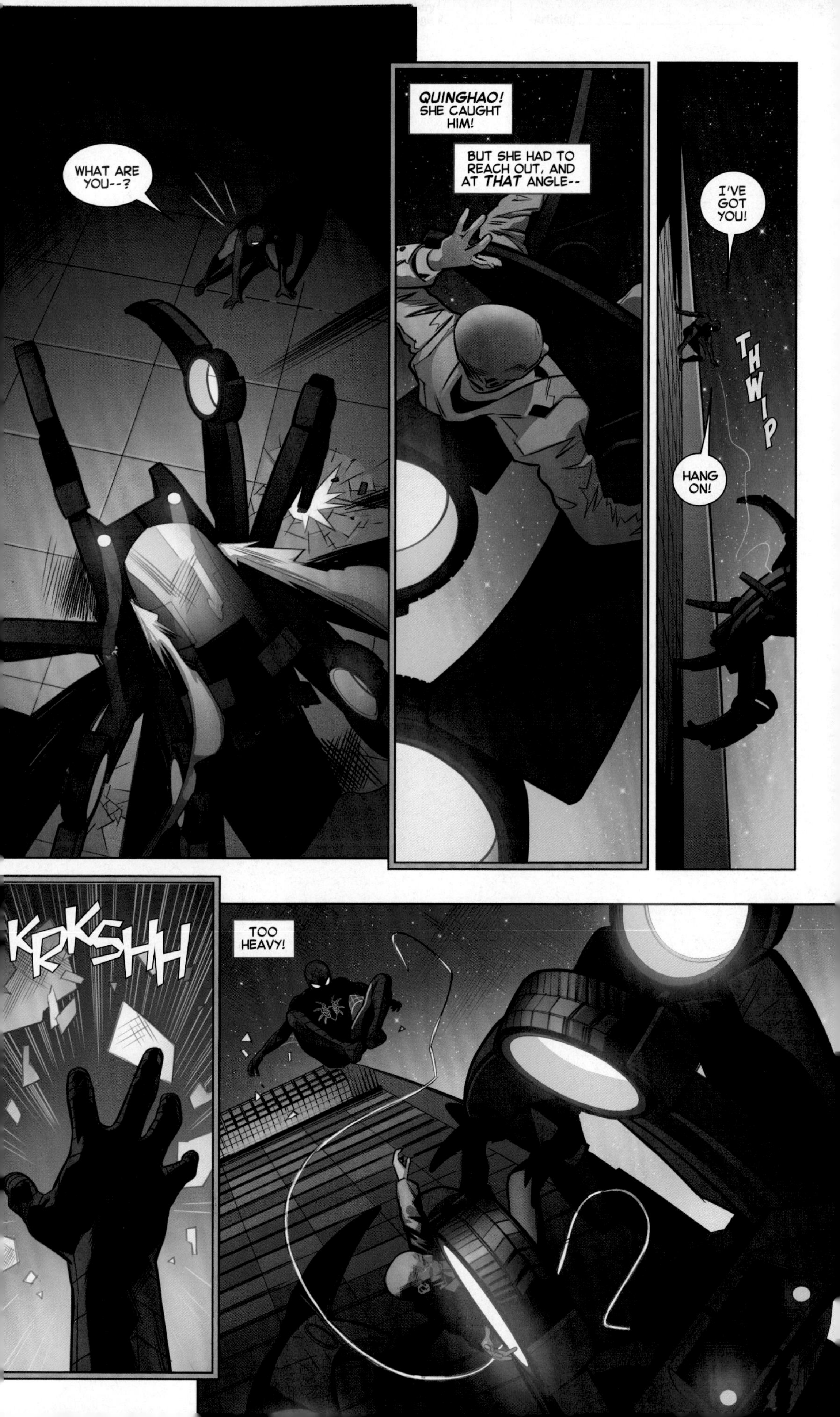
WHAT ARE YOU--?
QUINGHAO! SHE CAUGHT HIM!
BUT SHE HAD TO REACH OUT, AND AT THAT ANGLE--
I'VE GOT YOU!
THWIP
HANG ON!
KRKSHH
TOO HEAVY!

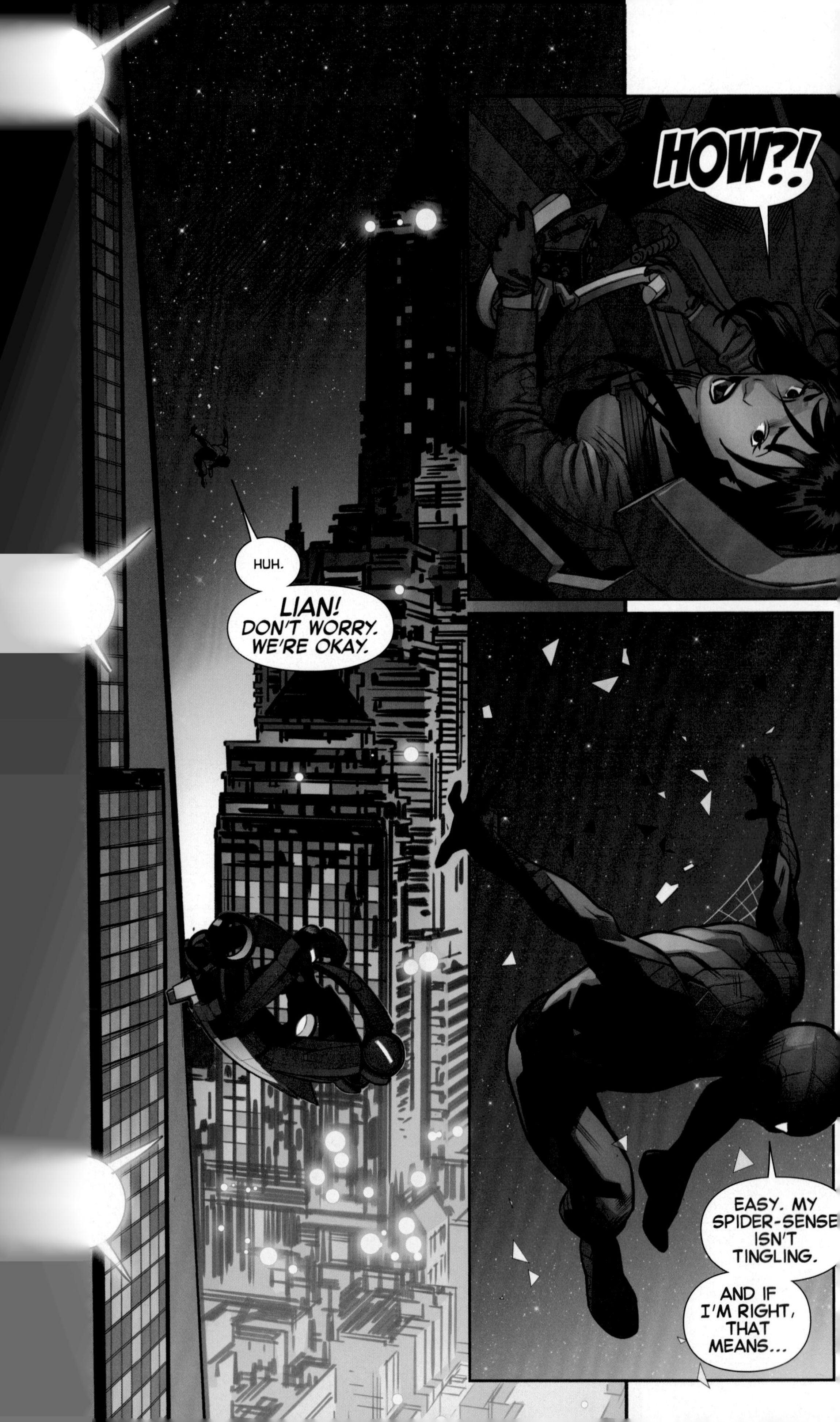
HOW?!
HUH.
LIAN! DON'T WORRY. WE'RE OKAY.
EASY. MY SPIDER-SENSE ISN'T TINGLING.
AND IF I'M RIGHT, THAT MEANS...

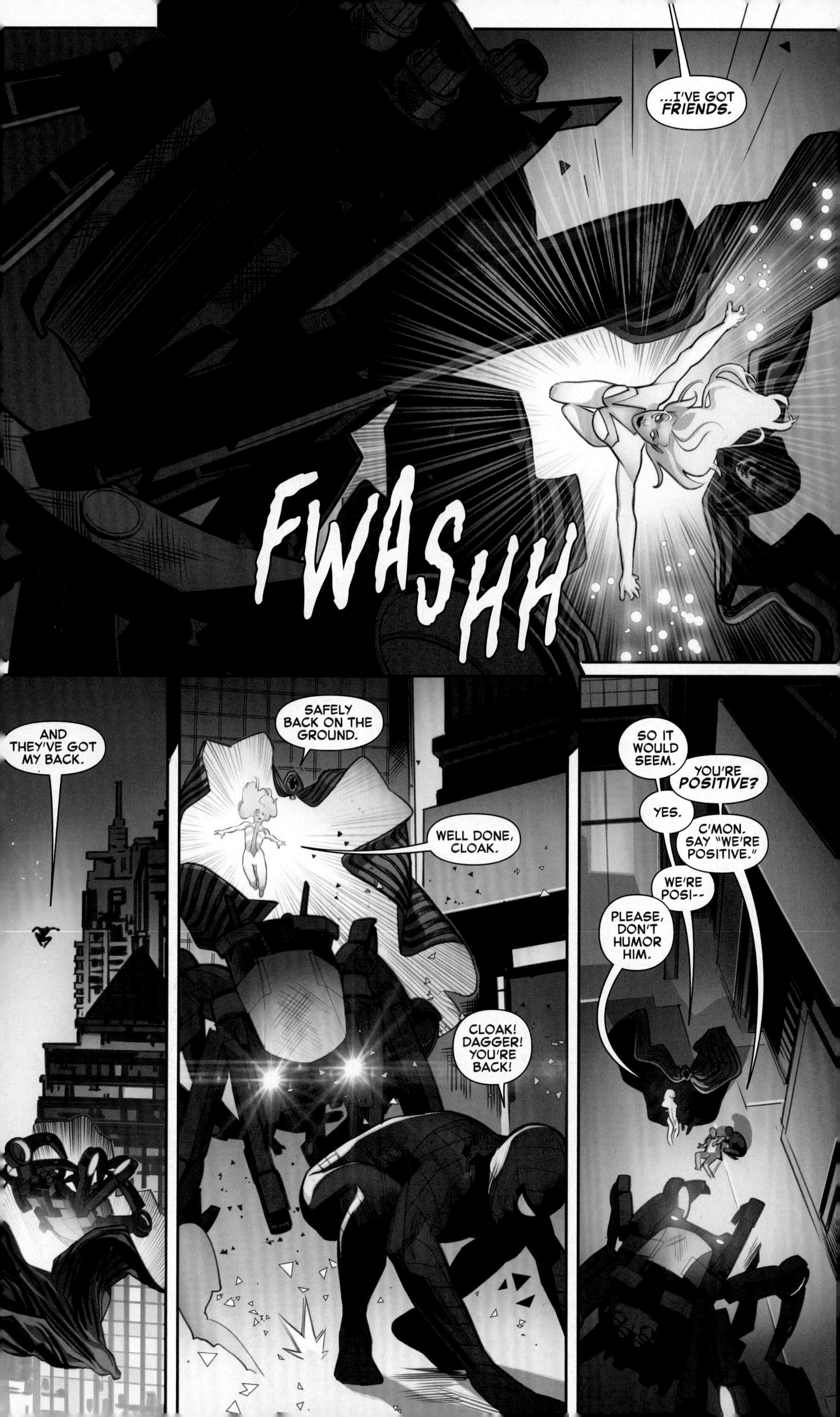
...I'VE GOT FRIENDS.
FWASHH
AND THEY'VE GOT MY BACK.
SAFELY BACK ON THE GROUND.
WELL DONE, CLOAK.
CLOAK! DAGGER! YOU'RE BACK!
SO IT WOULD SEEM.
YOU'RE POSITIVE?
YES.
C'MON. SAY "WE'RE POSITIVE."
WE'RE POSI--
PLEASE, DON'T HUMOR HIM.

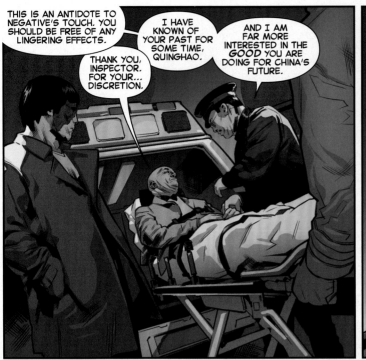

THIS IS AN ANTIDOTE TO NEGATIVE'S TOUCH. YOU SHOULD BE FREE OF ANY LINGERING EFFECTS.

THANK YOU, INSPECTOR. FOR YOUR... DISCRETION.

I HAVE KNOWN OF YOUR PAST FOR SOME TIME, QUINGHAO.

AND I AM FAR MORE INTERESTED IN THE *GOOD* YOU ARE DOING FOR CHINA'S FUTURE.

YOU ARE A LUCKY MAN, QUINGHAO. SOME OF US CARRY OUR MISTAKES WITH US FOR ALL TO SEE. MAYBE THAT'S HOW IT SHOULD BE.

I WON'T BE SHARING MY HARD WORK WITH A MAN LIKE YOU.

GOODBYE, SHEN.

WHAT HAPPENS TO ME NOW?

I'M FIRED? GOING TO JAIL? WHAT? JUST TELL ME MOTHER WILL BE--

LIAN, STOP...

I GAVE ZODIAC OUR SECURITY CODES. I TRIED TO *KILL* YOU. I--

I UNDERSTAND.

I KNOW WHAT IT MEANS TO RISK EVERYTHING TO HELP FAMILY. SO DOES PETER.

WE'D BE HYPOCRITES IF WE DIDN'T GIVE YOU A CHANCE...

...TO *WORK* WITH US. WE'RE GOING TO HELP YOUR MOM. AND YOU'RE GOING TO HELP US TAKE DOWN ZODIAC.

I WAS ONLY THEIR MOLE.

FINE. LET'S SEE WHAT YOU CAN "DIG UP" FOR THE GOOD GUYS.

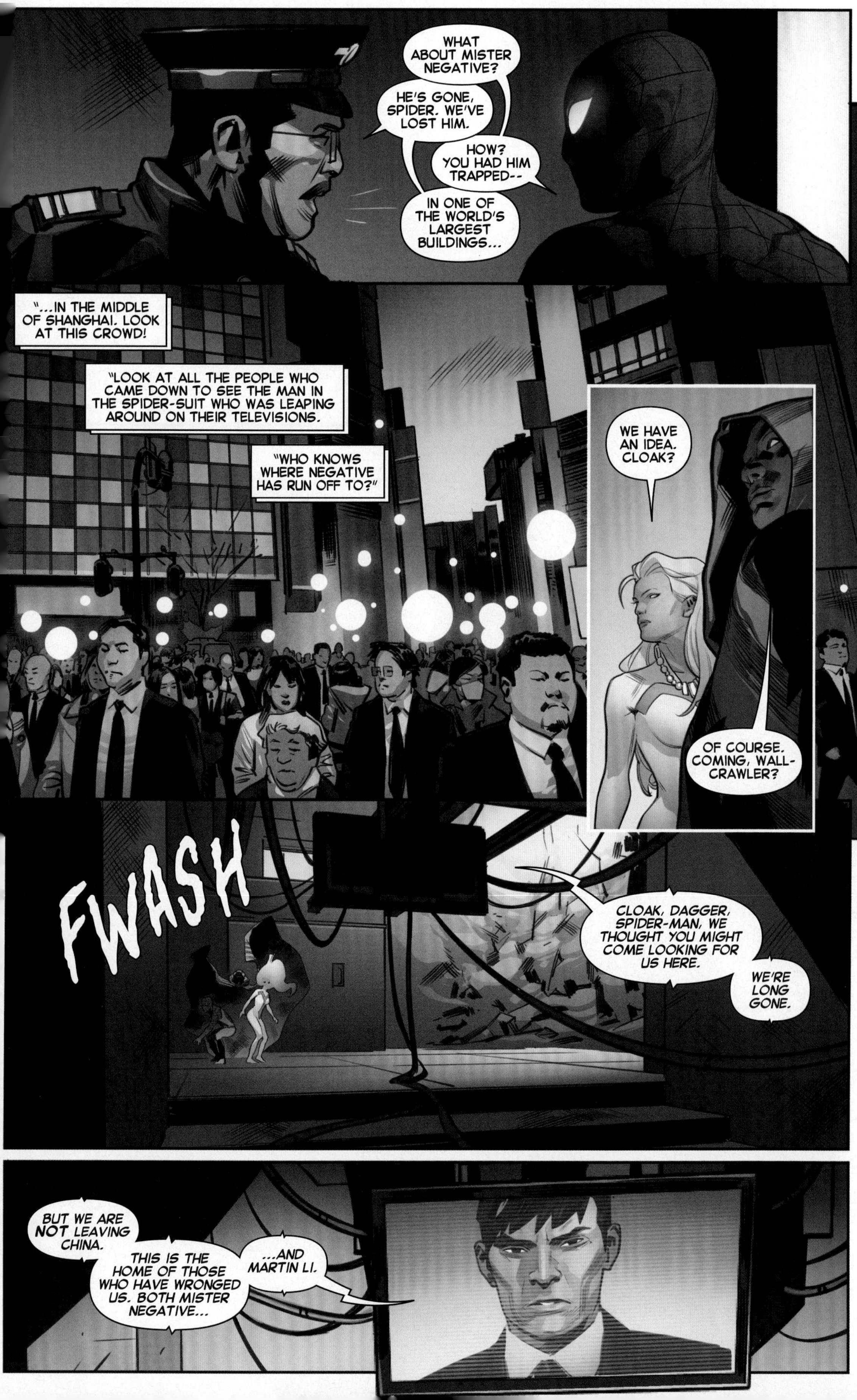
WHAT ABOUT MISTER NEGATIVE?
HE'S GONE, SPIDER. WE'VE LOST HIM.
HOW? YOU HAD HIM TRAPPED--
IN ONE OF THE WORLD'S LARGEST BUILDINGS...
"...IN THE MIDDLE OF SHANGHAI. LOOK AT THIS CROWD!
"LOOK AT ALL THE PEOPLE WHO CAME DOWN TO SEE THE MAN IN THE SPIDER-SUIT WHO WAS LEAPING AROUND ON THEIR TELEVISIONS.
"WHO KNOWS WHERE NEGATIVE HAS RUN OFF TO?"
WE HAVE AN IDEA. CLOAK?
OF COURSE. COMING, WALL-CRAWLER?
FWASH
CLOAK, DAGGER, SPIDER-MAN, WE THOUGHT YOU MIGHT COME LOOKING FOR US HERE.
WE'RE LONG GONE.
BUT WE ARE NOT LEAVING CHINA.
THIS IS THE HOME OF THOSE WHO HAVE WRONGED US. BOTH MISTER NEGATIVE...
...AND MARTIN LI.

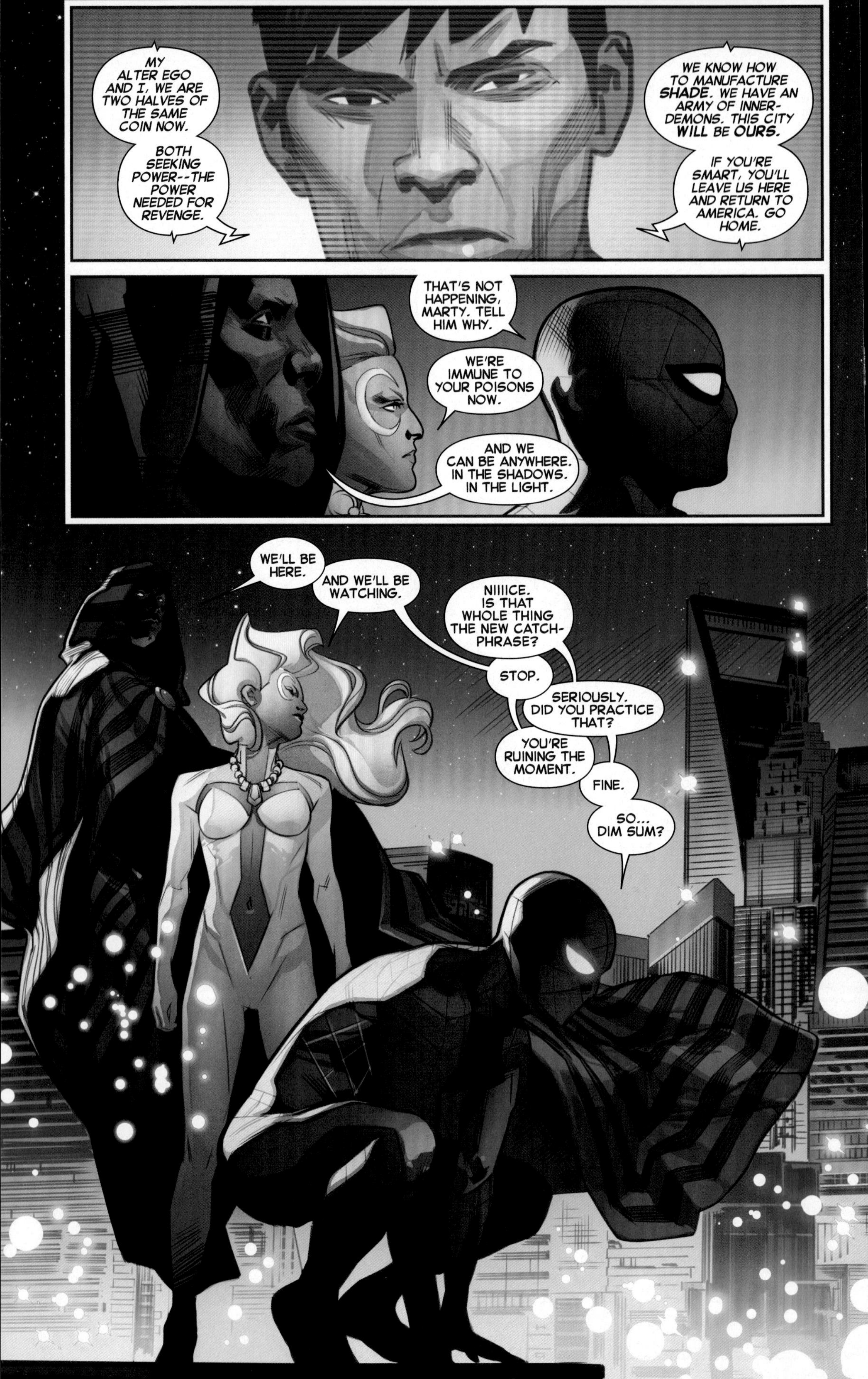
MY ALTER EGO AND I, WE ARE TWO HALVES OF THE SAME COIN NOW.
BOTH SEEKING POWER--THE POWER NEEDED FOR REVENGE.
WE KNOW HOW TO MANUFACTURE SHADE. WE HAVE AN ARMY OF INNER-DEMONS. THIS CITY WILL BE OURS.
IF YOU'RE SMART, YOU'LL LEAVE US HERE AND RETURN TO AMERICA. GO HOME.
THAT'S NOT HAPPENING, MARTY. TELL HIM WHY.
WE'RE IMMUNE TO YOUR POISONS NOW.
AND WE CAN BE ANYWHERE. IN THE SHADOWS. IN THE LIGHT.
WE'LL BE HERE.
AND WE'LL BE WATCHING.
NIIIICE. IS THAT WHOLE THING THE NEW CATCH-PHRASE?
STOP.
SERIOUSLY. DID YOU PRACTICE THAT?
YOU'RE RUINING THE MOMENT.
FINE.
SO... DIM SUM?

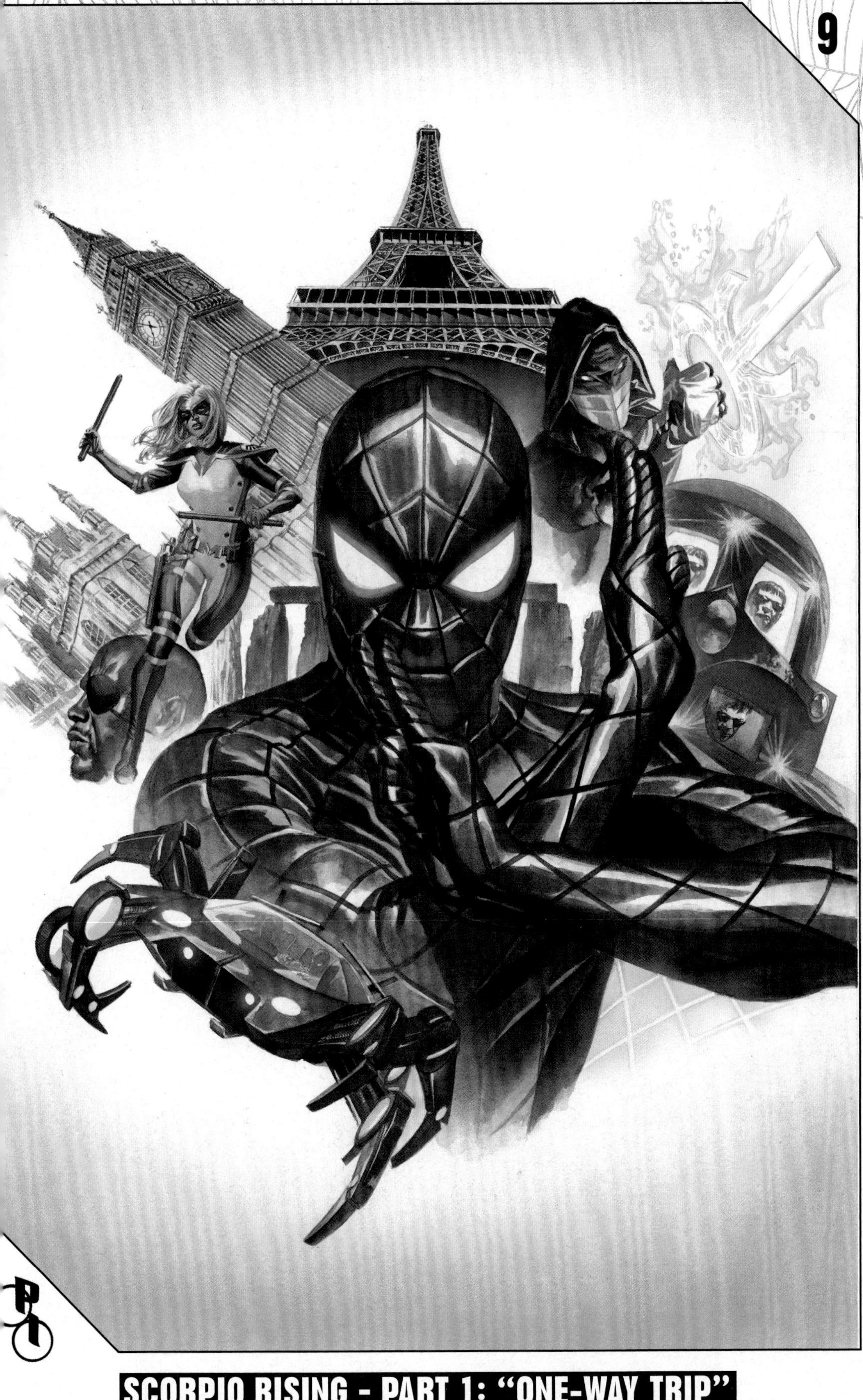

SCORPIO RISING - PART 1: "ONE-WAY TRIP"

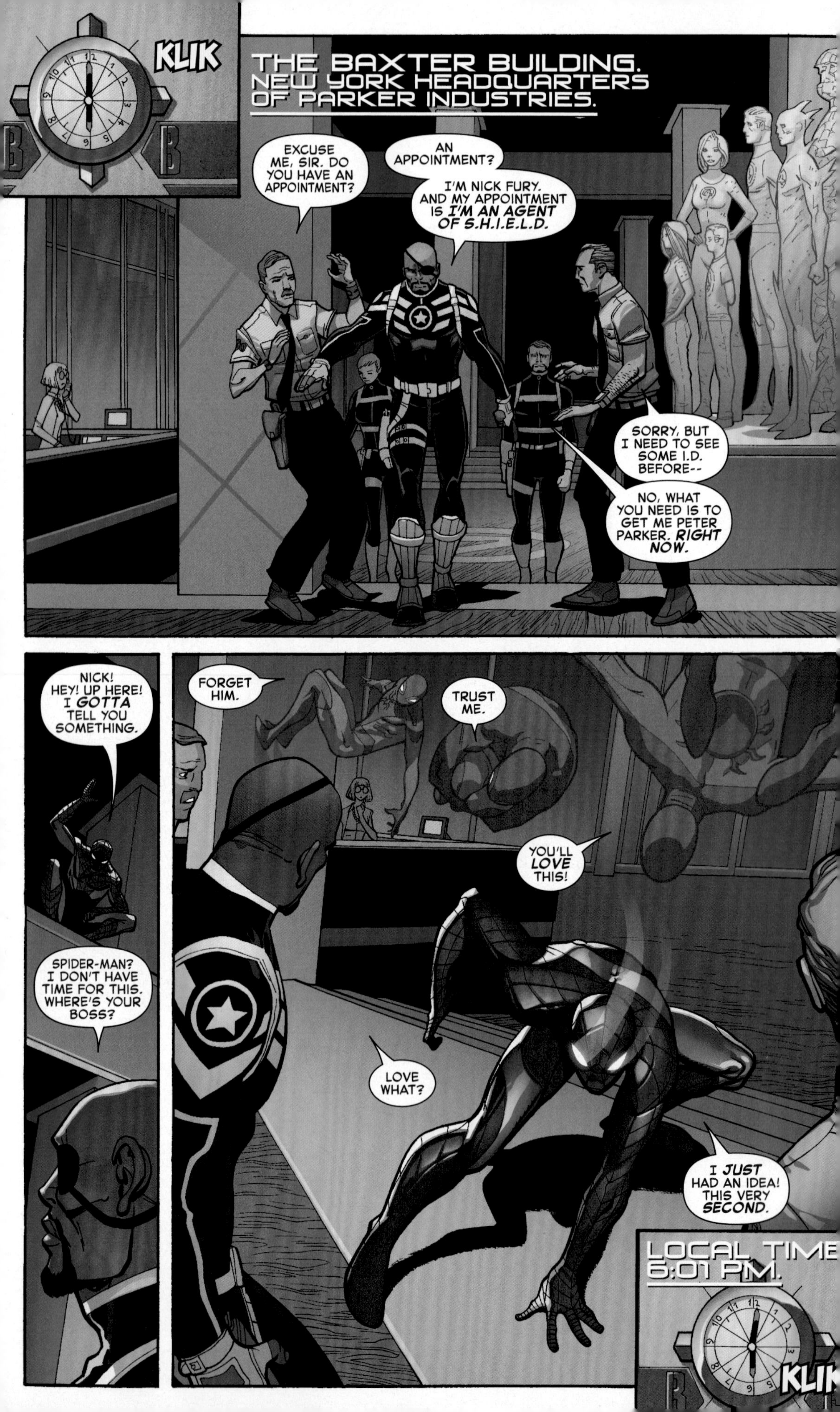
KLIK
THE BAXTER BUILDING. NEW YORK HEADQUARTERS OF PARKER INDUSTRIES.
EXCUSE ME, SIR. DO YOU HAVE AN APPOINTMENT?
AN APPOINTMENT?
I'M NICK FURY. AND MY APPOINTMENT IS I'M AN AGENT OF S.H.I.E.L.D.
SORRY, BUT I NEED TO SEE SOME I.D. BEFORE--
NO, WHAT YOU NEED IS TO GET ME PETER PARKER. RIGHT NOW.
NICK! HEY! UP HERE! I GOTTA TELL YOU SOMETHING.
SPIDER-MAN? I DON'T HAVE TIME FOR THIS. WHERE'S YOUR BOSS?
FORGET HIM.
TRUST ME.
YOU'LL LOVE THIS!
LOVE WHAT?
I JUST HAD AN IDEA! THIS VERY SECOND.
LOCAL TIME 6:01 PM.
KLIK

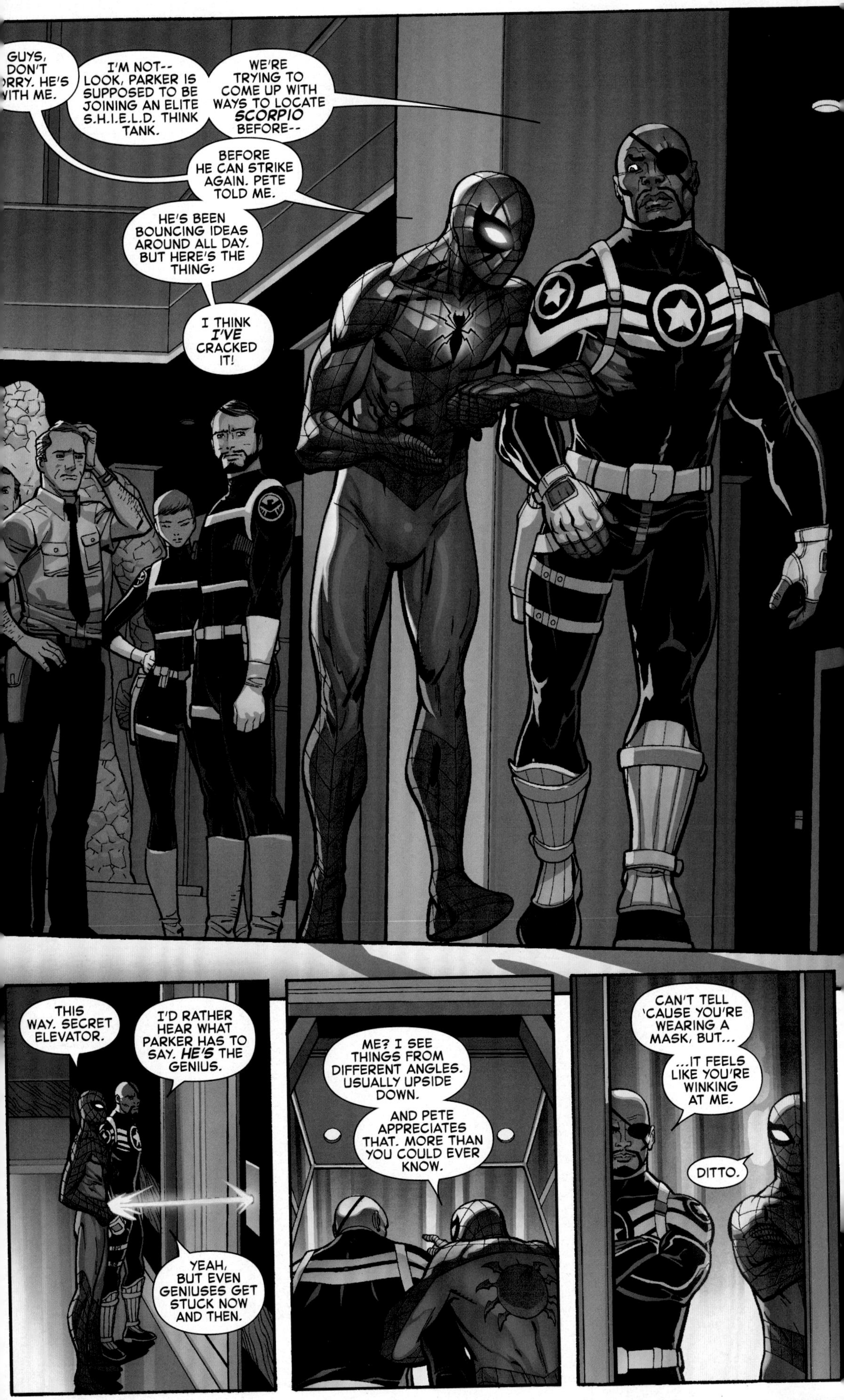
GUYS, DON'T ORRY. HE'S WITH ME.
I'M NOT-- LOOK, PARKER IS SUPPOSED TO BE JOINING AN ELITE S.H.I.E.L.D. THINK TANK.
WE'RE TRYING TO COME UP WITH WAYS TO LOCATE SCORPIO BEFORE--
BEFORE HE CAN STRIKE AGAIN. PETE TOLD ME.
HE'S BEEN BOUNCING IDEAS AROUND ALL DAY. BUT HERE'S THE THING:
I THINK I'VE CRACKED IT!
THIS WAY. SECRET ELEVATOR.
I'D RATHER HEAR WHAT PARKER HAS TO SAY. HE'S THE GENIUS.
YEAH, BUT EVEN GENIUSES GET STUCK NOW AND THEN.
ME? I SEE THINGS FROM DIFFERENT ANGLES. USUALLY UPSIDE DOWN.
AND PETE APPRECIATES THAT. MORE THAN YOU COULD EVER KNOW.
CAN'T TELL 'CAUSE YOU'RE WEARING A MASK, BUT...
...IT FEELS LIKE YOU'RE WINKING AT ME.
DITTO.

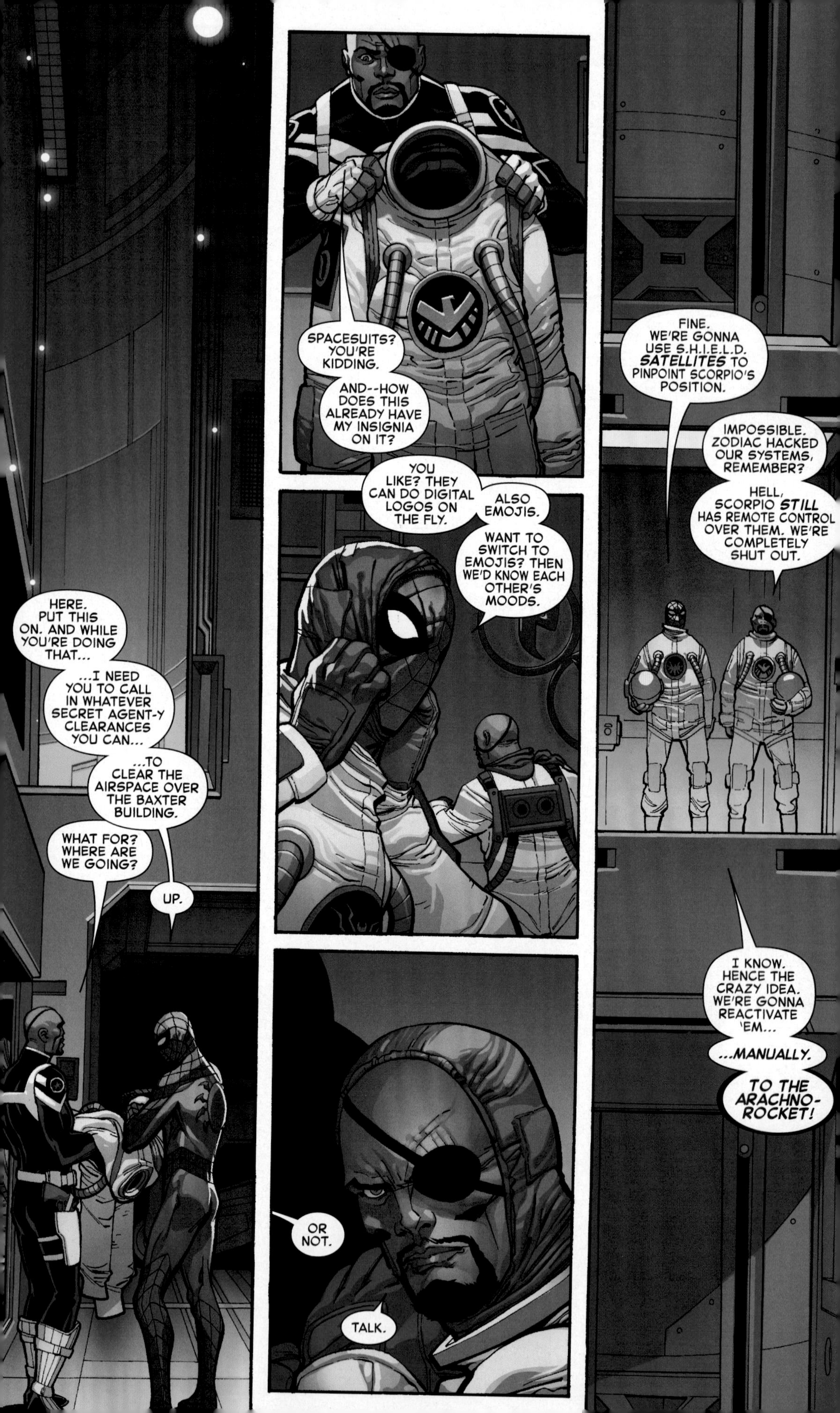
HERE. PUT THIS ON. AND WHILE YOU'RE DOING THAT...
...I NEED YOU TO CALL IN WHATEVER SECRET AGENT-Y CLEARANCES YOU CAN...
...TO CLEAR THE AIRSPACE OVER THE BAXTER BUILDING.
WHAT FOR? WHERE ARE WE GOING?
UP.
SPACESUITS? YOU'RE KIDDING.
AND--HOW DOES THIS ALREADY HAVE MY INSIGNIA ON IT?
YOU LIKE? THEY CAN DO DIGITAL LOGOS ON THE FLY.
ALSO EMOJIS.
WANT TO SWITCH TO EMOJIS? THEN WE'D KNOW EACH OTHER'S MOODS.
OR NOT.
TALK.
FINE. WE'RE GONNA USE S.H.I.E.L.D. SATELLITES TO PINPOINT SCORPIO'S POSITION.
IMPOSSIBLE. ZODIAC HACKED OUR SYSTEMS, REMEMBER?
HELL, SCORPIO STILL HAS REMOTE CONTROL OVER THEM. WE'RE COMPLETELY SHUT OUT.
I KNOW. HENCE THE CRAZY IDEA. WE'RE GONNA REACTIVATE 'EM...
...MANUALLY.
TO THE ARACHNO-ROCKET!

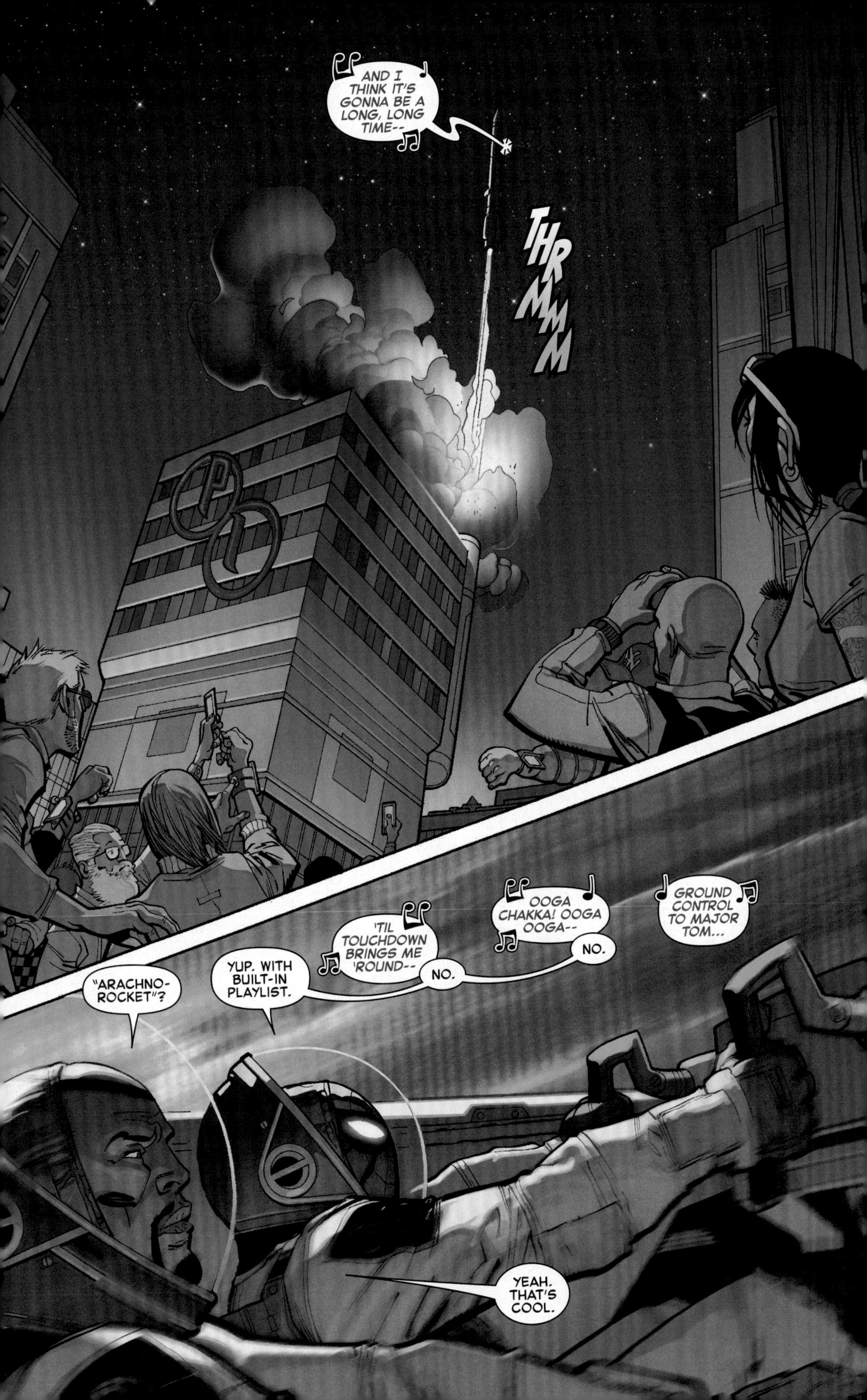
AND I THINK IT'S GONNA BE A LONG, LONG TIME--
THRMMM
"ARACHNO-ROCKET"?
YUP. WITH BUILT-IN PLAYLIST.
'TIL TOUCHDOWN BRINGS ME 'ROUND--
NO.
OOGA CHAKKA! OOGA OOGA--
NO.
GROUND CONTROL TO MAJOR TOM...
YEAH. THAT'S COOL.

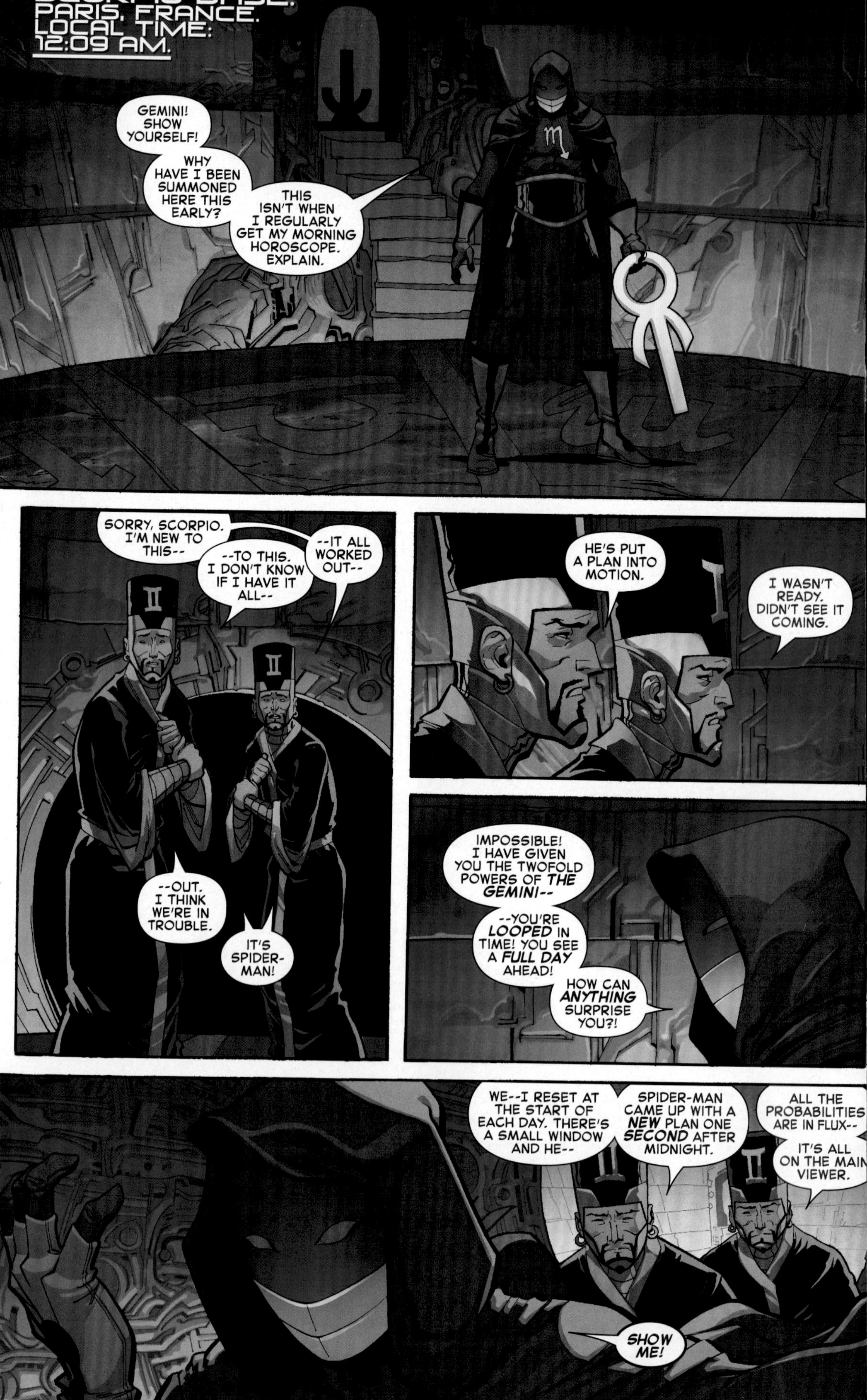

PARIS, FRANCE. LOCAL TIME: 12:09 AM.
GEMINI! SHOW YOURSELF!
WHY HAVE I BEEN SUMMONED HERE THIS EARLY?
THIS ISN'T WHEN I REGULARLY GET MY MORNING HOROSCOPE. EXPLAIN.
SORRY, SCORPIO. I'M NEW TO THIS--
--TO THIS. I DON'T KNOW IF I HAVE IT ALL--
--IT ALL WORKED OUT--
--OUT. I THINK WE'RE IN TROUBLE.
IT'S SPIDER-MAN!
HE'S PUT A PLAN INTO MOTION.
I WASN'T READY. DIDN'T SEE IT COMING.
IMPOSSIBLE! I HAVE GIVEN YOU THE TWOFOLD POWERS OF THE GEMINI--
--YOU'RE LOOPED IN TIME! YOU SEE A FULL DAY AHEAD!
HOW CAN ANYTHING SURPRISE YOU?!
WE--I RESET AT THE START OF EACH DAY. THERE'S A SMALL WINDOW AND HE--
SPIDER-MAN CAME UP WITH A NEW PLAN ONE SECOND AFTER MIDNIGHT.
ALL THE PROBABILITIES ARE IN FLUX--
IT'S ALL ON THE MAIN VIEWER.
SHOW ME!

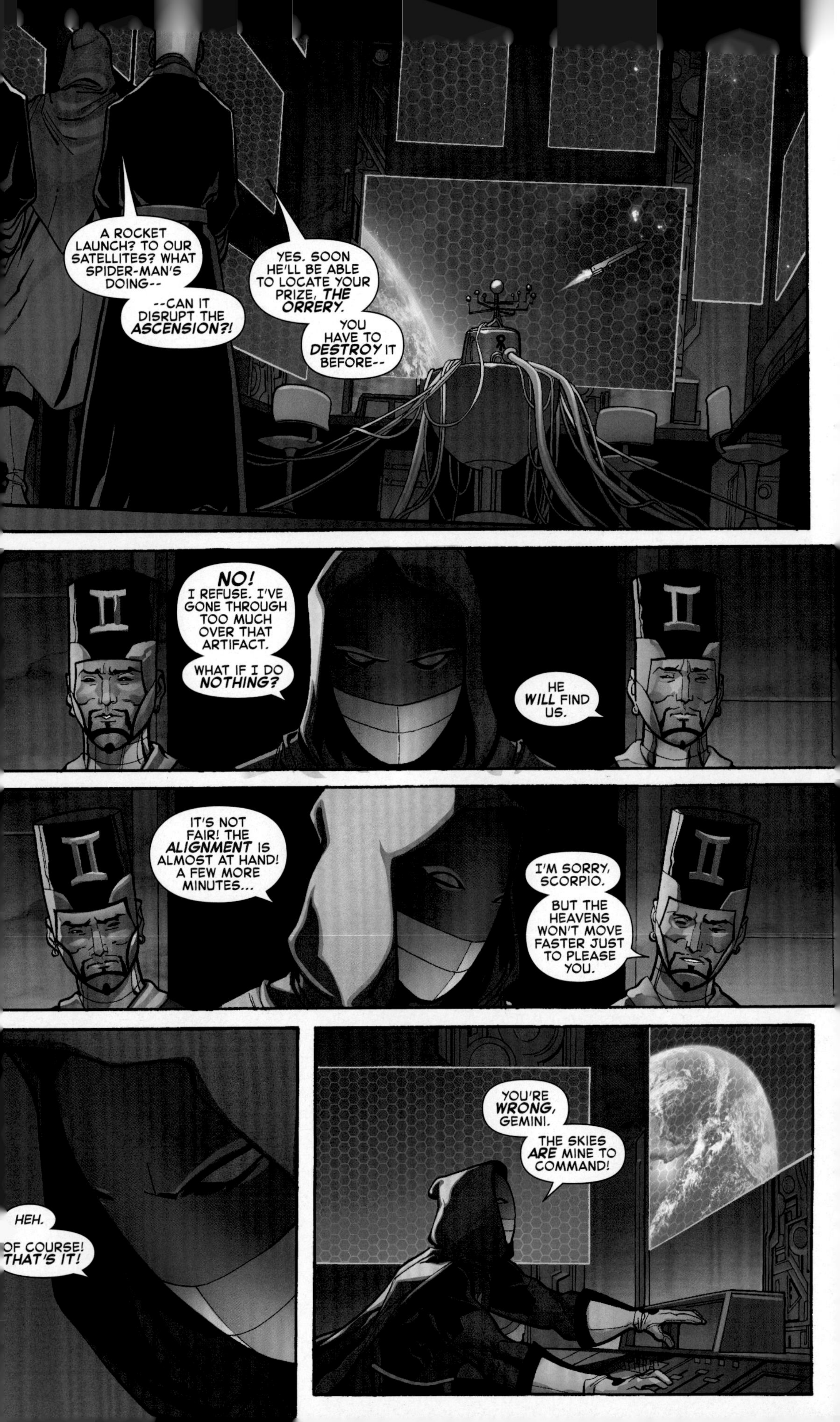

A ROCKET LAUNCH? TO OUR SATELLITES? WHAT SPIDER-MAN'S DOING--
--CAN IT DISRUPT THE ASCENSION?!
YES. SOON HE'LL BE ABLE TO LOCATE YOUR PRIZE, THE ORRERY.
YOU HAVE TO DESTROY IT BEFORE--
NO! I REFUSE. I'VE GONE THROUGH TOO MUCH OVER THAT ARTIFACT.
WHAT IF I DO NOTHING?
HE WILL FIND US.
IT'S NOT FAIR! THE ALIGNMENT IS ALMOST AT HAND! A FEW MORE MINUTES...
I'M SORRY, SCORPIO.
BUT THE HEAVENS WON'T MOVE FASTER JUST TO PLEASE YOU.
HEH.
OF COURSE! THAT'S IT!
YOU'RE WRONG, GEMINI.
THE SKIES ARE MINE TO COMMAND!

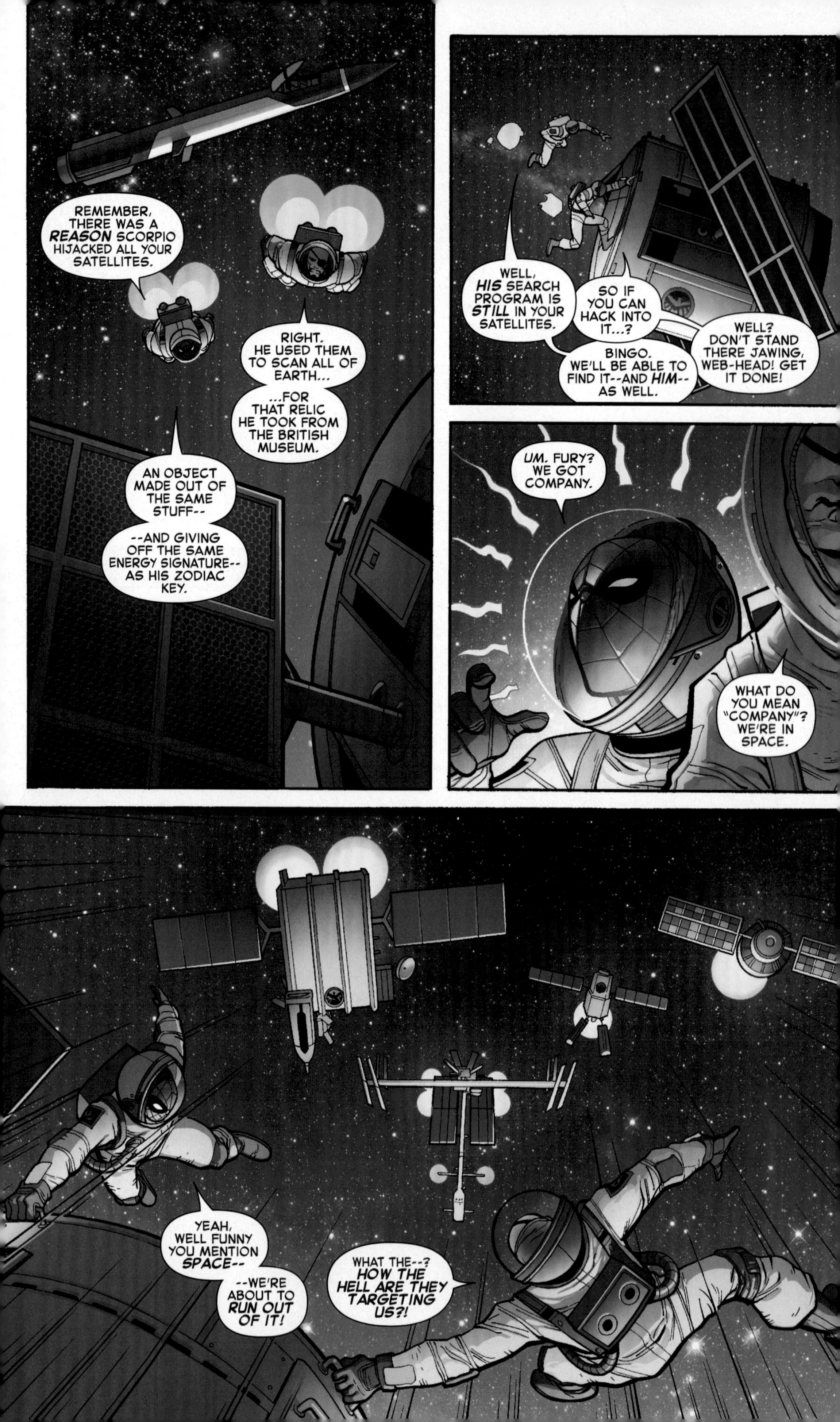

REMEMBER, THERE WAS A *REASON* SCORPIO HIJACKED ALL YOUR SATELLITES.
RIGHT. HE USED THEM TO SCAN ALL OF EARTH...
...FOR THAT RELIC HE TOOK FROM THE BRITISH MUSEUM.
AN OBJECT MADE OUT OF THE SAME STUFF--
--AND GIVING OFF THE SAME ENERGY SIGNATURE--AS HIS ZODIAC KEY.
WELL, *HIS* SEARCH PROGRAM IS *STILL* IN YOUR SATELLITES.
SO IF YOU CAN HACK INTO IT...?
BINGO. WE'LL BE ABLE TO FIND IT--AND *HIM*--AS WELL.
WELL? DON'T STAND THERE JAWING, WEB-HEAD! GET IT DONE!
UM. FURY? WE GOT COMPANY.
WHAT DO YOU MEAN "COMPANY"? WE'RE IN SPACE.
YEAH, WELL FUNNY YOU MENTION *SPACE*--
--WE'RE ABOUT TO *RUN OUT OF IT!*
WHAT THE--? *HOW THE HELL ARE THEY TARGETING US?!*

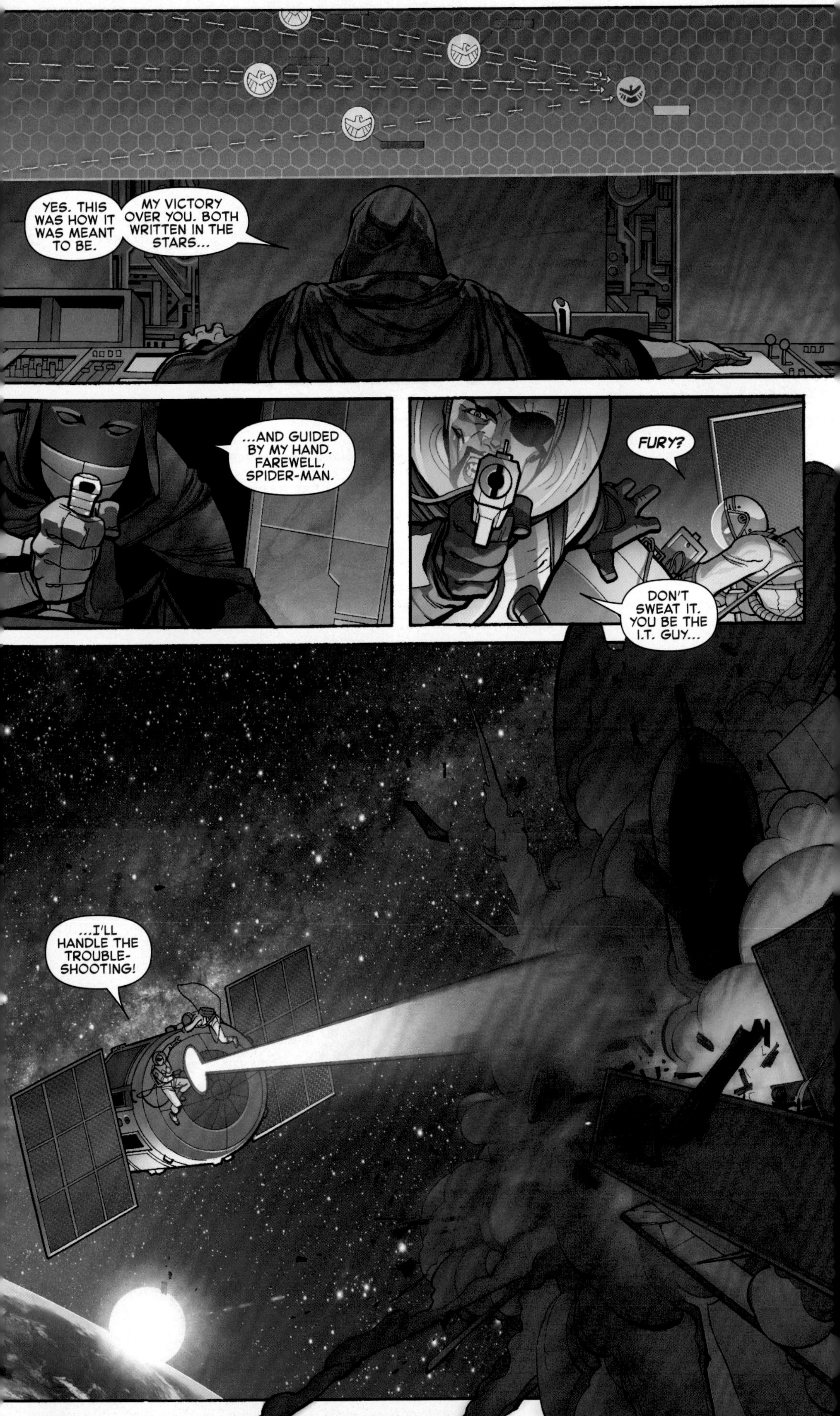
YES. THIS WAS HOW IT WAS MEANT TO BE.
MY VICTORY OVER YOU. BOTH WRITTEN IN THE STARS...
...AND GUIDED BY MY HAND. FAREWELL, SPIDER-MAN.
FURY?
DON'T SWEAT IT. YOU BE THE I.T. GUY...
...I'LL HANDLE THE TROUBLE-SHOOTING!

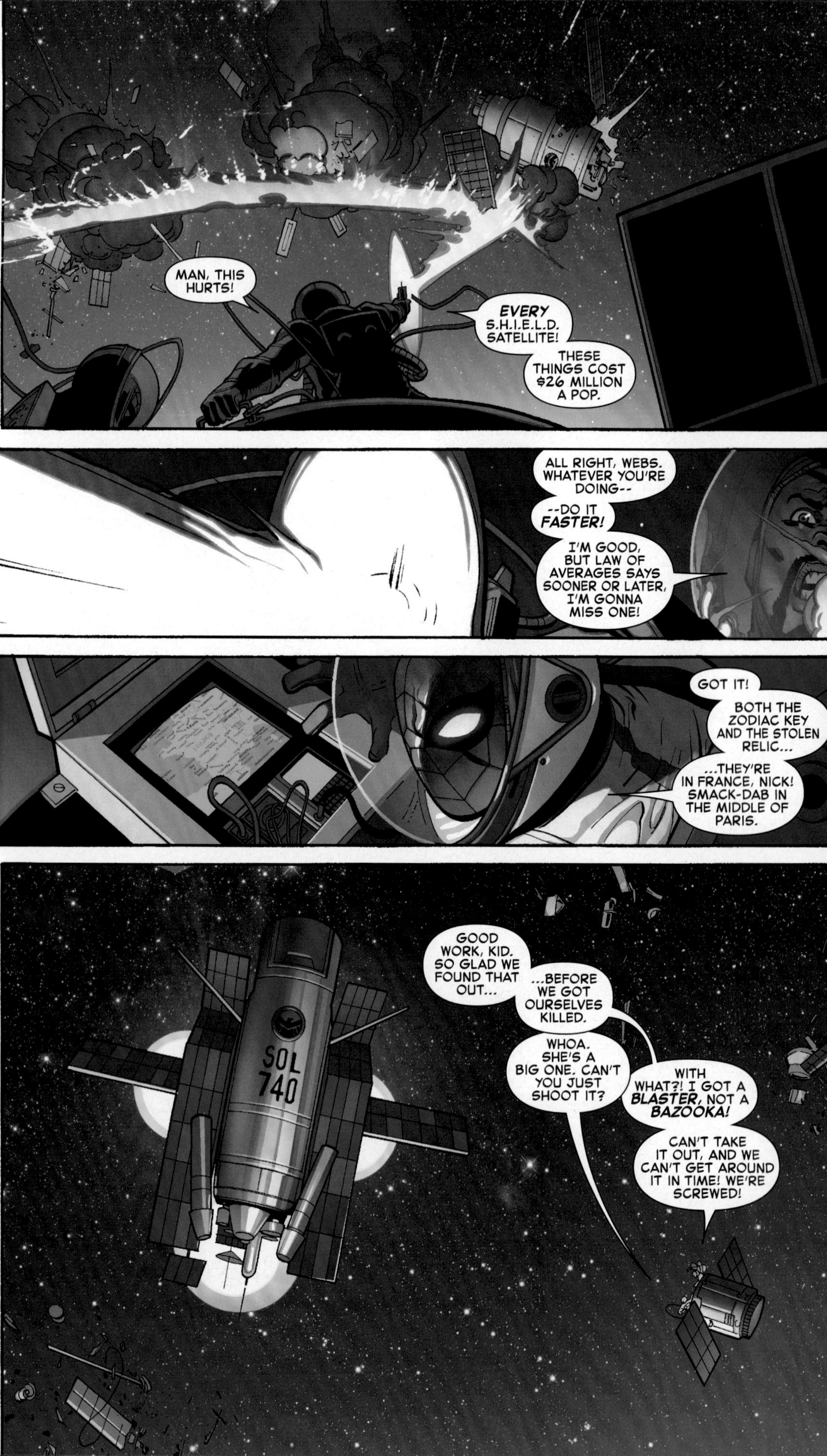
MAN, THIS HURTS!
EVERY S.H.I.E.L.D. SATELLITE!
THESE THINGS COST $26 MILLION A POP.
ALL RIGHT, WEBS. WHATEVER YOU'RE DOING--
--DO IT FASTER!
I'M GOOD, BUT LAW OF AVERAGES SAYS SOONER OR LATER, I'M GONNA MISS ONE!
GOT IT!
BOTH THE ZODIAC KEY AND THE STOLEN RELIC...
...THEY'RE IN FRANCE, NICK! SMACK-DAB IN THE MIDDLE OF PARIS.
GOOD WORK, KID. SO GLAD WE FOUND THAT OUT...
...BEFORE WE GOT OURSELVES KILLED.
WHOA. SHE'S A BIG ONE. CAN'T YOU JUST SHOOT IT?
WITH WHAT?! I GOT A BLASTER, NOT A BAZOOKA!
CAN'T TAKE IT OUT, AND WE CAN'T GET AROUND IT IN TIME! WE'RE SCREWED!
SOL 740

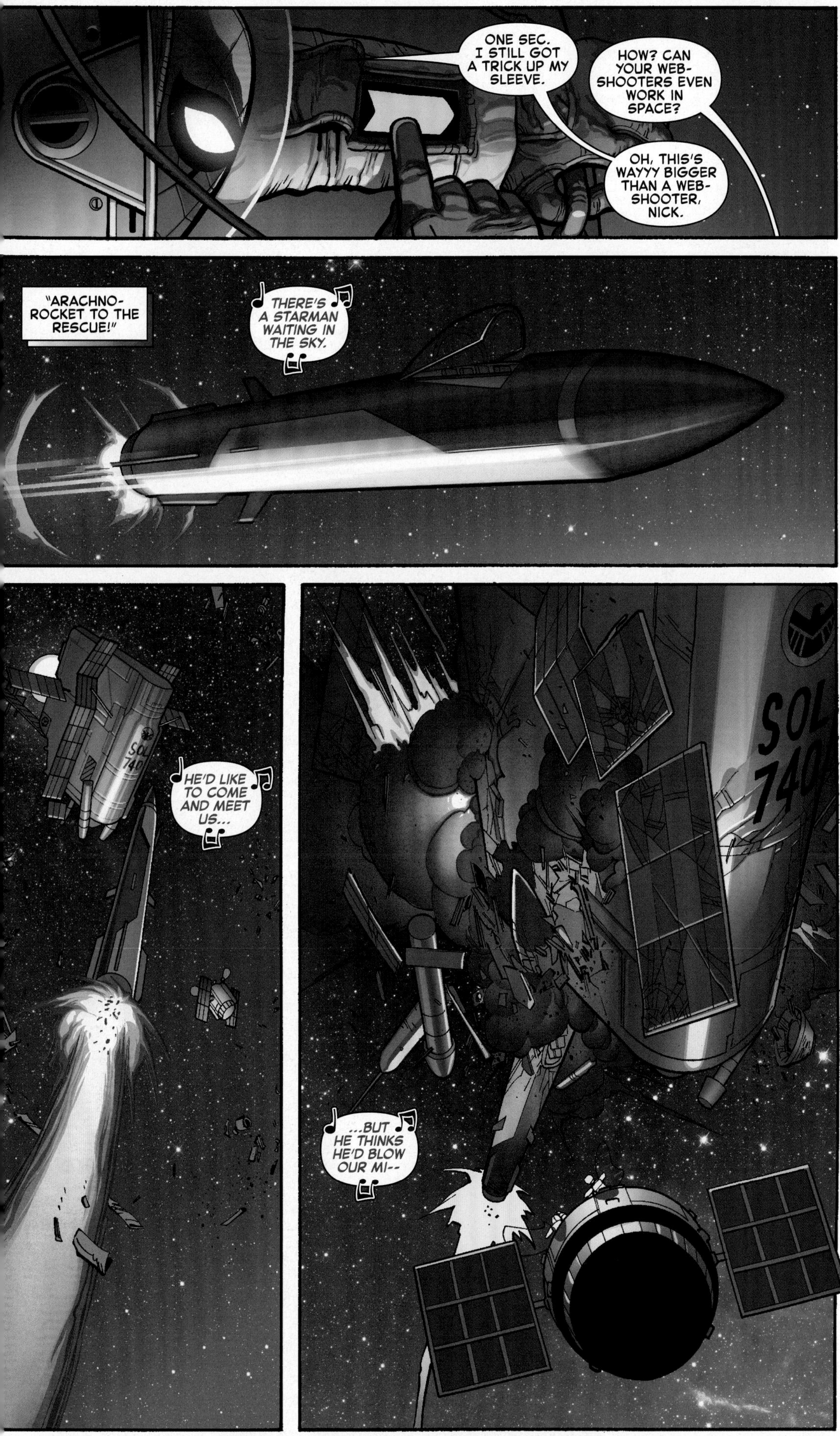
ONE SEC. I STILL GOT A TRICK UP MY SLEEVE.
HOW? CAN YOUR WEB-SHOOTERS EVEN WORK IN SPACE?
OH, THIS'S WAYYY BIGGER THAN A WEB-SHOOTER, NICK.
"ARACHNO-ROCKET TO THE RESCUE!"
THERE'S A STARMAN WAITING IN THE SKY.
SOL 740
HE'D LIKE TO COME AND MEET US...
SOL 740
...BUT HE THINKS HE'D BLOW OUR MI--

COOL. THERE YOU GO. ONE PROBLEM SOLVED.

"SOLVED"?! YOU CRAZY, WALL-HUGGING SPIDER-LOVER! THAT WAS OUR *RIDE!*

YOU'LL BE OKAY. LOOK. THE INTERNATIONAL SPACE STATION IS RIGHT OVER THERE.

YOU CAN SPACEWALK IT. JUST LIKE SANDRA BULLOCK IN *GRAVITY.* IT'LL BE EASY.

OKAY, *ONE,* NOT CRAZY ABOUT THE WHOLE *GRAVITY* SCENARIO. AND TWO...

...WHAT DO YOU MEAN I CAN SPACE-WALK IT? WHERE ARE *YOU* GOING?

PARIS.

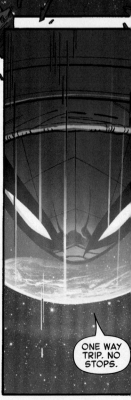

ONE WAY TRIP. NO STOPS.

HE--HE LIVES.

HIS ROCKET'S DESTROYED, BUT-- --HE'S STILL COMING!

IMPOSSIBLE! THIS IS SPIDER-MAN WE'RE TALKING ABOUT. *NOT THOR!*

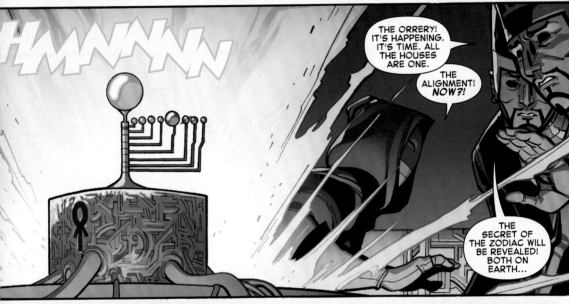

HMNNNN

THE ORRERY! IT'S HAPPENING. IT'S TIME. ALL THE HOUSES ARE ONE.

THE ALIGNMENT! *NOW?!*

THE SECRET OF THE ZODIAC WILL BE REVEALED! BOTH ON EARTH...

...AND IN HEAVEN.

STOP THAT. YOU'RE CREEPING ME OUT.

THERE IS A NEW CONSTELLATION IN THE SKY! A *THIRTEENTH* SIGN!

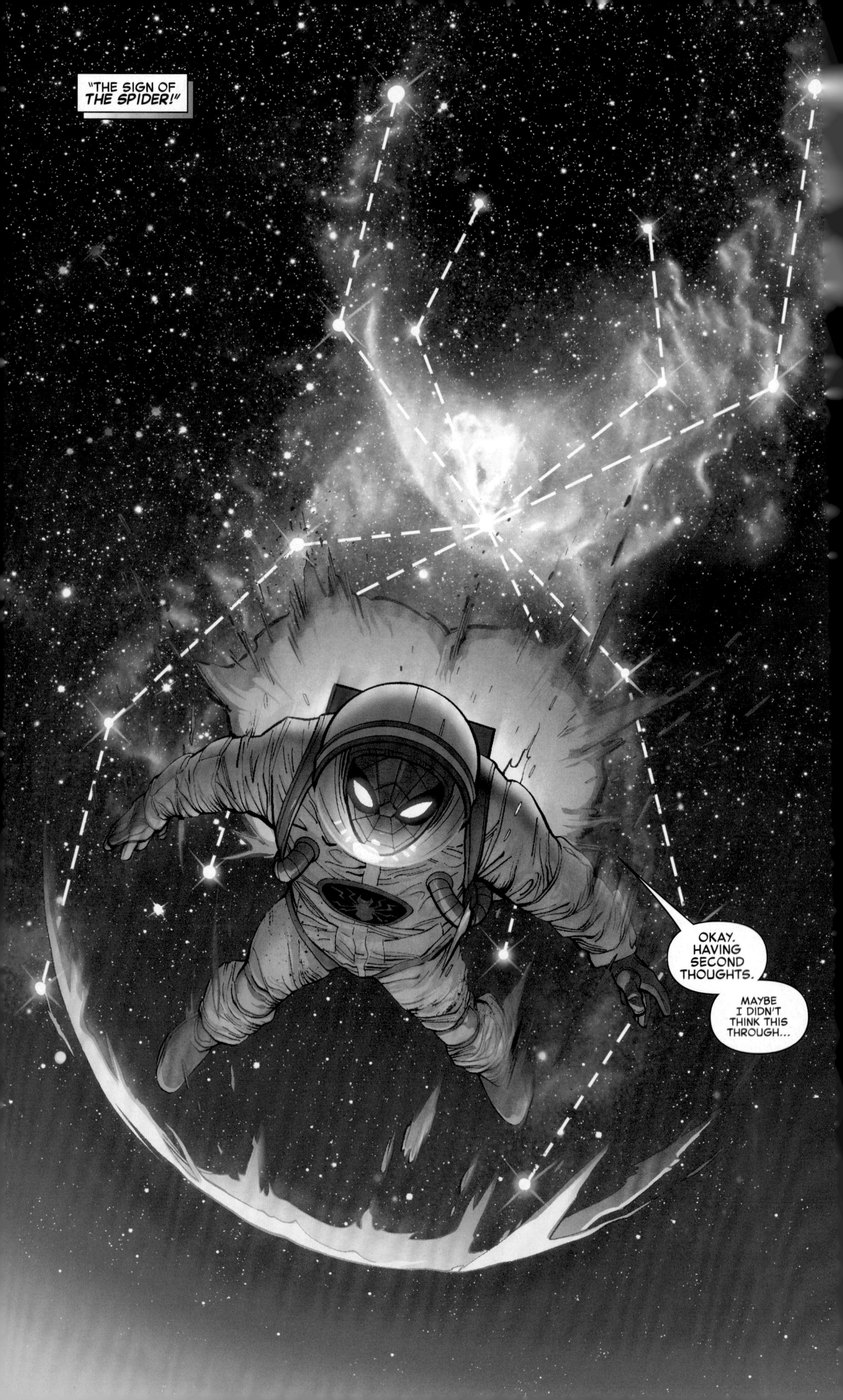
"THE SIGN OF THE SPIDER!"
OKAY. HAVING SECOND THOUGHTS.
MAYBE I DIDN'T THINK THIS THROUGH...

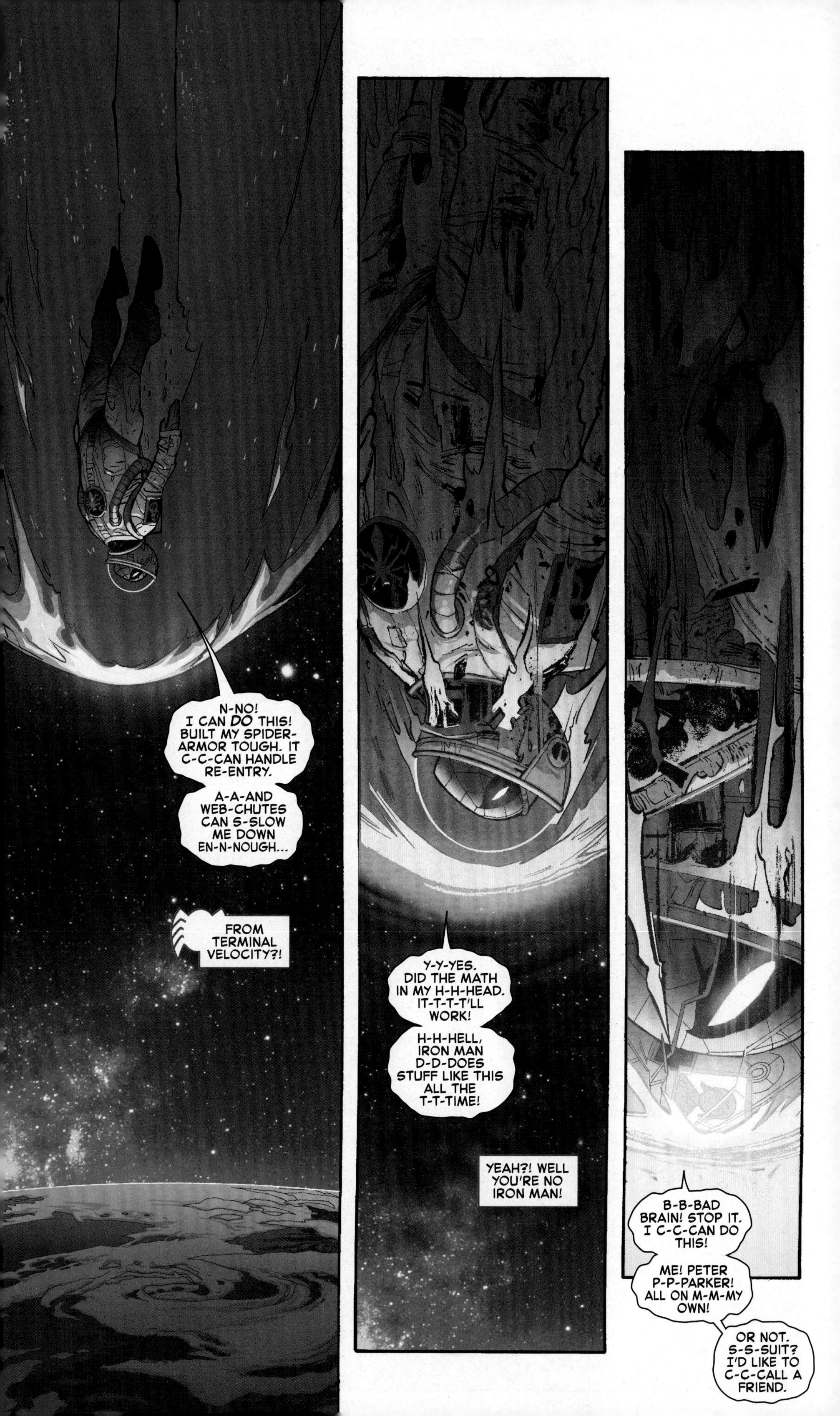
N-NO! I CAN *DO* THIS! BUILT MY SPIDER-ARMOR TOUGH. IT C-C-CAN HANDLE RE-ENTRY.
A-A-AND WEB-CHUTES CAN S-SLOW ME DOWN EN-N-NOUGH...
FROM TERMINAL VELOCITY?!
Y-Y-YES. DID THE MATH IN MY H-H-HEAD. IT-T-T-T'LL WORK!
H-H-HELL, IRON MAN D-D-DOES STUFF LIKE THIS ALL THE T-T-TIME!
YEAH?! WELL YOU'RE NO IRON MAN!
B-B-BAD BRAIN! STOP IT. I C-C-CAN DO THIS!
ME! PETER P-P-PARKER! ALL ON M-M-MY OWN!
OR NOT. S-S-SUIT? I'D LIKE TO C-C-CALL A FRIEND.

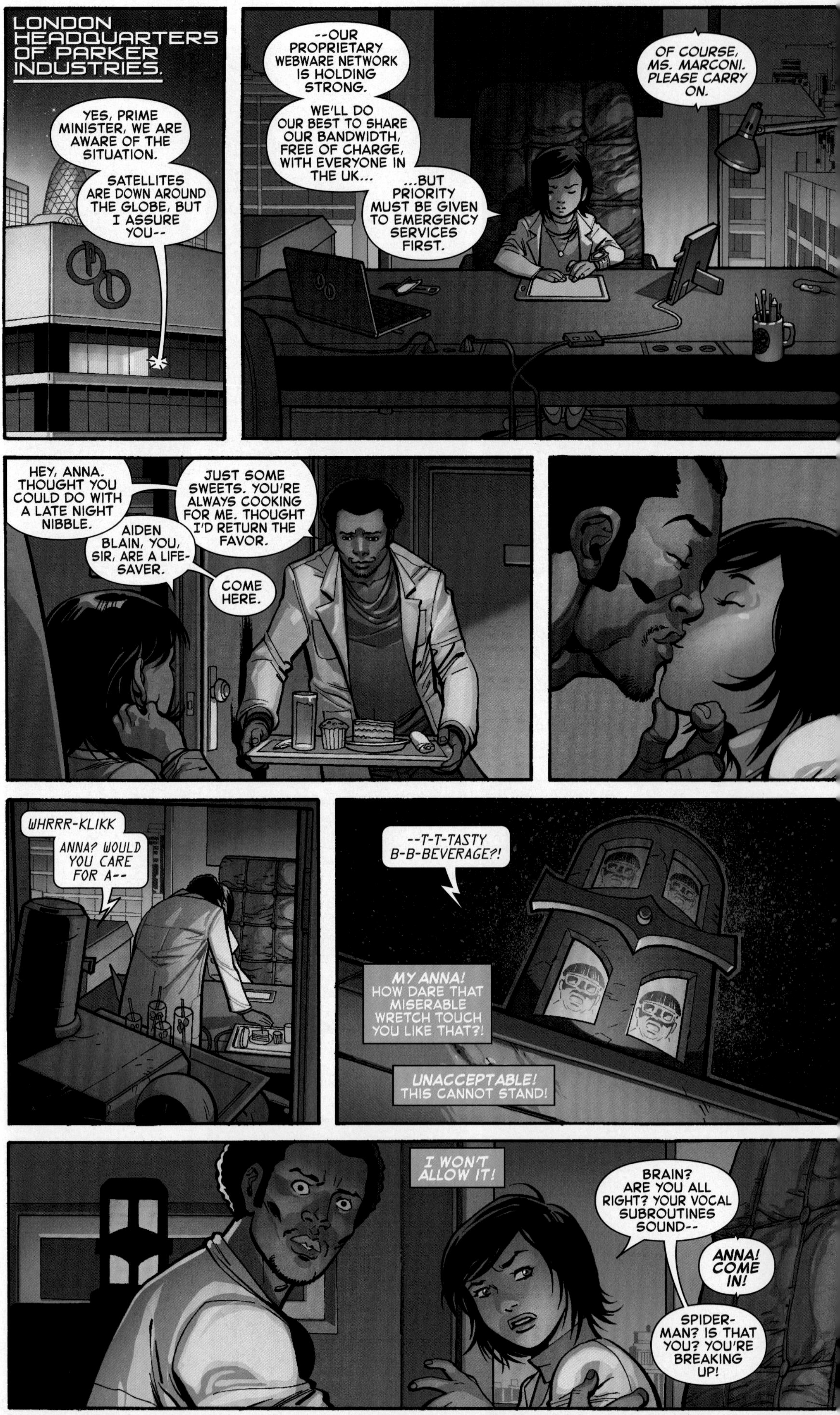
LONDON HEADQUARTERS OF PARKER INDUSTRIES.
YES, PRIME MINISTER, WE ARE AWARE OF THE SITUATION.
SATELLITES ARE DOWN AROUND THE GLOBE, BUT I ASSURE YOU--
--OUR PROPRIETARY WEBWARE NETWORK IS HOLDING STRONG.
WE'LL DO OUR BEST TO SHARE OUR BANDWIDTH, FREE OF CHARGE, WITH EVERYONE IN THE UK...
...BUT PRIORITY MUST BE GIVEN TO EMERGENCY SERVICES FIRST.
OF COURSE, MS. MARCONI. PLEASE CARRY ON.
HEY, ANNA. THOUGHT YOU COULD DO WITH A LATE NIGHT NIBBLE.
JUST SOME SWEETS. YOU'RE ALWAYS COOKING FOR ME. THOUGHT I'D RETURN THE FAVOR.
AIDEN BLAIN, YOU, SIR, ARE A LIFE-SAVER.
COME HERE.
WHRRR-KLIKK
ANNA? WOULD YOU CARE FOR A--
--T-T-TASTY B-B-BEVERAGE?!
MY ANNA! HOW DARE THAT MISERABLE WRETCH TOUCH YOU LIKE THAT?!
UNACCEPTABLE! THIS CANNOT STAND!
I WON'T ALLOW IT!
BRAIN? ARE YOU ALL RIGHT? YOUR VOCAL SUBROUTINES SOUND--
ANNA! COME IN!
SPIDER-MAN? IS THAT YOU? YOU'RE BREAKING UP!

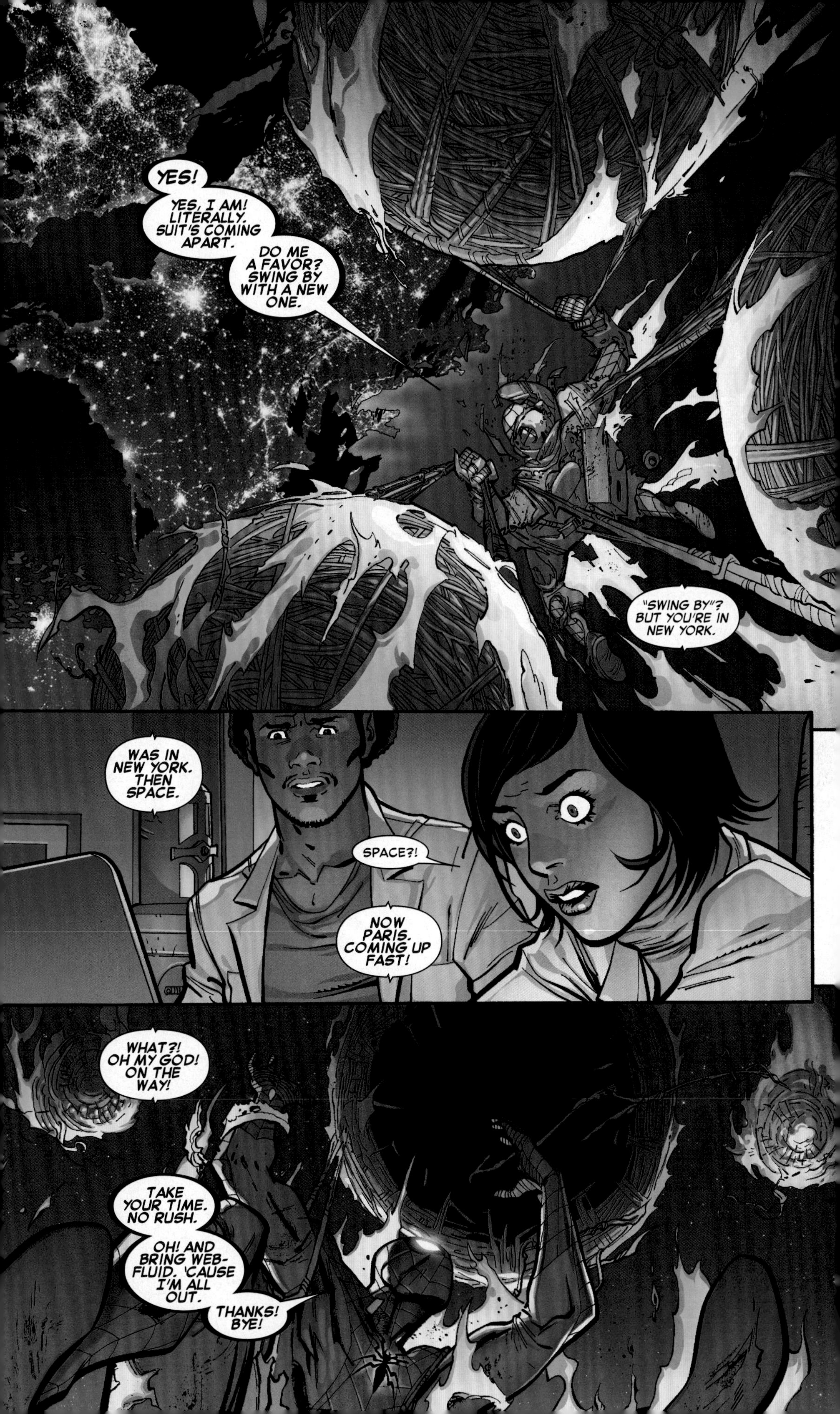
YES!
YES, I AM! LITERALLY. SUIT'S COMING APART.
DO ME A FAVOR? SWING BY WITH A NEW ONE.
"SWING BY"? BUT YOU'RE IN NEW YORK.
WAS IN NEW YORK. THEN SPACE.
SPACE?!
NOW PARIS. COMING UP FAST!
WHAT?! OH MY GOD! ON THE WAY!
TAKE YOUR TIME. NO RUSH.
OH! AND BRING WEB-FLUID. 'CAUSE I'M ALL OUT.
THANKS! BYE!

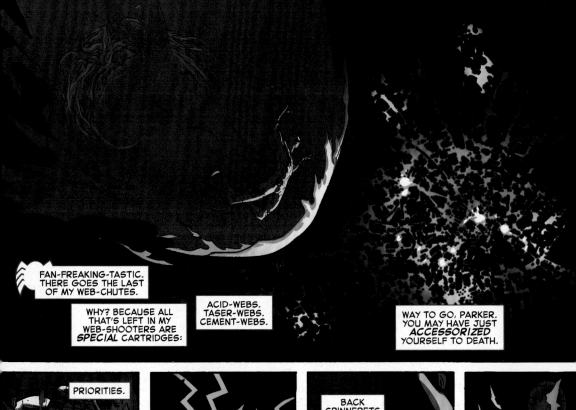

FAN-FREAKING-TASTIC. THERE GOES THE LAST OF MY WEB-CHUTES.

WHY? BECAUSE ALL THAT'S LEFT IN MY WEB-SHOOTERS ARE *SPECIAL* CARTRIDGES:

ACID-WEBS. TASER-WEBS. CEMENT-WEBS.

WAY TO GO, PARKER. YOU MAY HAVE JUST *ACCESSORIZED* YOURSELF TO DEATH.

PRIORITIES.

TEN

PARIS IS COMING UP FAST. ANYONE BELOW--

--IS GONNA NEED A WARNING!

S-SUIT... ACTIVATE EMERGENCY BEACON.

BACK SPINNERETS WORKING? GOOD!

EMERGENCY WEB-FOAM'S A GO.

WEEOOWEEOOWEEOOWEEOOWEEOO

WEEOOWEEOOWEEOOWEEOOWEEOO

THOUGHT I'D BE COMING IN SLOWER--

--BUT THIS "SHOULD" STILL WORK.

KEY WORD: SHOULD.

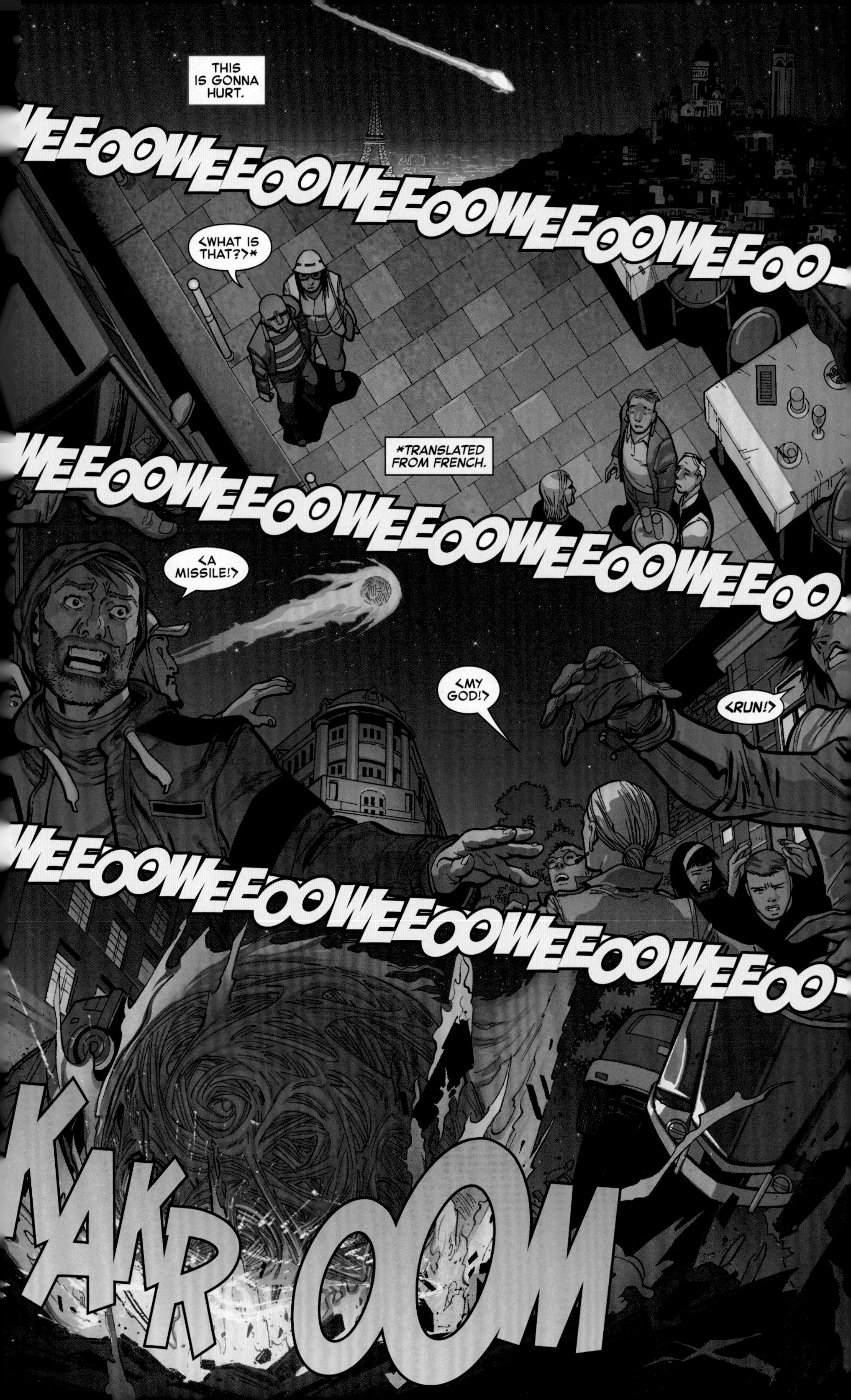
THIS IS GONNA HURT.
WEEOOWEEOOWEEOOWEEOOWEEOO-
<WHAT IS THAT?>*
*TRANSLATED FROM FRENCH.
WEEOOWEEOOWEEOOWEEOOWEEOO-
<A MISSILE!>
<MY GOD!>
<RUN!>
WEEOOWEEOOWEEOOWEEOOWEEOO-
KAKROOOM

OW.

YES! I'M ONE BIG BRUISE. SUIT'S A WRECK. BUT *I DID IT!*

SON OF A BISCUIT! FELL ALL THE WAY FROM *SPACE* AND SURVIVED!

EVERYONE OKAY OUT THERE? HANG ON, I'LL BE RIGHT--

--OUT?

UM. WHAT IS THAT? IS SOMEONE OUT--

TSSSS

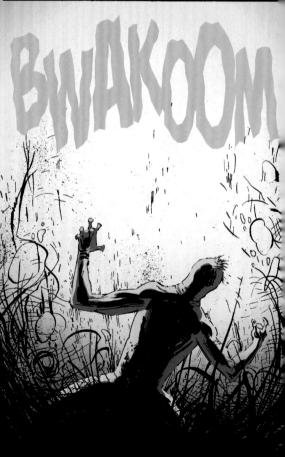

BWAKOOM

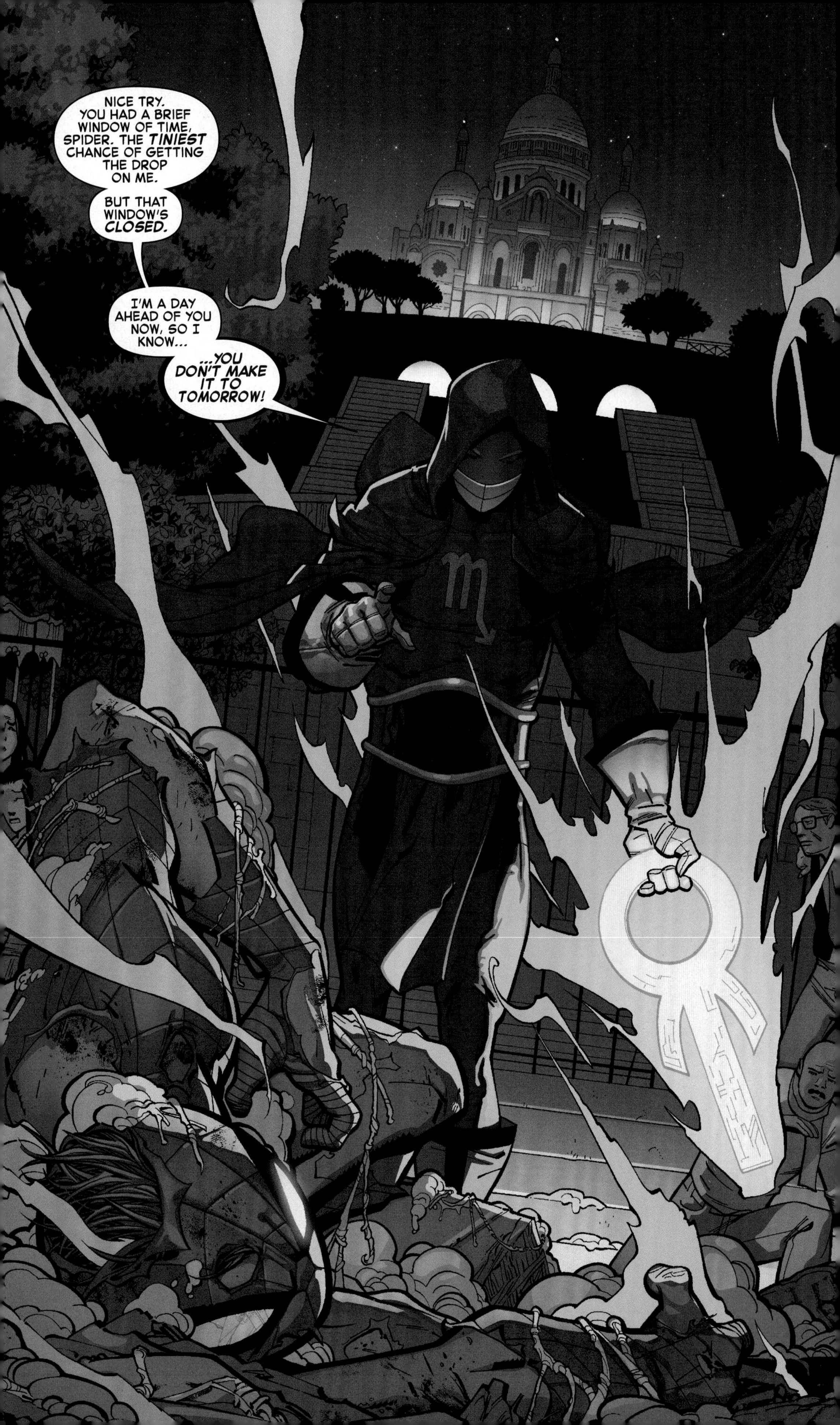
NICE TRY. YOU HAD A BRIEF WINDOW OF TIME, SPIDER. THE *TINIEST* CHANCE OF GETTING THE DROP ON ME.
BUT THAT WINDOW'S *CLOSED.*
I'M A DAY AHEAD OF YOU NOW, SO I KNOW...
...YOU DON'T MAKE IT TO TOMORROW!

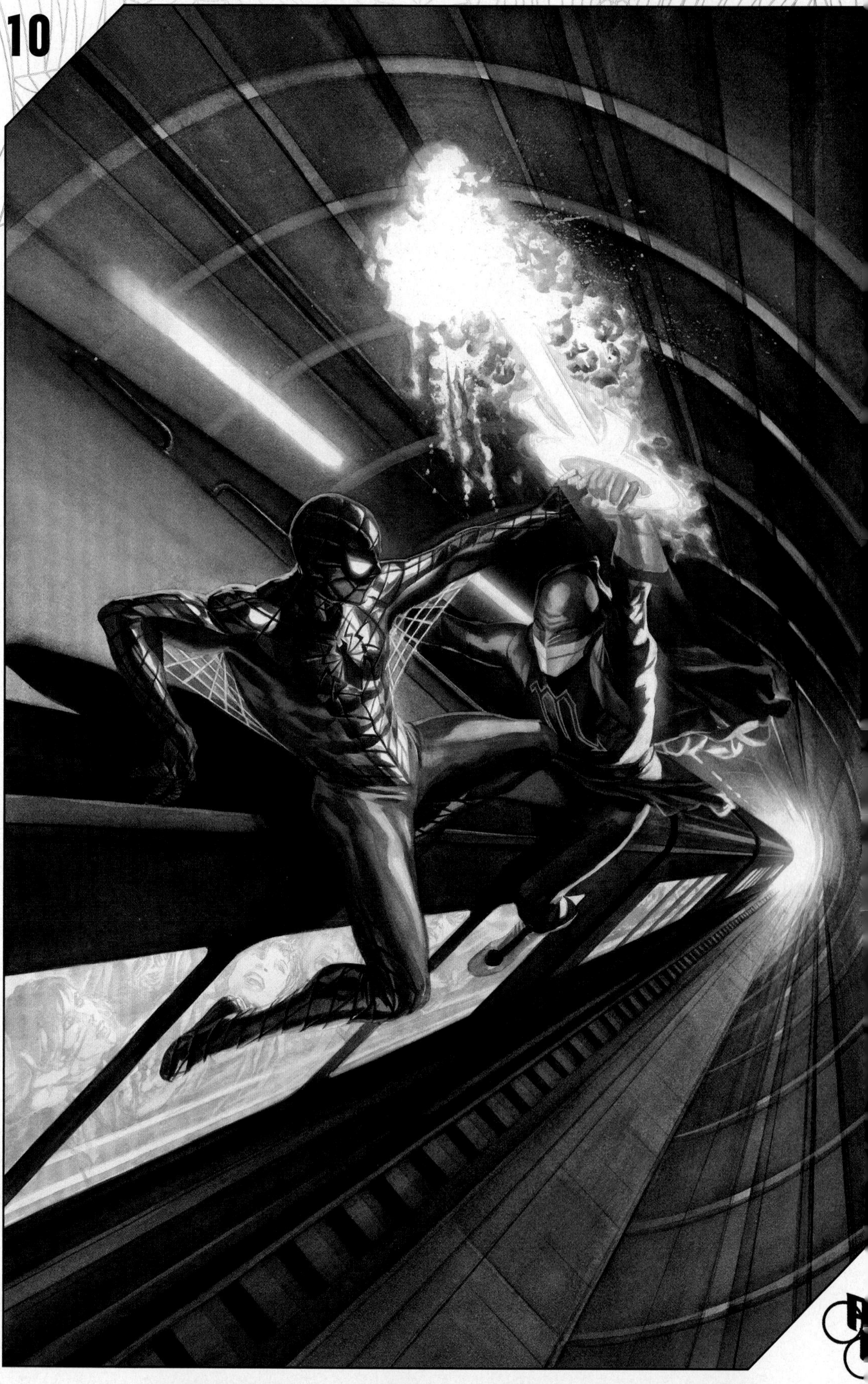

SCORPIO RISING - PART 2: "POWER PLAY"

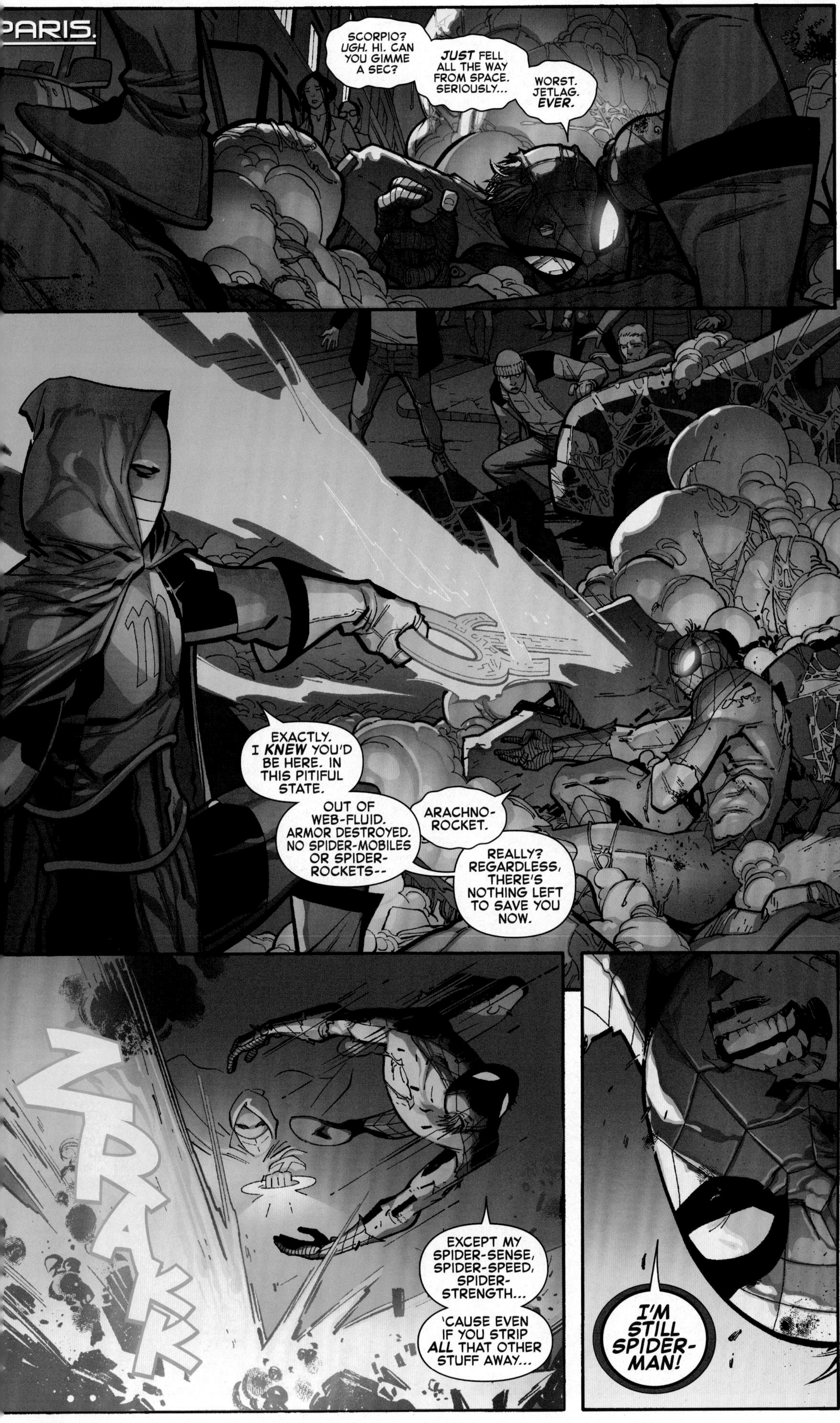
PARIS.
SCORPIO? UGH. HI. CAN YOU GIMME A SEC?
JUST FELL ALL THE WAY FROM SPACE. SERIOUSLY...
WORST. JETLAG. EVER.
EXACTLY. I KNEW YOU'D BE HERE. IN THIS PITIFUL STATE.
OUT OF WEB-FLUID. ARMOR DESTROYED. NO SPIDER-MOBILES OR SPIDER-ROCKETS--
ARACHNO-ROCKET.
REALLY? REGARDLESS, THERE'S NOTHING LEFT TO SAVE YOU NOW.
ZRAKK
EXCEPT MY SPIDER-SENSE, SPIDER-SPEED, SPIDER-STRENGTH...
'CAUSE EVEN IF YOU STRIP ALL THAT OTHER STUFF AWAY...
I'M STILL SPIDER-MAN!

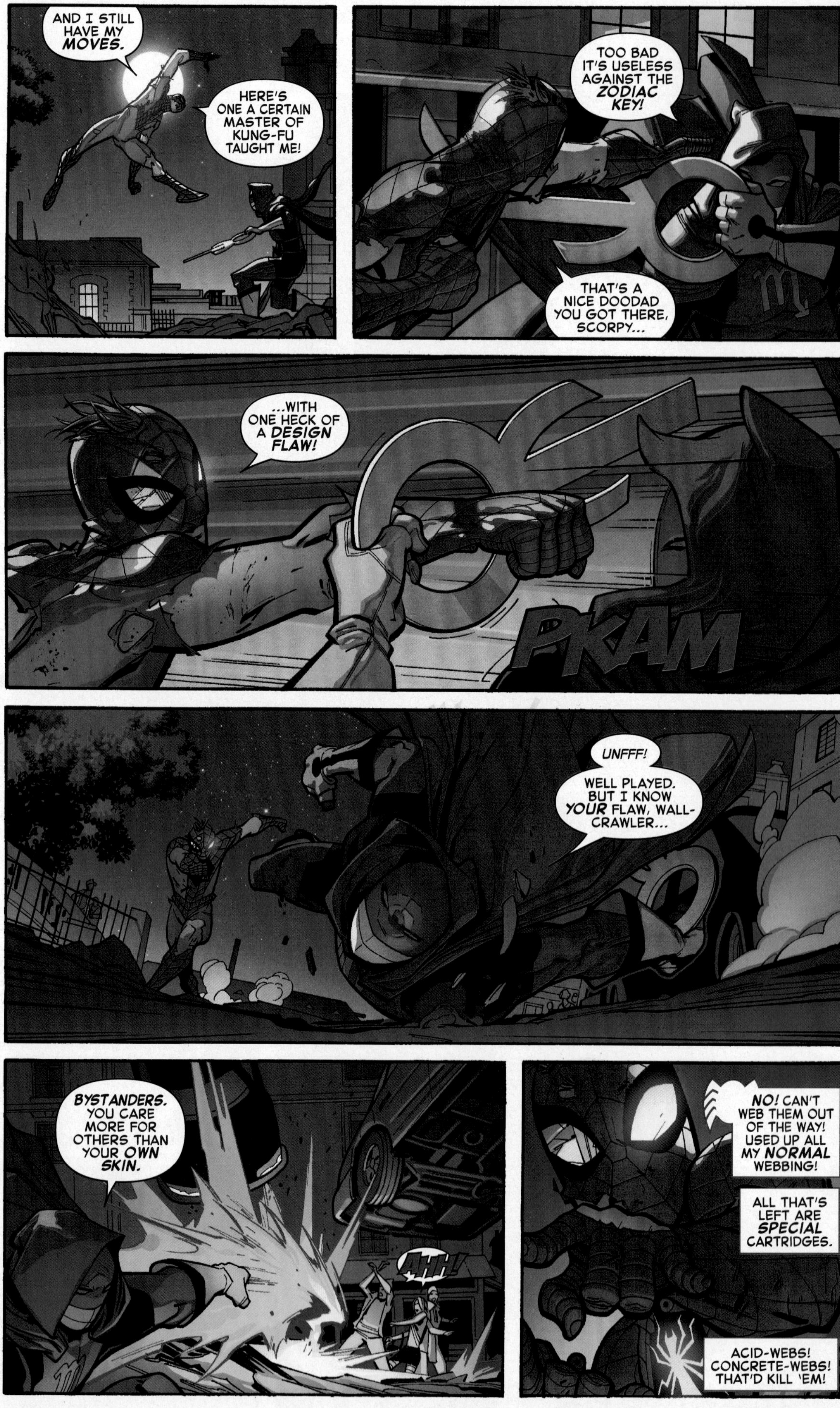

AND I STILL HAVE MY MOVES.
HERE'S ONE A CERTAIN MASTER OF KUNG-FU TAUGHT ME!
TOO BAD IT'S USELESS AGAINST THE ZODIAC KEY!
THAT'S A NICE DOODAD YOU GOT THERE, SCORPY...
...WITH ONE HECK OF A DESIGN FLAW!
PKAM
UNFFF!
WELL PLAYED. BUT I KNOW YOUR FLAW, WALL-CRAWLER...
BYSTANDERS. YOU CARE MORE FOR OTHERS THAN YOUR OWN SKIN.
AHH!
NO! CAN'T WEB THEM OUT OF THE WAY! USED UP ALL MY NORMAL WEBBING!
ALL THAT'S LEFT ARE SPECIAL CARTRIDGES.
ACID-WEBS! CONCRETE-WEBS! THAT'D KILL 'EM!

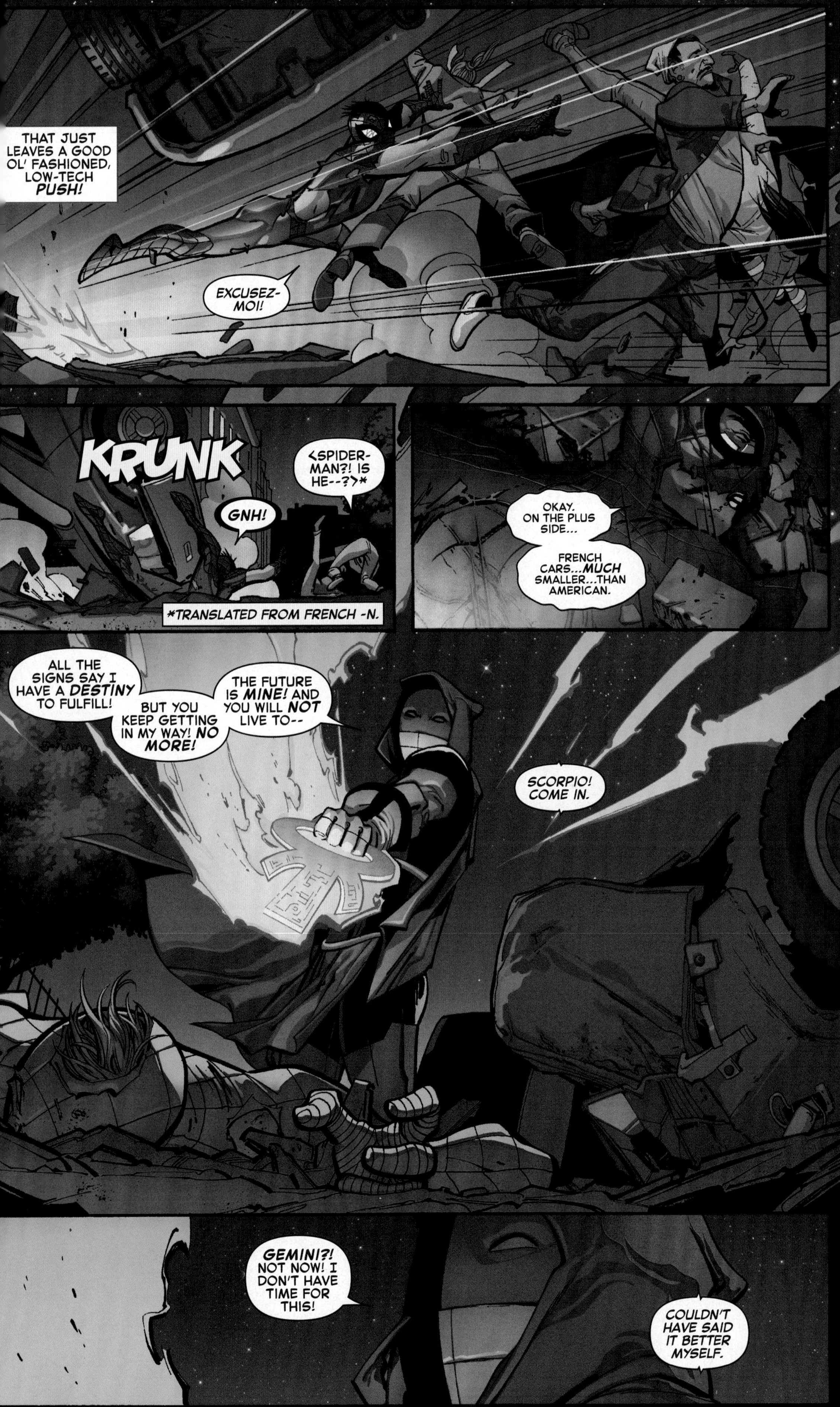
THAT JUST LEAVES A GOOD OL' FASHIONED, LOW-TECH PUSH!
EXCUSEZ-MOI!
KRUNK
<SPIDER-MAN?! IS HE--?>*
GNH!
*TRANSLATED FROM FRENCH -N.
OKAY. ON THE PLUS SIDE...
FRENCH CARS...MUCH SMALLER...THAN AMERICAN.
ALL THE SIGNS SAY I HAVE A DESTINY TO FULFILL!
BUT YOU KEEP GETTING IN MY WAY! NO MORE!
THE FUTURE IS MINE! AND YOU WILL NOT LIVE TO--
SCORPIO! COME IN.
GEMINI?! NOT NOW! I DON'T HAVE TIME FOR THIS!
COULDN'T HAVE SAID IT BETTER MYSELF.

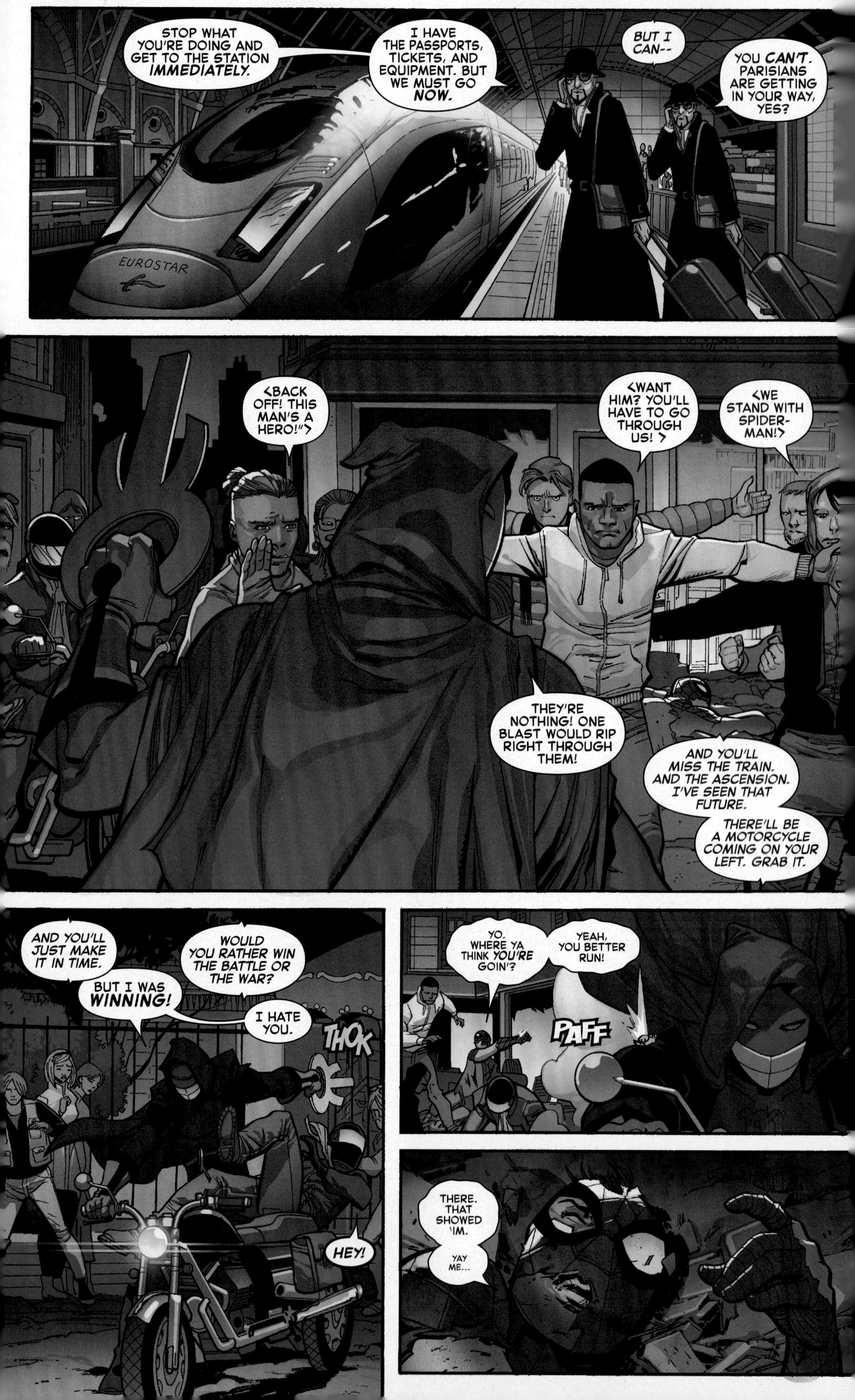
STOP WHAT YOU'RE DOING AND GET TO THE STATION *IMMEDIATELY.*
I HAVE THE PASSPORTS, TICKETS, AND EQUIPMENT. BUT WE MUST GO *NOW.*
BUT I CAN--
YOU **CAN'T.** PARISIANS ARE GETTING IN YOUR WAY, YES?
EUROSTAR
<BACK OFF! THIS MAN'S A HERO!">
<WANT HIM? YOU'LL HAVE TO GO THROUGH US! >
<WE STAND WITH SPIDER-MAN!>
THEY'RE NOTHING! ONE BLAST WOULD RIP RIGHT THROUGH THEM!
AND YOU'LL MISS THE TRAIN. AND THE ASCENSION. I'VE SEEN THAT FUTURE.
THERE'LL BE A MOTORCYCLE COMING ON YOUR LEFT. GRAB IT.
AND YOU'LL JUST MAKE IT IN TIME.
WOULD YOU RATHER WIN THE BATTLE OR THE WAR?
BUT I WAS **WINNING!**
I HATE YOU.
THOK
HEY!
YO. WHERE YA THINK *YOU'RE* GOIN'?
YEAH, YOU BETTER RUN!
PAFF
THERE. THAT SHOWED 'IM.
YAY ME...

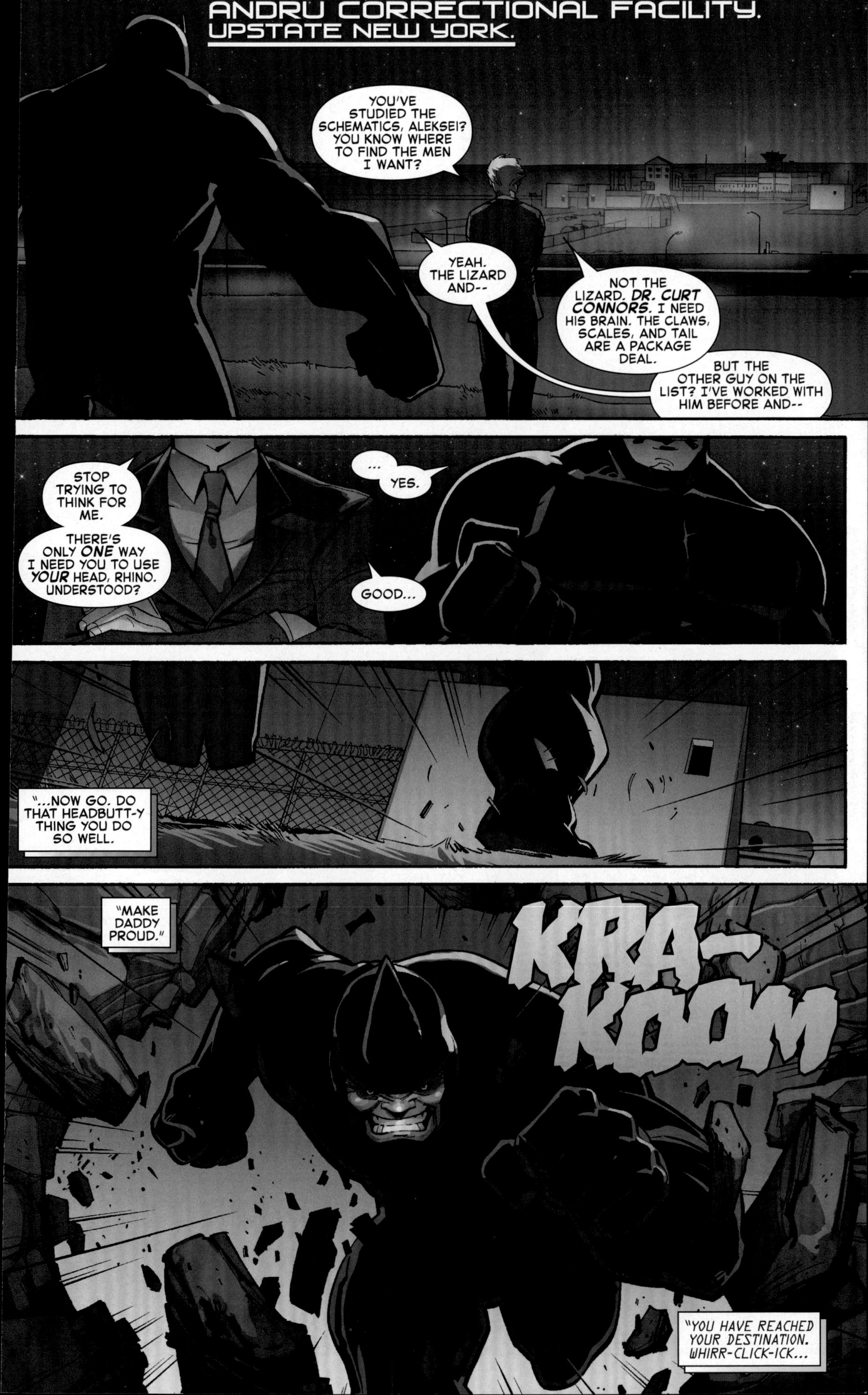
ANDRU CORRECTIONAL FACILITY. UPSTATE NEW YORK.
YOU'VE STUDIED THE SCHEMATICS, ALEKSEI? YOU KNOW WHERE TO FIND THE MEN I WANT?
YEAH. THE LIZARD AND--
NOT THE LIZARD. DR. CURT CONNORS. I NEED HIS BRAIN. THE CLAWS, SCALES, AND TAIL ARE A PACKAGE DEAL.
BUT THE OTHER GUY ON THE LIST? I'VE WORKED WITH HIM BEFORE AND--
STOP TRYING TO THINK FOR ME.
THERE'S ONLY ONE WAY I NEED YOU TO USE YOUR HEAD, RHINO. UNDERSTOOD?
...
YES.
GOOD...
"...NOW GO. DO THAT HEADBUTT-Y THING YOU DO SO WELL.
"MAKE DADDY PROUD."
KRA-KOOM
"YOU HAVE REACHED YOUR DESTINATION. WHIRR-CLICK-ICK...

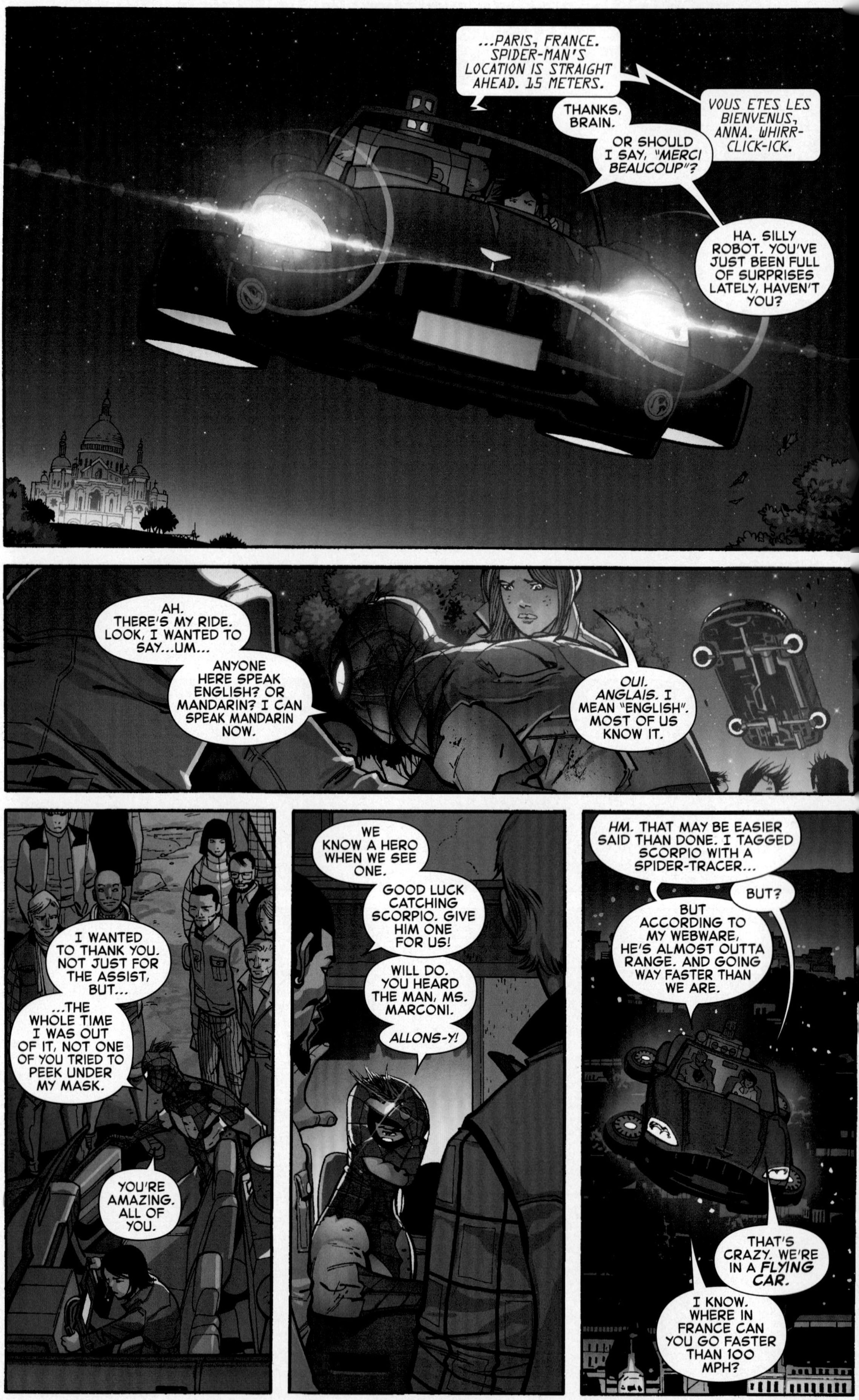
...PARIS, FRANCE. SPIDER-MAN'S LOCATION IS STRAIGHT AHEAD. 15 METERS.
THANKS, BRAIN.
OR SHOULD I SAY, "MERCI BEAUCOUP"?
VOUS ETES LES BIENVENUS, ANNA. WHIRR-CLICK-ICK.
HA. SILLY ROBOT. YOU'VE JUST BEEN FULL OF SURPRISES LATELY, HAVEN'T YOU?
AH. THERE'S MY RIDE. LOOK, I WANTED TO SAY...UM...
ANYONE HERE SPEAK ENGLISH? OR MANDARIN? I CAN SPEAK MANDARIN NOW.
OUI. ANGLAIS. I MEAN "ENGLISH". MOST OF US KNOW IT.
I WANTED TO THANK YOU. NOT JUST FOR THE ASSIST, BUT...
...THE WHOLE TIME I WAS OUT OF IT, NOT ONE OF YOU TRIED TO PEEK UNDER MY MASK.
YOU'RE AMAZING. ALL OF YOU.
WE KNOW A HERO WHEN WE SEE ONE.
GOOD LUCK CATCHING SCORPIO. GIVE HIM ONE FOR US!
WILL DO. YOU HEARD THE MAN, MS. MARCONI.
ALLONS-Y!
HM. THAT MAY BE EASIER SAID THAN DONE. I TAGGED SCORPIO WITH A SPIDER-TRACER...
BUT?
BUT ACCORDING TO MY WEBWARE, HE'S ALMOST OUTTA RANGE. AND GOING WAY FASTER THAN WE ARE.
THAT'S CRAZY. WE'RE IN A FLYING CAR.
I KNOW. WHERE IN FRANCE CAN YOU GO FASTER THAN 100 MPH?

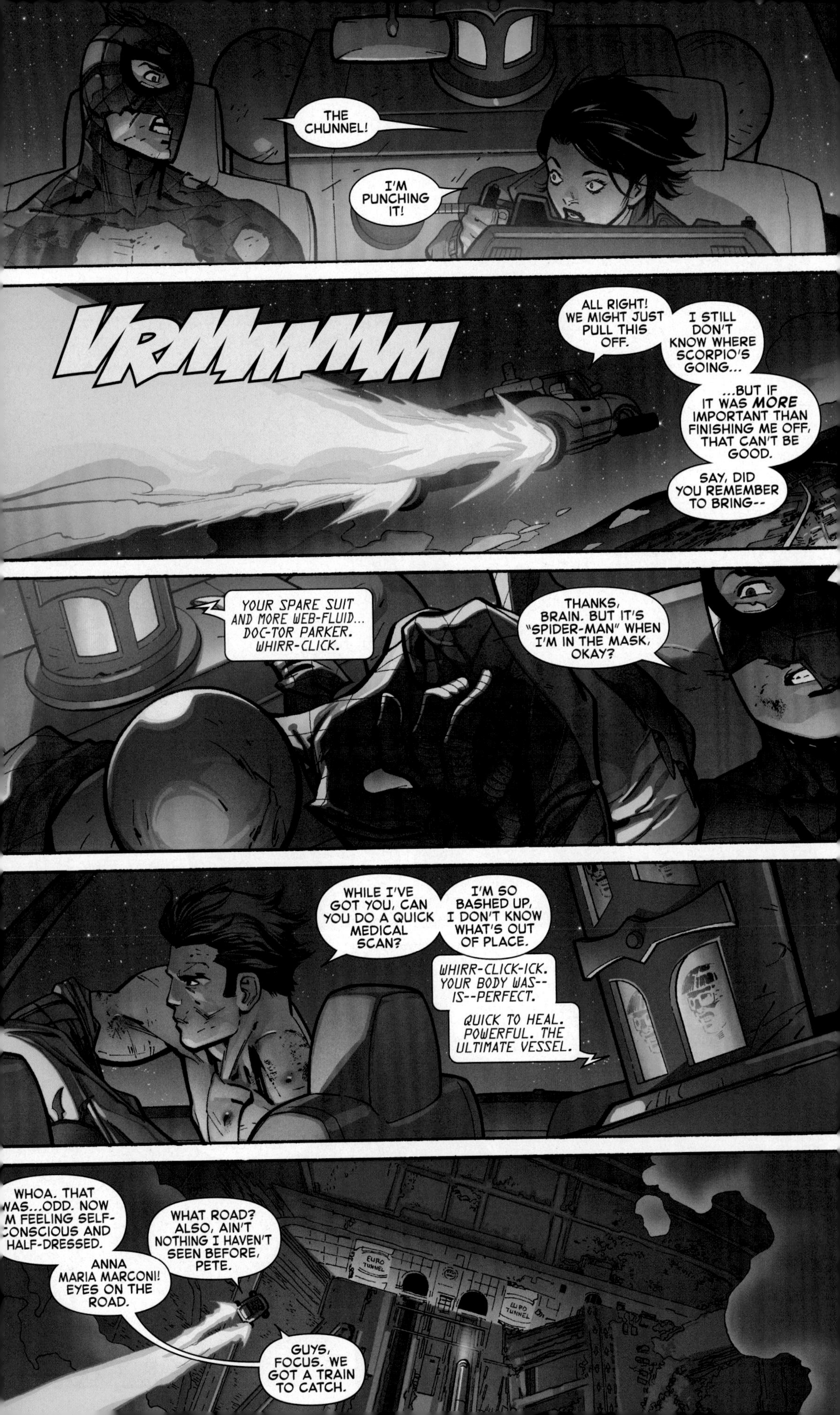
THE CHUNNEL!
I'M PUNCHING IT!
VRMMMMM
ALL RIGHT! WE MIGHT JUST PULL THIS OFF.
I STILL DON'T KNOW WHERE SCORPIO'S GOING...
...BUT IF IT WAS MORE IMPORTANT THAN FINISHING ME OFF, THAT CAN'T BE GOOD.
SAY, DID YOU REMEMBER TO BRING--
YOUR SPARE SUIT AND MORE WEB-FLUID... DOC-TOR PARKER. WHIRR-CLICK.
THANKS, BRAIN. BUT IT'S "SPIDER-MAN" WHEN I'M IN THE MASK, OKAY?
WHILE I'VE GOT YOU, CAN YOU DO A QUICK MEDICAL SCAN?
I'M SO BASHED UP, I DON'T KNOW WHAT'S OUT OF PLACE.
WHIRR-CLICK-ICK. YOUR BODY WAS--IS--PERFECT.
QUICK TO HEAL. POWERFUL. THE ULTIMATE VESSEL.
WHOA. THAT WAS...ODD. NOW I'M FEELING SELF-CONSCIOUS AND HALF-DRESSED.
WHAT ROAD? ALSO, AIN'T NOTHING I HAVEN'T SEEN BEFORE, PETE.
ANNA MARIA MARCONI! EYES ON THE ROAD.
GUYS, FOCUS. WE GOT A TRAIN TO CATCH.
EURO TUNNEL
EURO TUNNEL

TERRY? WHAT'RE YOU DOING, MAN?

TAKE THAT STUPID HAT OFF YOUR HEAD, AND STOP THE DAMN TRAIN!

SORRY, BUT THAT'S NOT YOUR CO-WORKER ANYMORE. THE MASK HAS REWRITTEN HIM.

HE'S PART OF MY FAMILY NOW. MY NEW CANCER.

AS FOR YOU, MR. RICHARDSON, YOU'RE A LEO, RIGHT?

I CAN ALWAYS TELL.

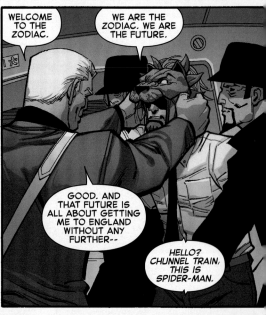

WELCOME TO THE ZODIAC.

WE ARE THE ZODIAC. WE ARE THE FUTURE.

GOOD. AND THAT FUTURE IS ALL ABOUT GETTING ME TO ENGLAND WITHOUT ANY FURTHER--

HELLO? CHUNNEL TRAIN, THIS IS SPIDER-MAN.

I'M COMING TO YOU OVER A SECURE S.H.I.E.L.D. CHANNEL.

WE BELIEVE SOME OF YOUR PASSENGERS MIGHT BE ZODIAC TERRORISTS. REMAIN CALM. I'M ON THE WAY.

SPIDER-MAN? AGAIN?! GEMINI, YOU'RE LOOPED IN TIME. WHY DIDN'T YOU FORESEE THIS?

I HAVE TROUBLE READING INTO MY OWN FUTURE, REMEMBER?

THAT'S WHY YOU WERE ABLE TO POISON THE LAST GEMINI.

YOU'RE NOT GOING TO POISON ME NOW, ARE YOU?

NO. JUST TELL ME HOW HE FOUND US SO QUICKLY.

HM. IN ONE VERSION OF TODAY, HE PUT A SPIDER-TRACER ON YOU. IF YOU TAKE IT OFF--

LET HIM COME. I'LL BE READY FOR HIM.

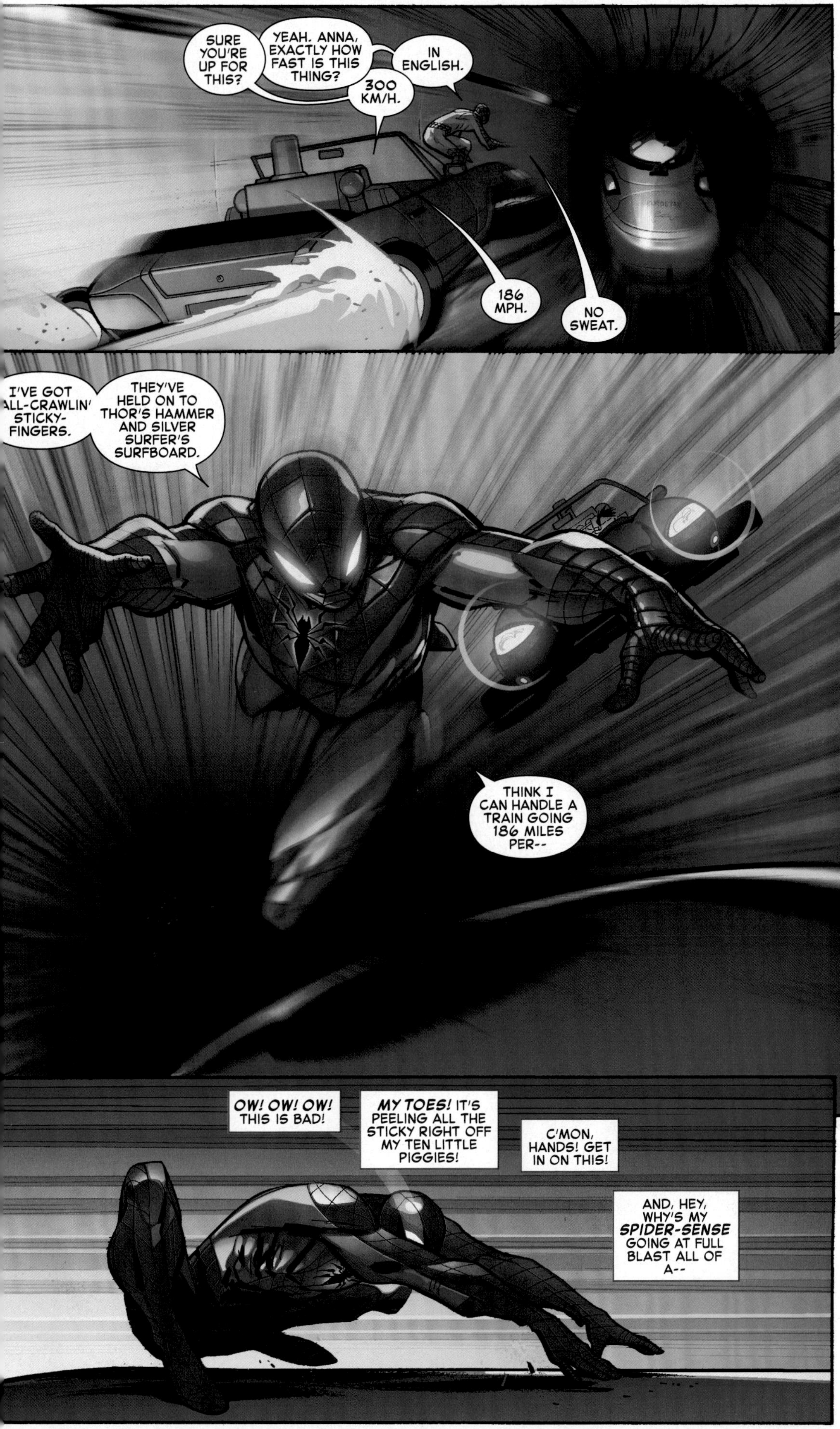
SURE YOU'RE UP FOR THIS?
YEAH. ANNA, EXACTLY HOW FAST IS THIS THING?
IN ENGLISH.
300 KM/H.
186 MPH.
NO SWEAT.
I'VE GOT WALL-CRAWLIN' STICKY-FINGERS.
THEY'VE HELD ON TO THOR'S HAMMER AND SILVER SURFER'S SURFBOARD.
THINK I CAN HANDLE A TRAIN GOING 186 MILES PER--
OW! OW! OW! THIS IS BAD!
MY TOES! IT'S PEELING ALL THE STICKY RIGHT OFF MY TEN LITTLE PIGGIES!
C'MON, HANDS! GET IN ON THIS!
AND, HEY, WHY'S MY SPIDER-SENSE GOING AT FULL BLAST ALL OF A--

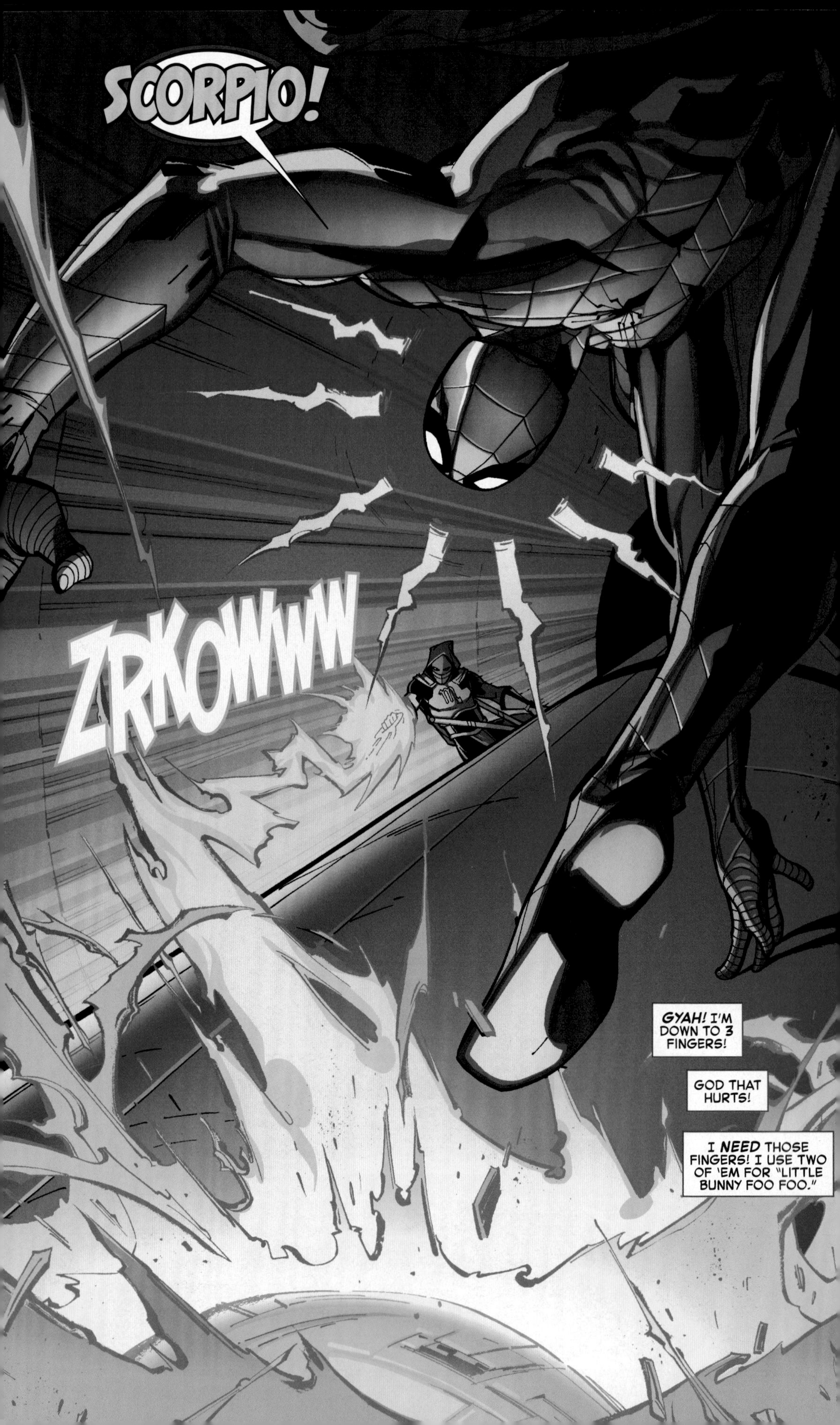
SCORPIO!
ZRKOWWW
GYAH! I'M DOWN TO 3 FINGERS!
GOD THAT HURTS!
I NEED THOSE FINGERS! I USE TWO OF 'EM FOR "LITTLE BUNNY FOO FOO."

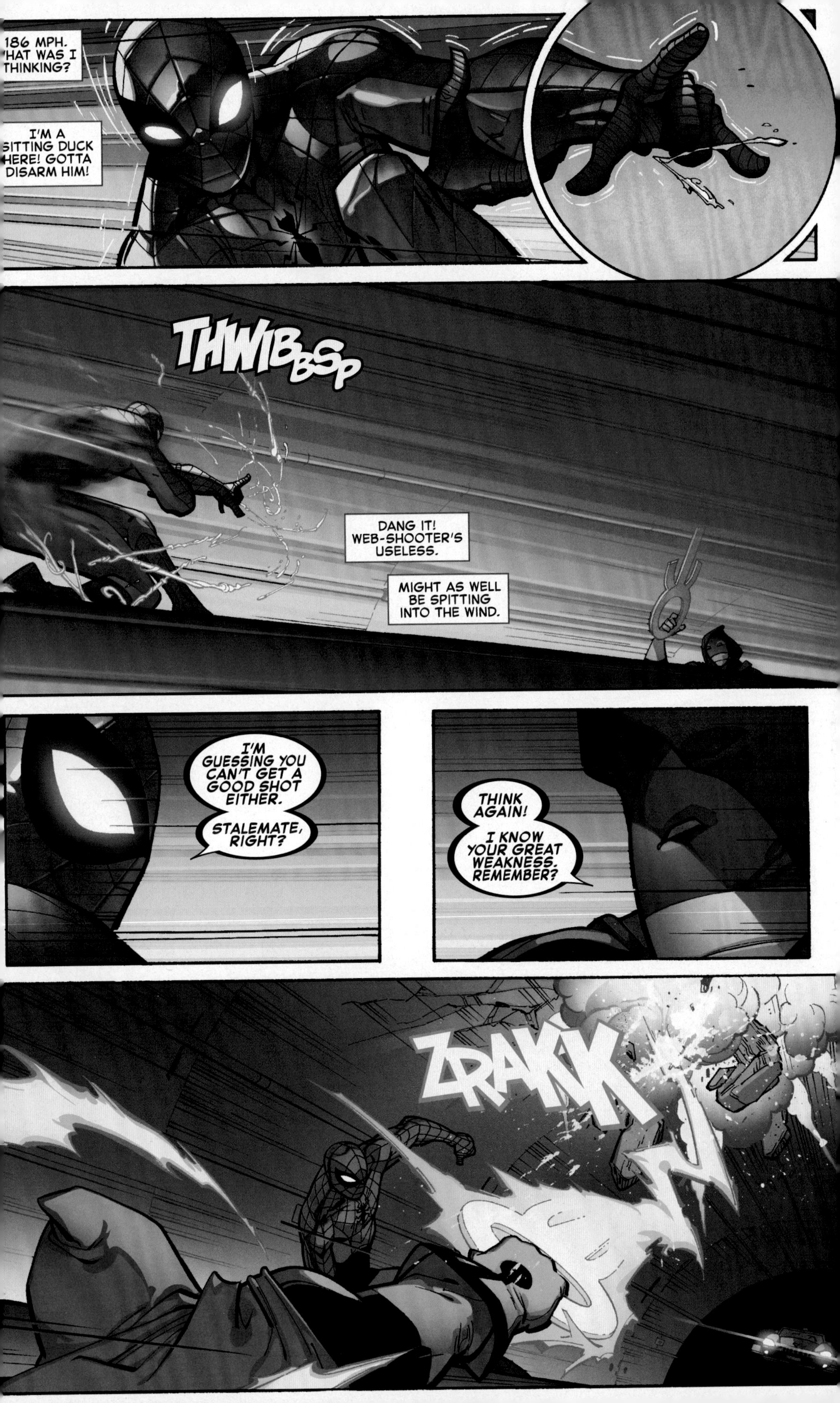
186 MPH. WHAT WAS I THINKING?
I'M A SITTING DUCK HERE! GOTTA DISARM HIM!
THWIBBSP
DANG IT! WEB-SHOOTER'S USELESS.
MIGHT AS WELL BE SPITTING INTO THE WIND.
I'M GUESSING YOU CAN'T GET A GOOD SHOT EITHER.
STALEMATE, RIGHT?
THINK AGAIN!
I KNOW YOUR GREAT WEAKNESS. REMEMBER?
ZRAKK

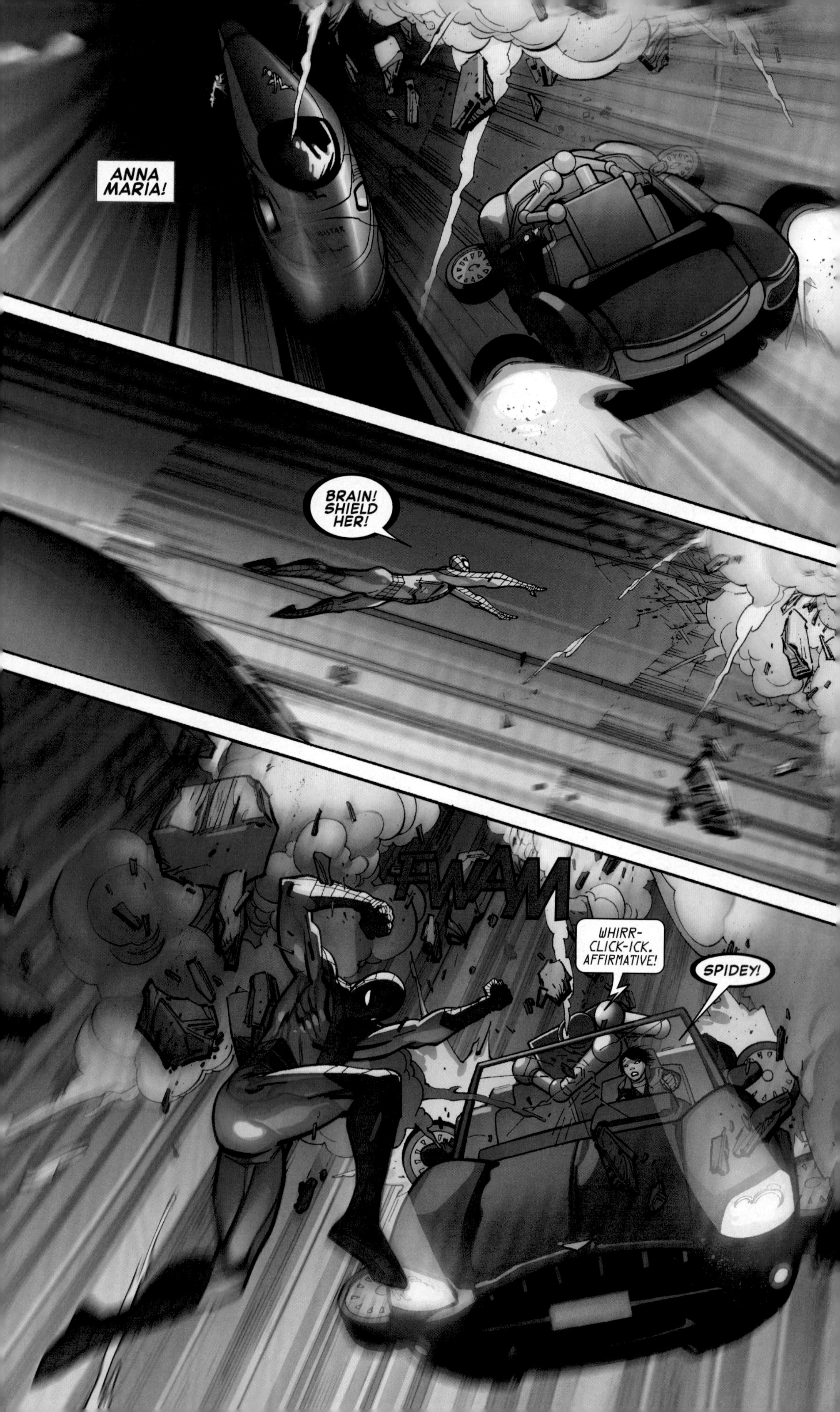
ANNA MARIA!
BRAIN! SHIELD HER!
FWAM
WHIRR-CLICK-ICK. AFFIRMATIVE!
SPIDEY!

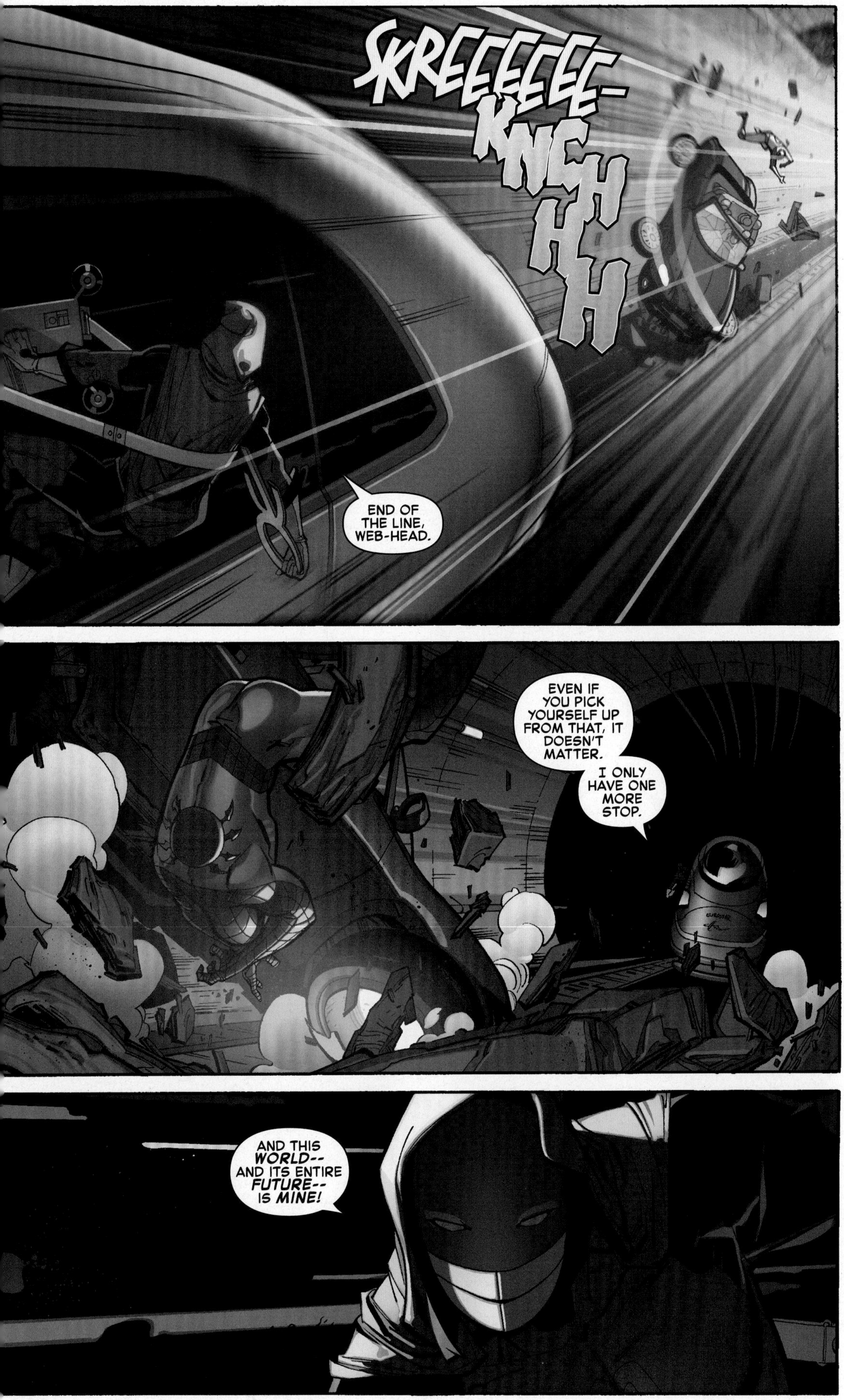
SKREEEEEE-KNGHHHH
END OF THE LINE, WEB-HEAD.
EVEN IF YOU PICK YOURSELF UP FROM THAT, IT DOESN'T MATTER.
I ONLY HAVE ONE MORE STOP.
AND THIS WORLD-- AND ITS ENTIRE FUTURE-- IS MINE!

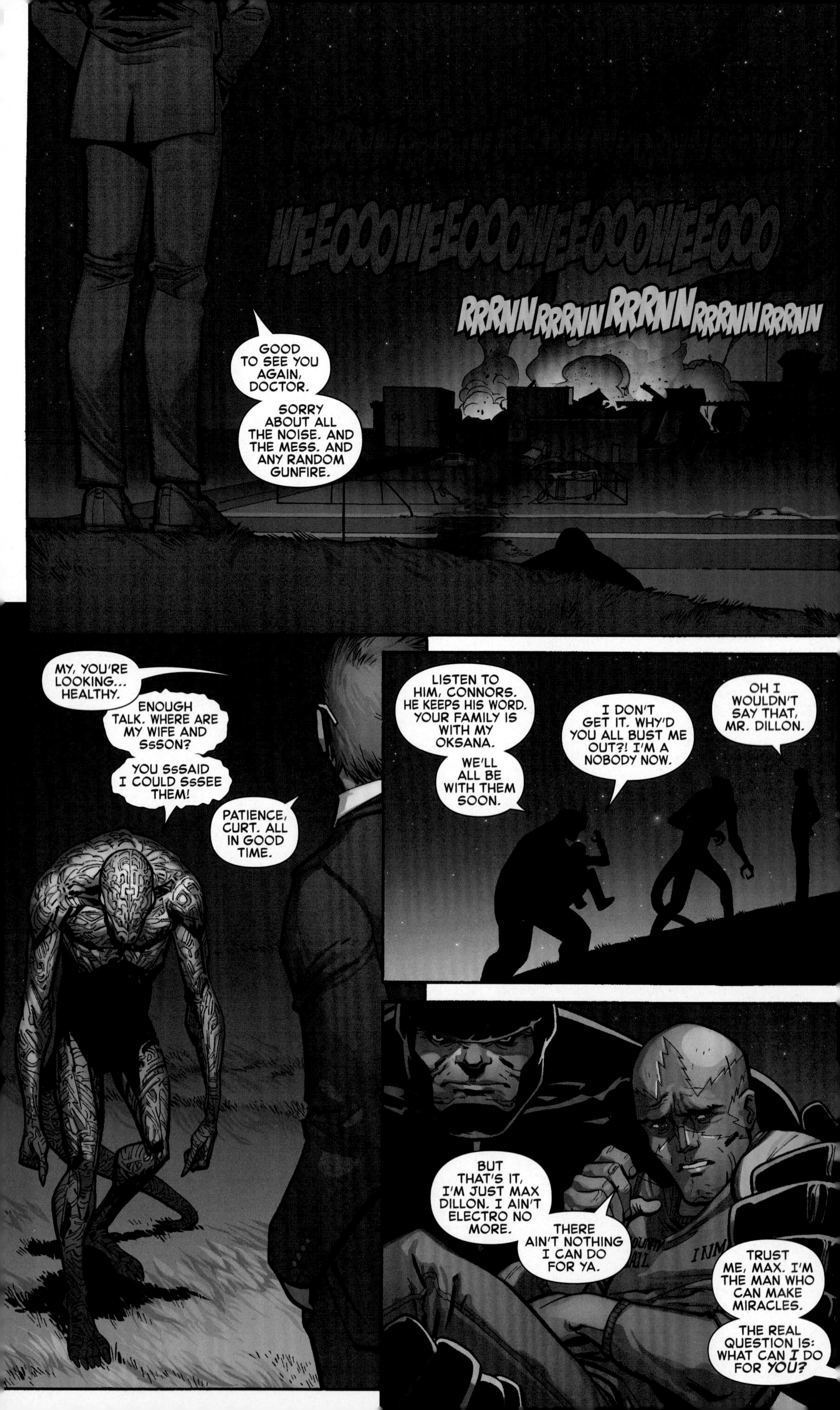
WEE-OOO WEE-OOO WEE-OOO WEE-OOO
RRRNN RRRNN RRRNN RRRNN RRRNN
GOOD TO SEE YOU AGAIN, DOCTOR.
SORRY ABOUT ALL THE NOISE. AND THE MESS. AND ANY RANDOM GUNFIRE.
MY, YOU'RE LOOKING... HEALTHY.
ENOUGH TALK. WHERE ARE MY WIFE AND SsSON?
YOU SsSAID I COULD SsSEE THEM!
PATIENCE, CURT. ALL IN GOOD TIME.
LISTEN TO HIM, CONNORS. HE KEEPS HIS WORD. YOUR FAMILY IS WITH MY OKSANA.
WE'LL ALL BE WITH THEM SOON.
I DON'T GET IT. WHY'D YOU ALL BUST ME OUT?! I'M A NOBODY NOW.
OH I WOULDN'T SAY THAT, MR. DILLON.
BUT THAT'S IT, I'M JUST MAX DILLON. I AIN'T ELECTRO NO MORE.
THERE AIN'T NOTHING I CAN DO FOR YA.
TRUST ME, MAX. I'M THE MAN WHO CAN MAKE MIRACLES.
THE REAL QUESTION IS: WHAT CAN *I* DO FOR *YOU?*

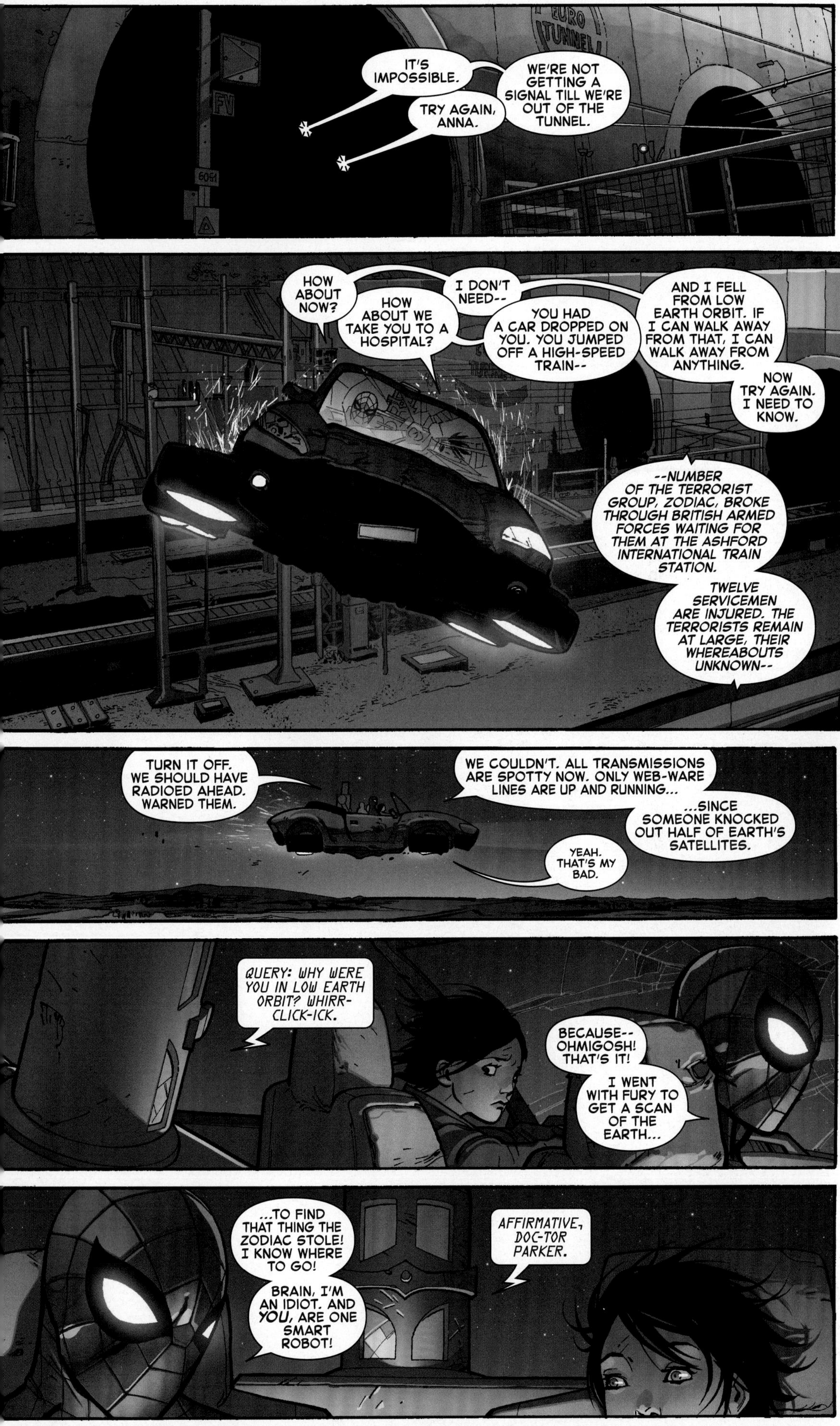
EURO TUNNEL
IT'S IMPOSSIBLE.
TRY AGAIN, ANNA.
WE'RE NOT GETTING A SIGNAL TILL WE'RE OUT OF THE TUNNEL.
HOW ABOUT NOW?
I DON'T NEED--
HOW ABOUT WE TAKE YOU TO A HOSPITAL?
YOU HAD A CAR DROPPED ON YOU. YOU JUMPED OFF A HIGH-SPEED TRAIN--
AND I FELL FROM LOW EARTH ORBIT. IF I CAN WALK AWAY FROM THAT, I CAN WALK AWAY FROM ANYTHING.
NOW TRY AGAIN. I NEED TO KNOW.
--NUMBER OF THE TERRORIST GROUP, ZODIAC, BROKE THROUGH BRITISH ARMED FORCES WAITING FOR THEM AT THE ASHFORD INTERNATIONAL TRAIN STATION.
TWELVE SERVICEMEN ARE INJURED. THE TERRORISTS REMAIN AT LARGE, THEIR WHEREABOUTS UNKNOWN--
TURN IT OFF. WE SHOULD HAVE RADIOED AHEAD. WARNED THEM.
WE COULDN'T. ALL TRANSMISSIONS ARE SPOTTY NOW. ONLY WEB-WARE LINES ARE UP AND RUNNING...
...SINCE SOMEONE KNOCKED OUT HALF OF EARTH'S SATELLITES.
YEAH. THAT'S MY BAD.
QUERY: WHY WERE YOU IN LOW EARTH ORBIT? WHIRR-CLICK-ICK.
BECAUSE-- OHMIGOSH! THAT'S IT!
I WENT WITH FURY TO GET A SCAN OF THE EARTH...
...TO FIND THAT THING THE ZODIAC STOLE! I KNOW WHERE TO GO!
BRAIN, I'M AN IDIOT. AND YOU, ARE ONE SMART ROBOT!
AFFIRMATIVE, DOC-TOR PARKER.

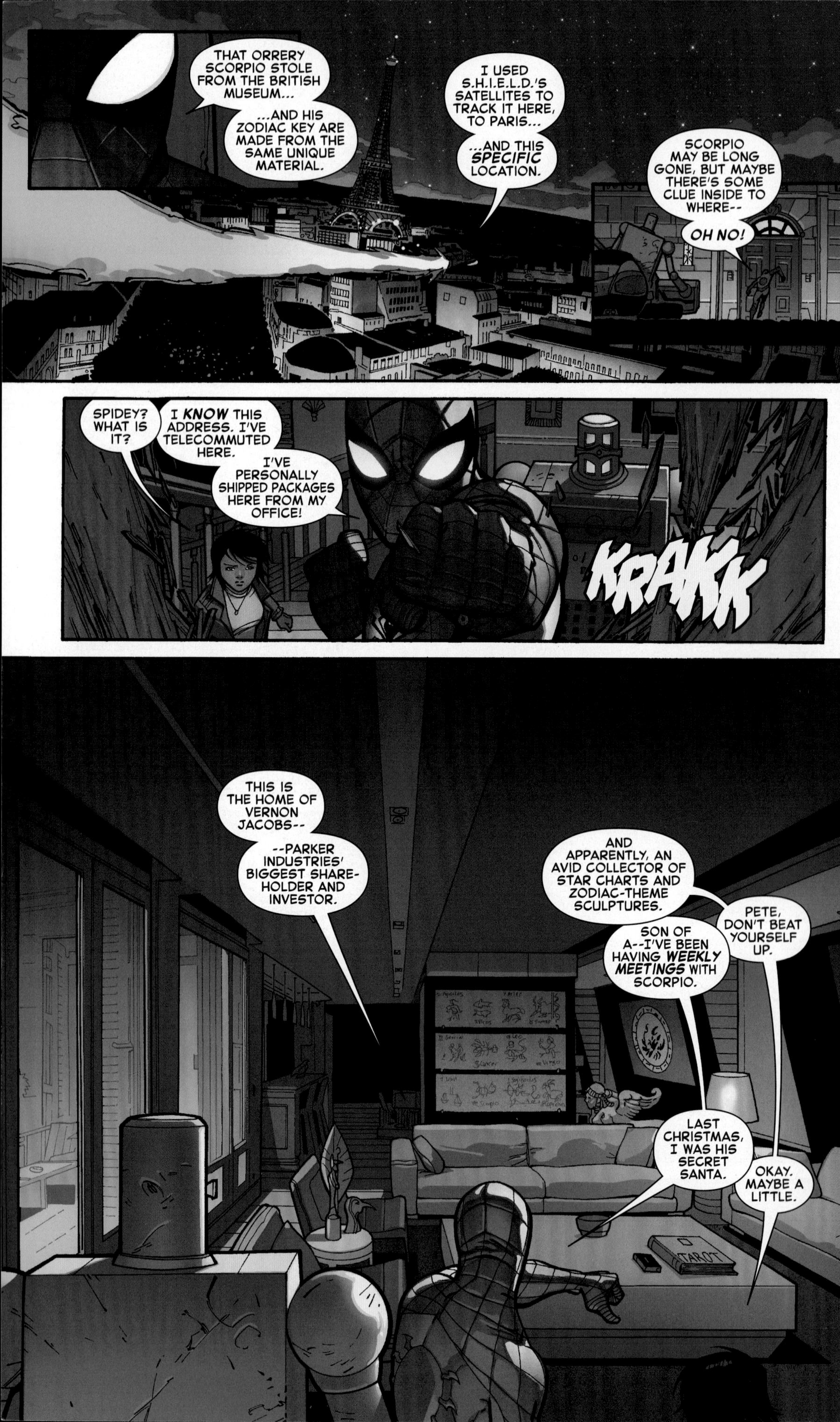
THAT ORRERY SCORPIO STOLE FROM THE BRITISH MUSEUM...
...AND HIS ZODIAC KEY ARE MADE FROM THE SAME UNIQUE MATERIAL.
I USED S.H.I.E.L.D.'S SATELLITES TO TRACK IT HERE, TO PARIS...
...AND THIS SPECIFIC LOCATION.
SCORPIO MAY BE LONG GONE, BUT MAYBE THERE'S SOME CLUE INSIDE TO WHERE--
OH NO!
SPIDEY? WHAT IS IT?
I KNOW THIS ADDRESS. I'VE TELECOMMUTED HERE.
I'VE PERSONALLY SHIPPED PACKAGES HERE FROM MY OFFICE!
KRAKK
THIS IS THE HOME OF VERNON JACOBS--
--PARKER INDUSTRIES' BIGGEST SHARE-HOLDER AND INVESTOR.
AND APPARENTLY, AN AVID COLLECTOR OF STAR CHARTS AND ZODIAC-THEME SCULPTURES.
SON OF A--I'VE BEEN HAVING WEEKLY MEETINGS WITH SCORPIO.
PETE, DON'T BEAT YOURSELF UP.
LAST CHRISTMAS, I WAS HIS SECRET SANTA.
OKAY. MAYBE A LITTLE.
TAROT

MY SPIDEY-LENSES ARE PICKING UP TRACES OF BOTH THE KEY AND THE ORRERY.

JACOBS MUST'VE KEPT THEM BACK HERE.

BRAIN, YOU SCANNING ANYTHING?

AN ENTRANCE TO SUB-LEVELS. WHIRR-CLICK-ICK.

ASTRO-TURF. WHO NEEDS A FAKE HILL IN THEIR HOUSE?

THIS DOME? IT'S AN ENORMOUS, CURVED SCREEN.

IT'S A PRIVATE PLANETARIUM.

WHIRR-CLICK-ICK. THERE IS MORE THIS WAY.

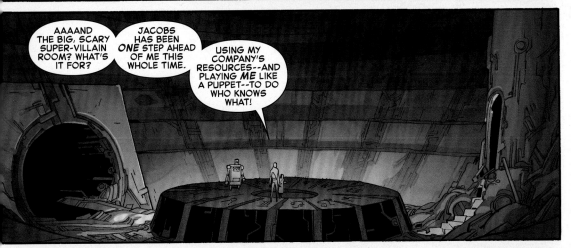

AAAAND THE BIG, SCARY SUPER-VILLAIN ROOM? WHAT'S IT FOR?

JACOBS HAS BEEN ONE STEP AHEAD OF ME THIS WHOLE TIME.

USING MY COMPANY'S RESOURCES--AND PLAYING ME LIKE A PUPPET--TO DO WHO KNOWS WHAT!

THERE'S TOO MUCH TO GO THROUGH HERE. AND NOT ENOUGH TIME. I MIGHT ALREADY BE TOO LATE. WHAT DO I DO?

ASK FOR HELP.

I JUST DID.

NOT ME.

IF HE CAN USE YOUR COMPANY, SO CAN YOU.

THE BEST PART OF IT. CALL IN EVERYONE.

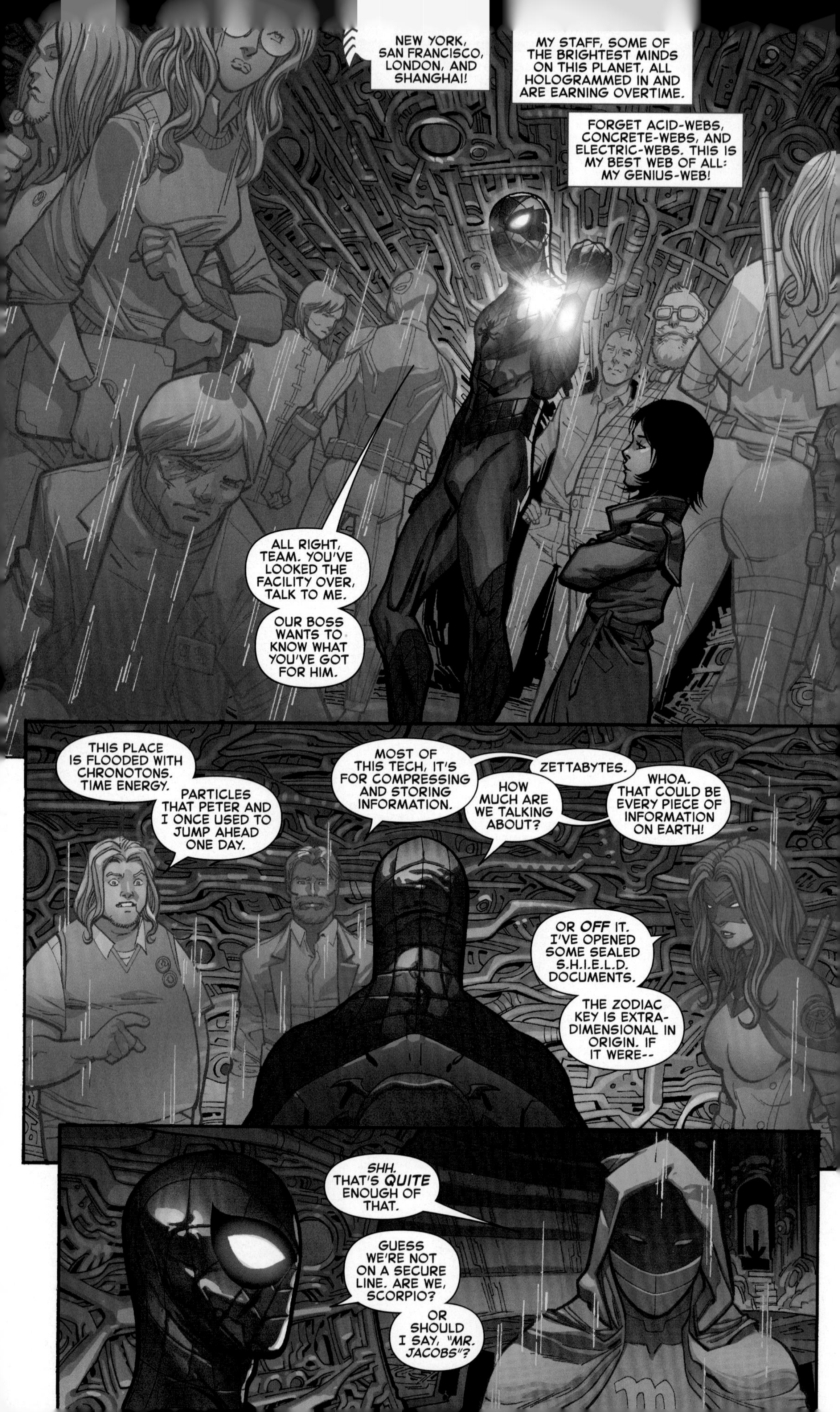
NEW YORK, SAN FRANCISCO, LONDON, AND SHANGHAI!
MY STAFF, SOME OF THE BRIGHTEST MINDS ON THIS PLANET, ALL HOLOGRAMMED IN AND ARE EARNING OVERTIME.
FORGET ACID-WEBS, CONCRETE-WEBS, AND ELECTRIC-WEBS. THIS IS MY BEST WEB OF ALL: MY GENIUS-WEB!
ALL RIGHT, TEAM. YOU'VE LOOKED THE FACILITY OVER, TALK TO ME.
OUR BOSS WANTS TO KNOW WHAT YOU'VE GOT FOR HIM.
THIS PLACE IS FLOODED WITH CHRONOTONS. TIME ENERGY.
PARTICLES THAT PETER AND I ONCE USED TO JUMP AHEAD ONE DAY.
MOST OF THIS TECH, IT'S FOR COMPRESSING AND STORING INFORMATION.
HOW MUCH ARE WE TALKING ABOUT?
ZETTABYTES.
WHOA. THAT COULD BE EVERY PIECE OF INFORMATION ON EARTH!
OR *OFF* IT. I'VE OPENED SOME SEALED S.H.I.E.L.D. DOCUMENTS.
THE ZODIAC KEY IS EXTRA-DIMENSIONAL IN ORIGIN. IF IT WERE--
SHH. THAT'S ***QUITE*** ENOUGH OF THAT.
GUESS WE'RE NOT ON A SECURE LINE. ARE WE, SCORPIO?
OR SHOULD I SAY, "*MR. JACOBS*"?

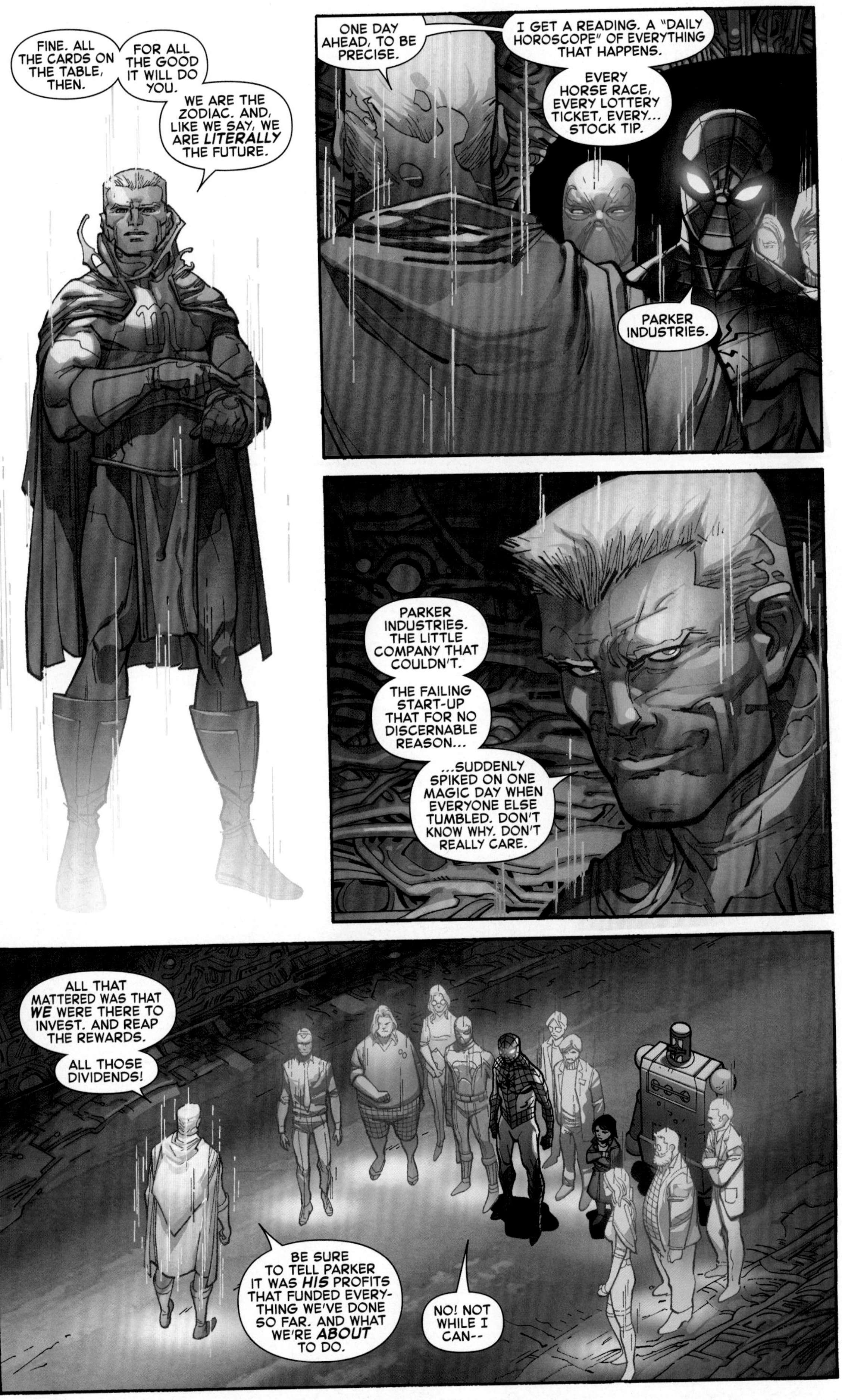

FINE. ALL THE CARDS ON THE TABLE, THEN.
FOR ALL THE GOOD IT WILL DO YOU.
WE ARE THE ZODIAC. AND, LIKE WE SAY, WE ARE *LITERALLY* THE FUTURE.
ONE DAY AHEAD, TO BE PRECISE.
I GET A READING. A "DAILY HOROSCOPE" OF EVERYTHING THAT HAPPENS.
EVERY HORSE RACE, EVERY LOTTERY TICKET, EVERY... STOCK TIP.
PARKER INDUSTRIES.
PARKER INDUSTRIES. THE LITTLE COMPANY THAT COULDN'T.
THE FAILING START-UP THAT FOR NO DISCERNABLE REASON...
...SUDDENLY SPIKED ON ONE MAGIC DAY WHEN EVERYONE ELSE TUMBLED. DON'T KNOW WHY. DON'T REALLY CARE.
ALL THAT MATTERED WAS THAT *WE* WERE THERE TO INVEST. AND REAP THE REWARDS.
ALL THOSE DIVIDENDS!
BE SURE TO TELL PARKER IT WAS *HIS* PROFITS THAT FUNDED EVERYTHING WE'VE DONE SO FAR. AND WHAT WE'RE *ABOUT* TO DO.
NO! NOT WHILE I CAN--

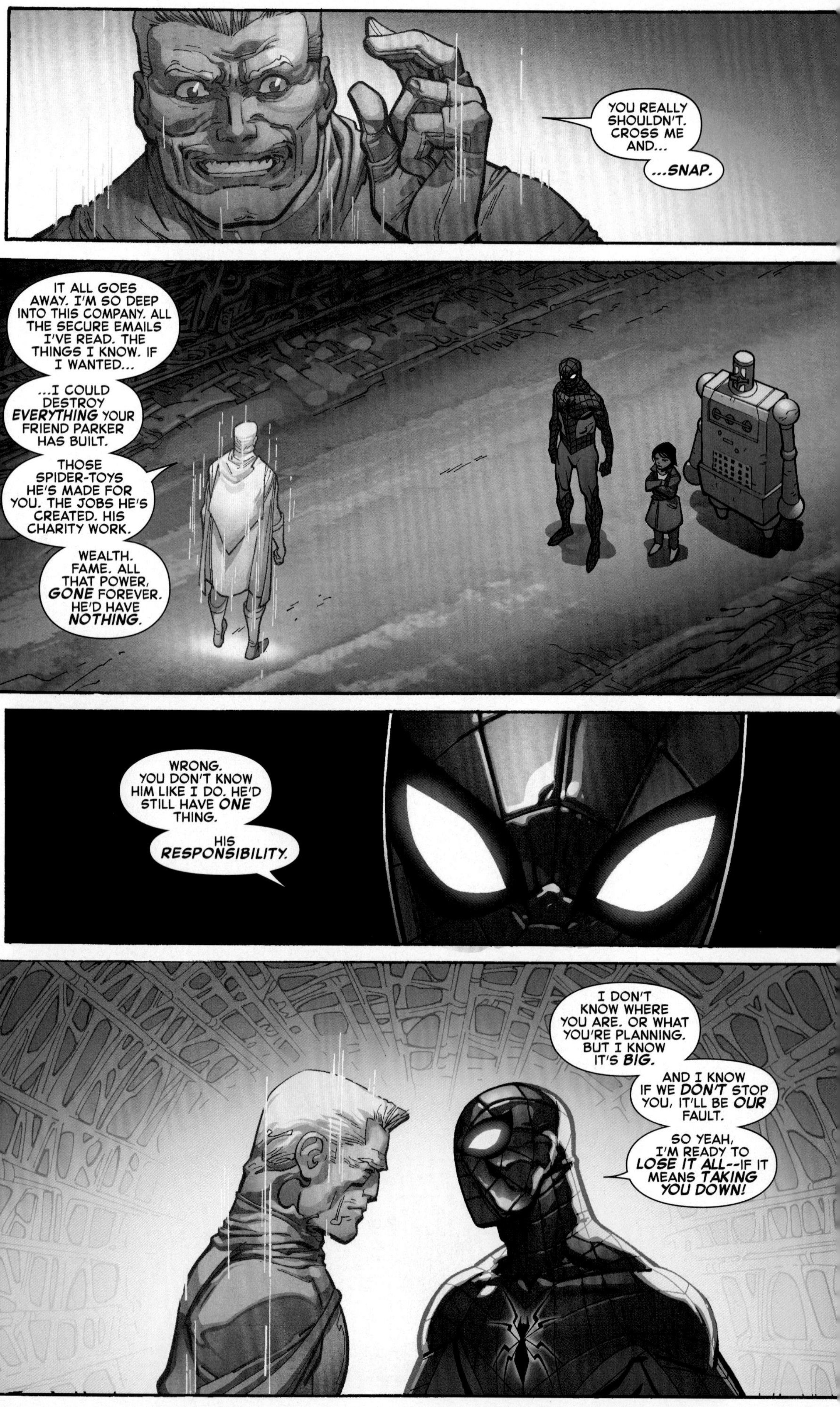

YOU REALLY SHOULDN'T. CROSS ME AND...
...SNAP.
IT ALL GOES AWAY. I'M SO DEEP INTO THIS COMPANY. ALL THE SECURE EMAILS I'VE READ. THE THINGS I KNOW. IF I WANTED...
...I COULD DESTROY EVERYTHING YOUR FRIEND PARKER HAS BUILT.
THOSE SPIDER-TOYS HE'S MADE FOR YOU. THE JOBS HE'S CREATED. HIS CHARITY WORK.
WEALTH. FAME. ALL THAT POWER, GONE FOREVER. HE'D HAVE NOTHING.
WRONG. YOU DON'T KNOW HIM LIKE I DO. HE'D STILL HAVE ONE THING.
HIS RESPONSIBILITY.
I DON'T KNOW WHERE YOU ARE. OR WHAT YOU'RE PLANNING. BUT I KNOW IT'S BIG.
AND I KNOW IF WE DON'T STOP YOU, IT'LL BE OUR FAULT.
SO YEAH, I'M READY TO LOSE IT ALL--IF IT MEANS TAKING YOU DOWN!

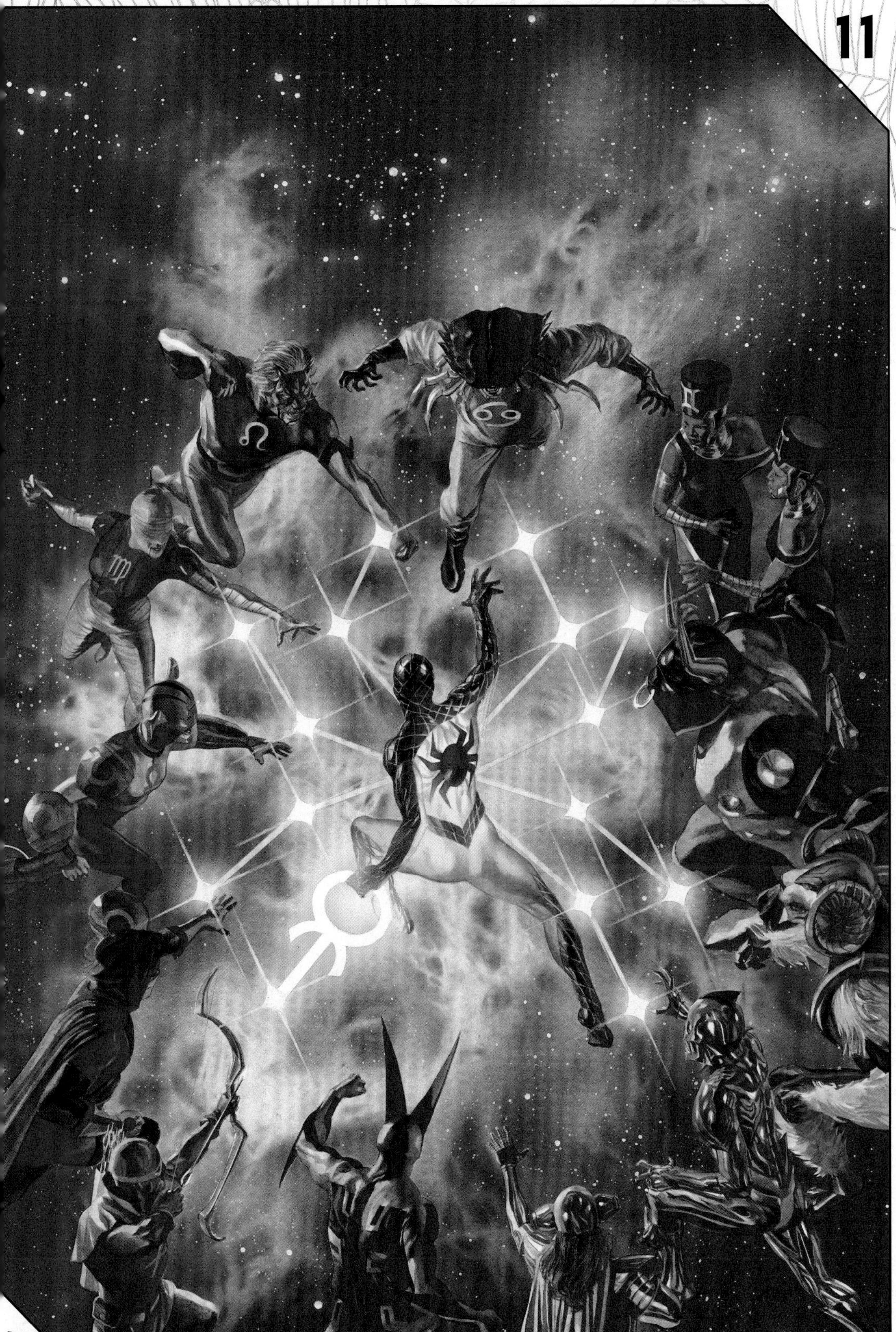

SCORPIO RISING - PART 3: "SIGNS FROM ABOVE"

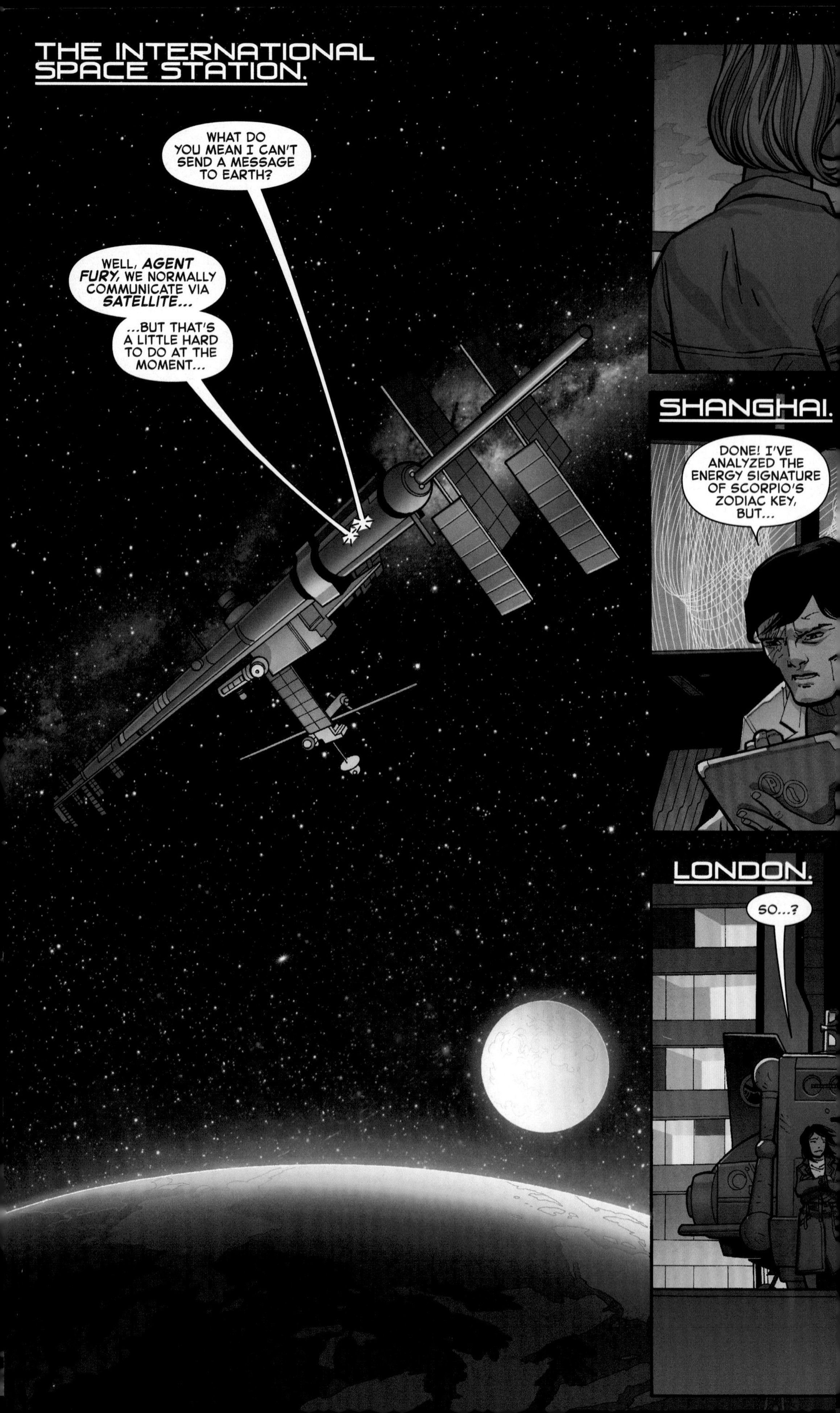

THE INTERNATIONAL SPACE STATION.
WHAT DO YOU MEAN I CAN'T SEND A MESSAGE TO EARTH?
WELL, AGENT FURY, WE NORMALLY COMMUNICATE VIA SATELLITE...
...BUT THAT'S A LITTLE HARD TO DO AT THE MOMENT...
SHANGHAI.
DONE! I'VE ANALYZED THE ENERGY SIGNATURE OF SCORPIO'S ZODIAC KEY, BUT...
LONDON.
SO...?

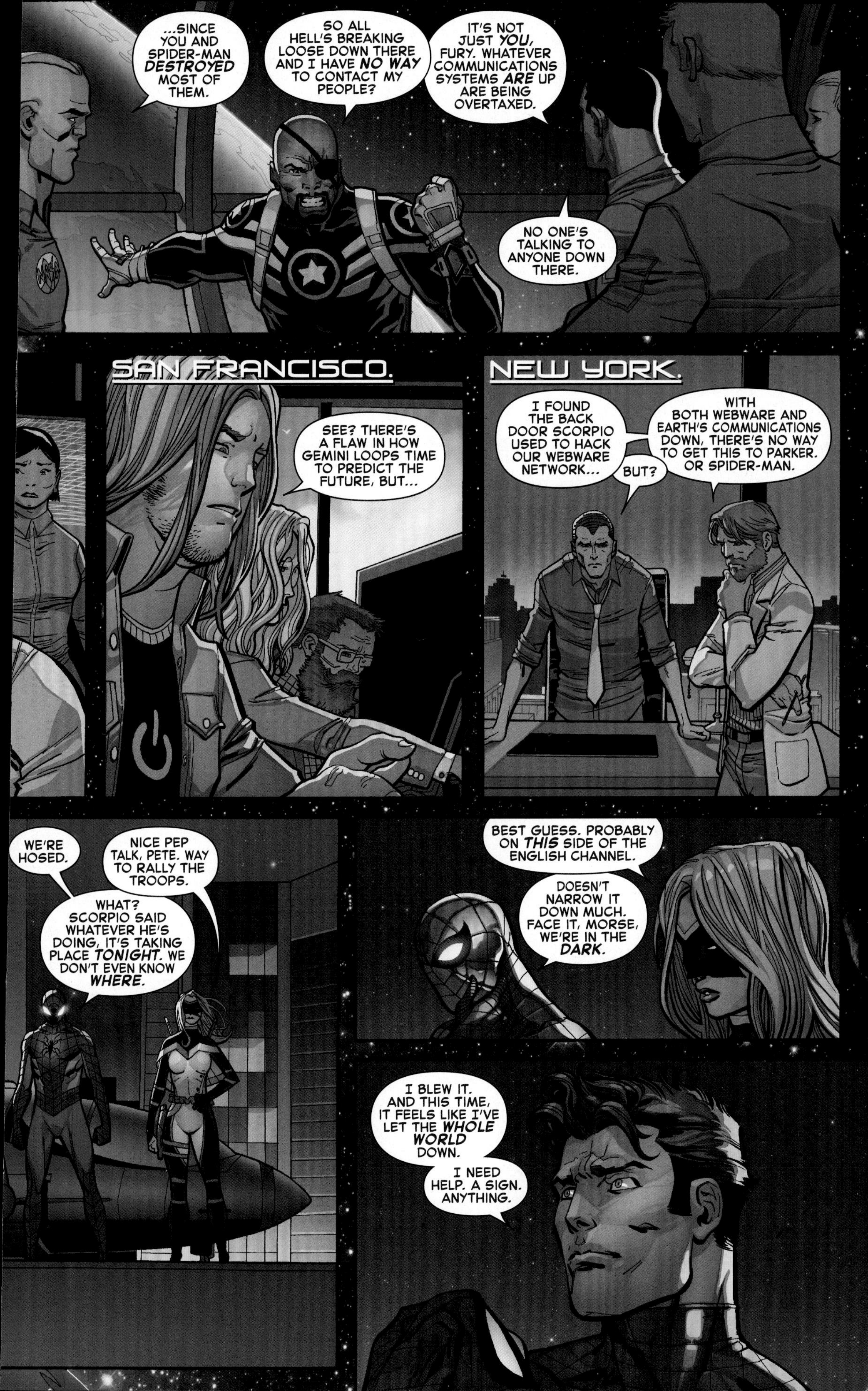
...SINCE YOU AND SPIDER-MAN *DESTROYED* MOST OF THEM.
SO ALL HELL'S BREAKING LOOSE DOWN THERE AND I HAVE *NO WAY* TO CONTACT MY PEOPLE?
IT'S NOT JUST *YOU*, FURY. WHATEVER COMMUNICATIONS SYSTEMS *ARE* UP ARE BEING OVERTAXED.
NO ONE'S TALKING TO ANYONE DOWN THERE.
SAN FRANCISCO.
SEE? THERE'S A FLAW IN HOW GEMINI LOOPS TIME TO PREDICT THE FUTURE, BUT...
NEW YORK.
I FOUND THE BACK DOOR SCORPIO USED TO HACK OUR WEBWARE NETWORK...
BUT?
WITH BOTH WEBWARE AND EARTH'S COMMUNICATIONS DOWN, THERE'S NO WAY TO GET THIS TO PARKER. OR SPIDER-MAN.
WE'RE HOSED.
NICE PEP TALK, PETE. WAY TO RALLY THE TROOPS.
WHAT? SCORPIO SAID WHATEVER HE'S DOING, IT'S TAKING PLACE *TONIGHT*. WE DON'T EVEN KNOW *WHERE*.
BEST GUESS. PROBABLY ON *THIS* SIDE OF THE ENGLISH CHANNEL.
DOESN'T NARROW IT DOWN MUCH. FACE IT, MORSE, WE'RE IN THE *DARK*.
I BLEW IT. AND THIS TIME, IT FEELS LIKE I'VE LET THE *WHOLE WORLD* DOWN.
I NEED HELP. A SIGN. ANYTHING.

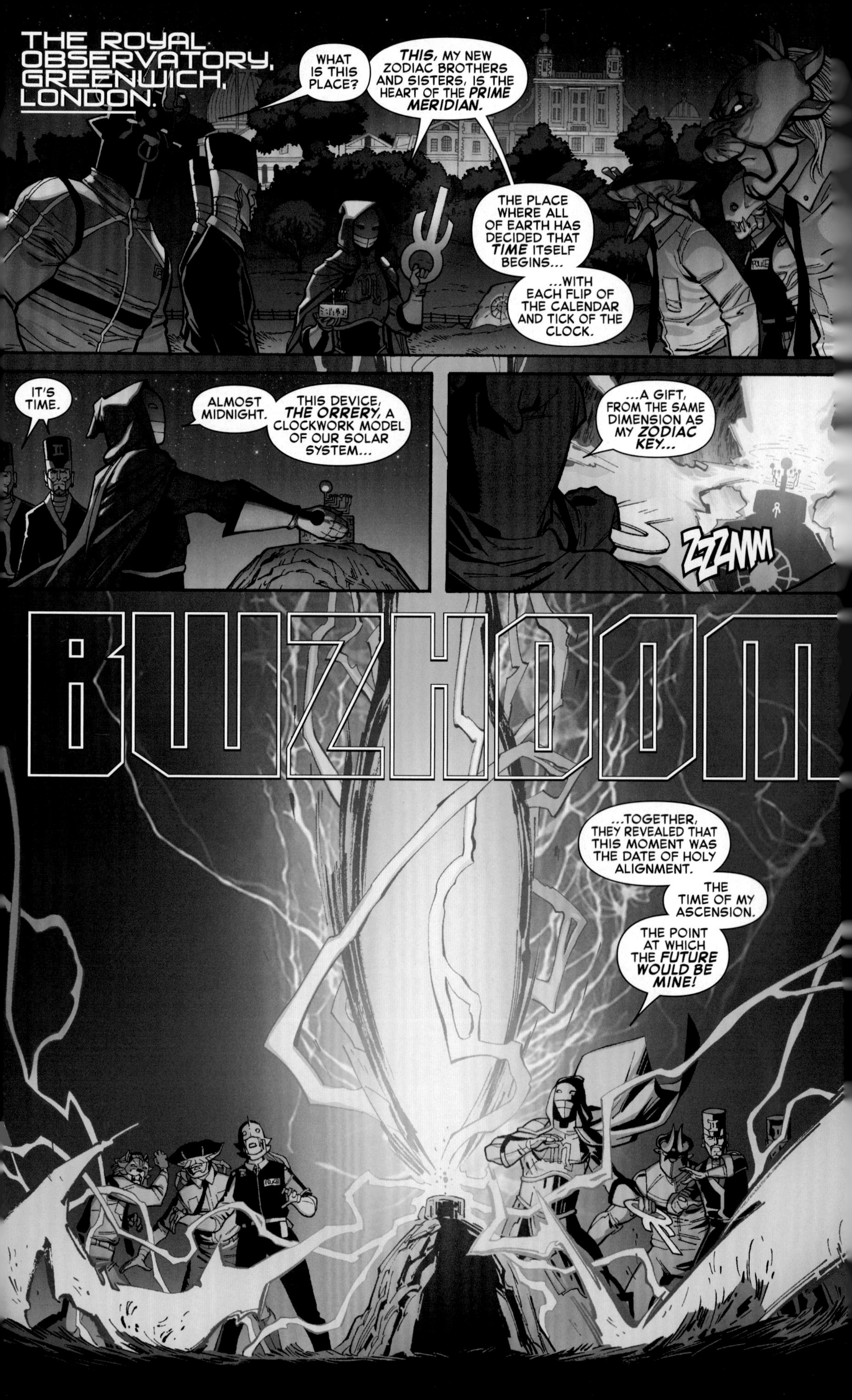
THE ROYAL OBSERVATORY, GREENWICH, LONDON.
WHAT IS THIS PLACE?
THIS, MY NEW ZODIAC BROTHERS AND SISTERS, IS THE HEART OF THE PRIME MERIDIAN.
THE PLACE WHERE ALL OF EARTH HAS DECIDED THAT TIME ITSELF BEGINS...
...WITH EACH FLIP OF THE CALENDAR AND TICK OF THE CLOCK.
IT'S TIME.
ALMOST MIDNIGHT.
THIS DEVICE, THE ORRERY, A CLOCKWORK MODEL OF OUR SOLAR SYSTEM...
...A GIFT, FROM THE SAME DIMENSION AS MY ZODIAC KEY...
ZZZMM
BWZHOOM
...TOGETHER, THEY REVEALED THAT THIS MOMENT WAS THE DATE OF HOLY ALIGNMENT.
THE TIME OF MY ASCENSION.
THE POINT AT WHICH THE FUTURE WOULD BE MINE!

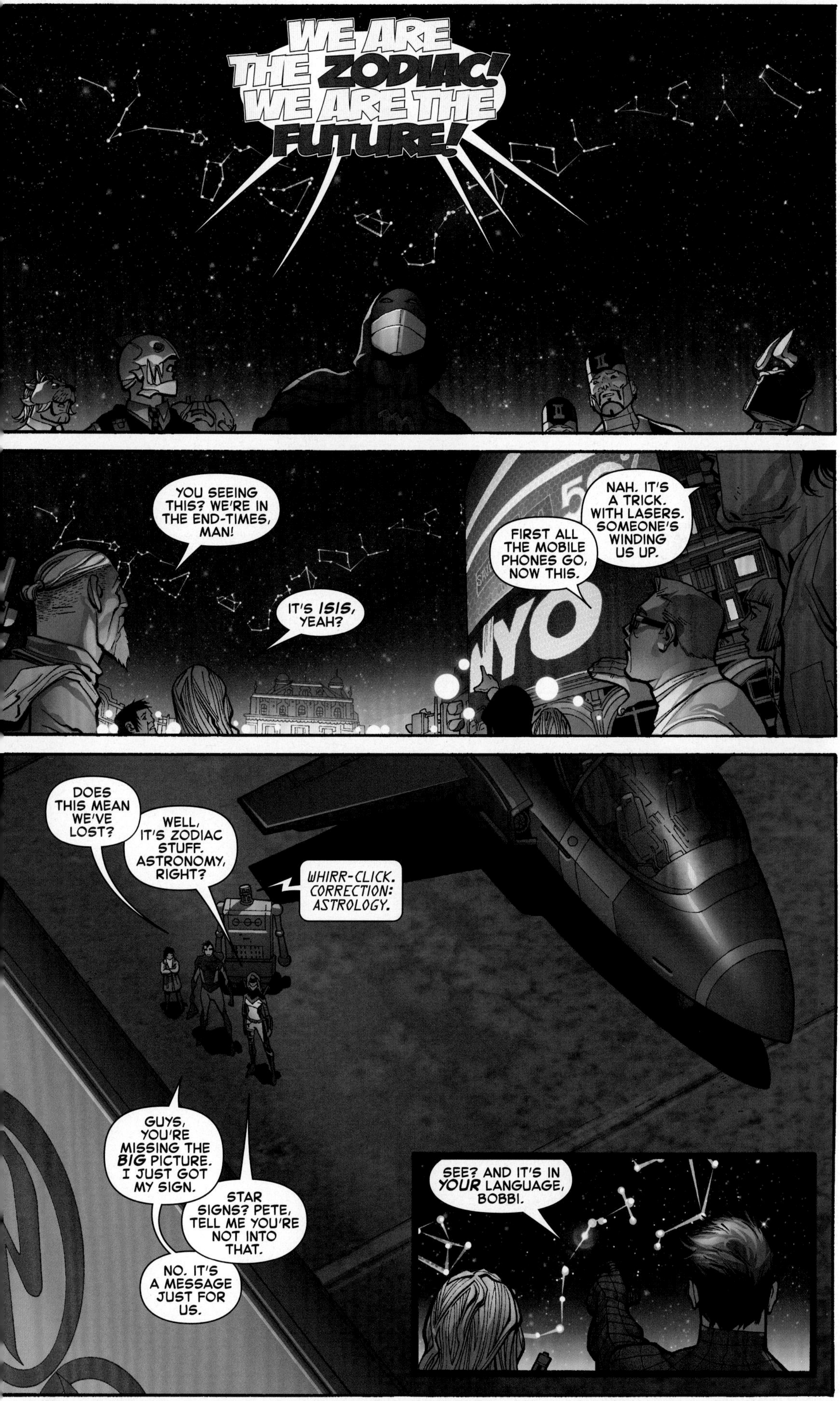
WE ARE THE ZODIAC! WE ARE THE FUTURE!
YOU SEEING THIS? WE'RE IN THE END-TIMES, MAN!
IT'S *ISIS*, YEAH?
NAH. IT'S A TRICK. WITH LASERS. SOMEONE'S WINDING US UP.
FIRST ALL THE MOBILE PHONES GO, NOW THIS.
DOES THIS MEAN WE'VE LOST?
WELL, IT'S ZODIAC STUFF. ASTRONOMY, RIGHT?
WHIRR-CLICK. CORRECTION: ASTROLOGY.
GUYS, YOU'RE MISSING THE *BIG* PICTURE. I JUST GOT MY SIGN.
STAR SIGNS? PETE, TELL ME YOU'RE NOT INTO THAT.
NO. IT'S A MESSAGE JUST FOR US.
SEE? AND IT'S IN *YOUR* LANGUAGE, BOBBI.

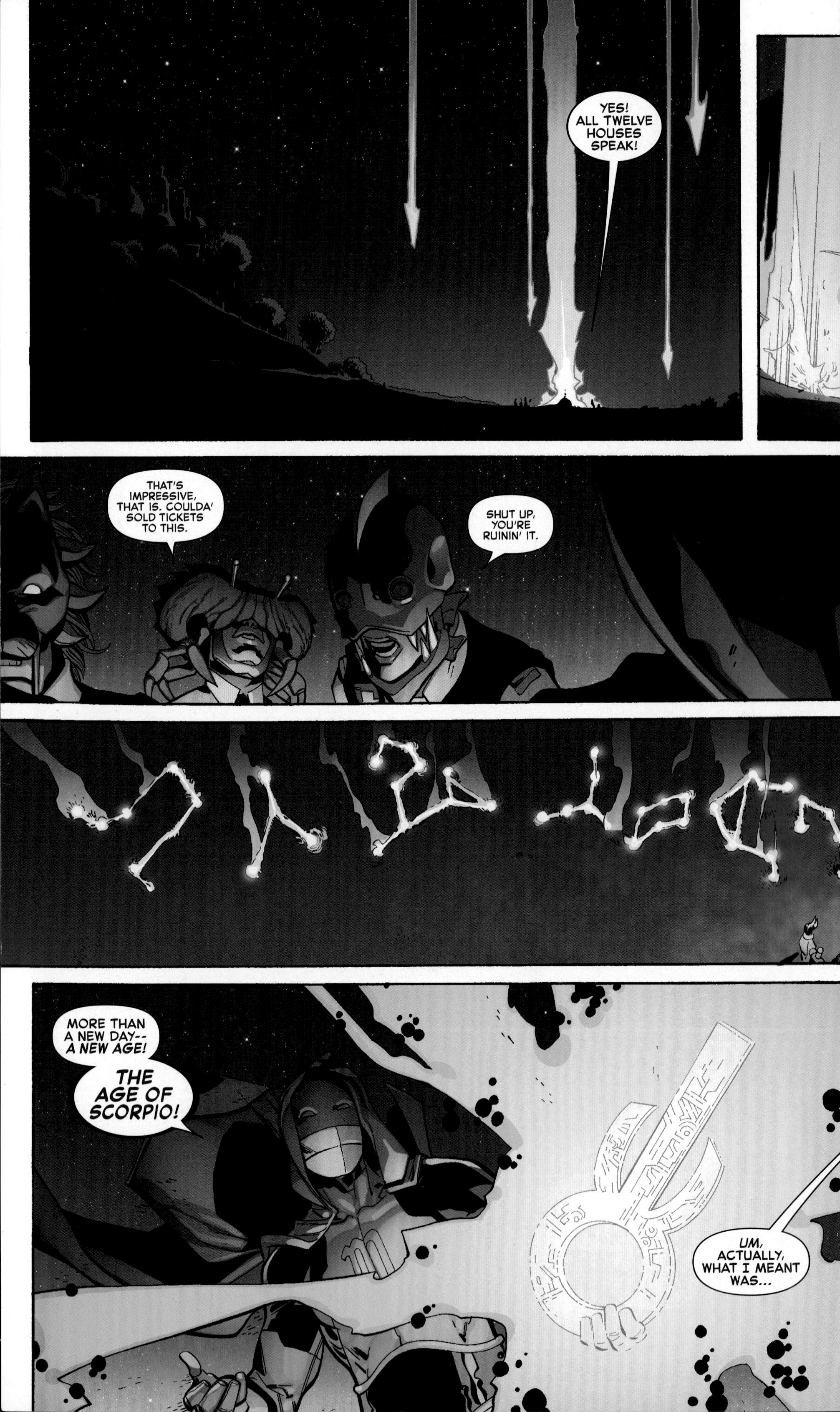
YES! ALL TWELVE HOUSES SPEAK!
THAT'S IMPRESSIVE, THAT IS. COULDA' SOLD TICKETS TO THIS.
SHUT UP, YOU'RE RUININ' IT.
MORE THAN A NEW DAY-- A NEW AGE!
THE AGE OF SCORPIO!
UM, ACTUALLY, WHAT I MEANT WAS...

BLAZE A TRAIL! SHOW ME!

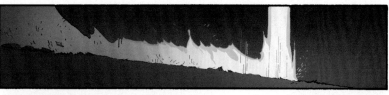

THE DOORWAY.

AT LAST, IT IS REVEALED.

MIDNIGHT. THE DAY IS OVER.

A NEW DAY BEGINS.

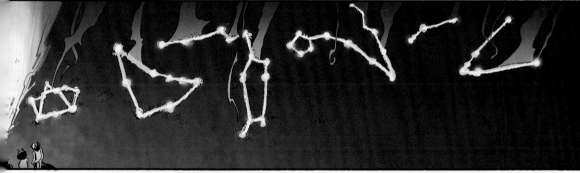

...I HAVE TO LOOP IN TIME AGAIN.

OR I CAN'T TELL YOU WHAT WILL HAPPEN ONE DAY INTO--

IT'S GONE. I DON'T KNOW WHAT'S NEXT.

WHO CARES?

BUT WHAT IF SPIDER-MAN INTERFERES AGAIN?

HERE! I'LL SAVE YOU THE TROUBLE!

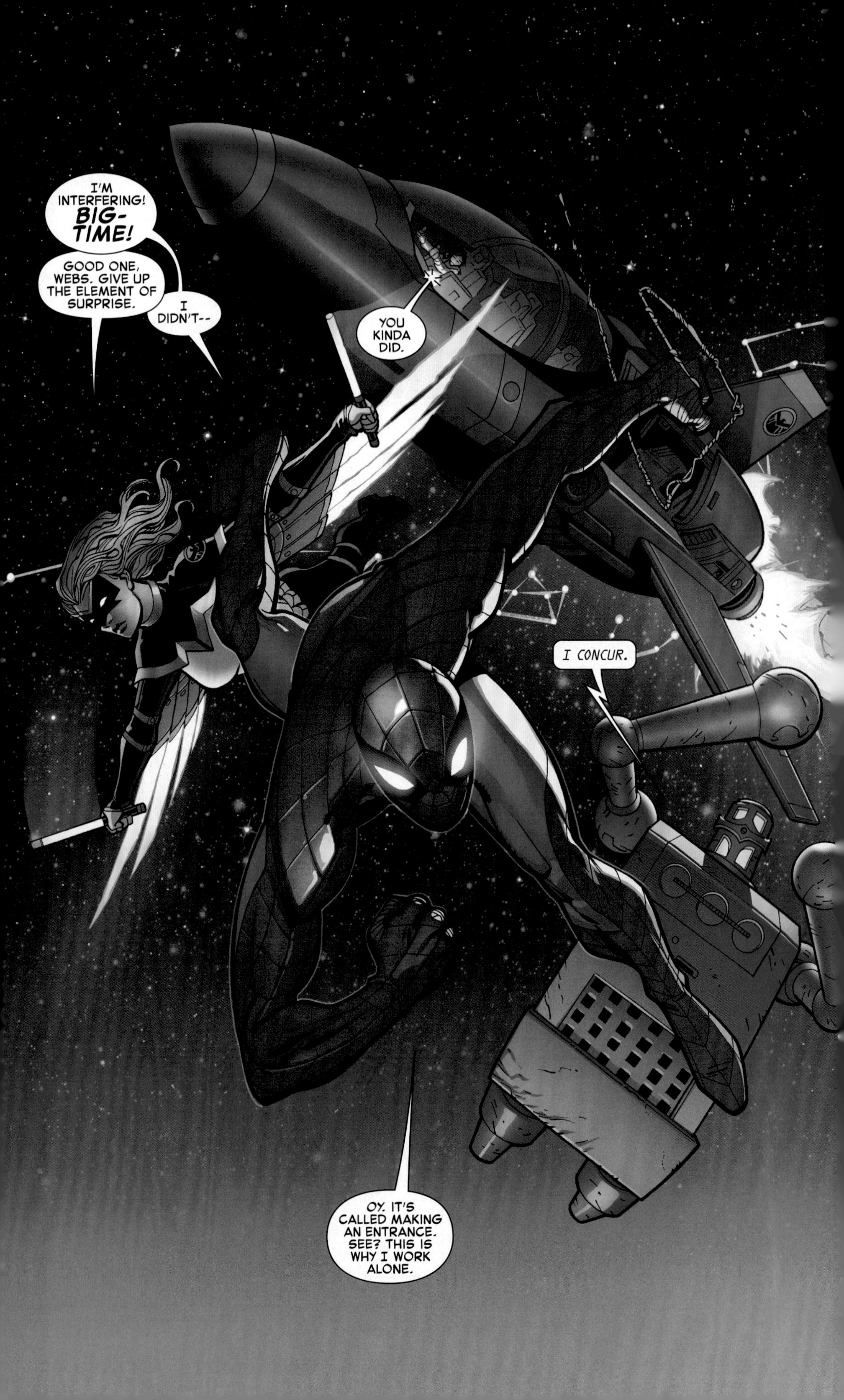
I'M INTERFERING! BIG-TIME!
GOOD ONE, WEBS. GIVE UP THE ELEMENT OF SURPRISE.
I DIDN'T--
YOU KINDA DID.
I CONCUR.
OY. IT'S CALLED MAKING AN ENTRANCE. SEE? THIS IS WHY I WORK ALONE.

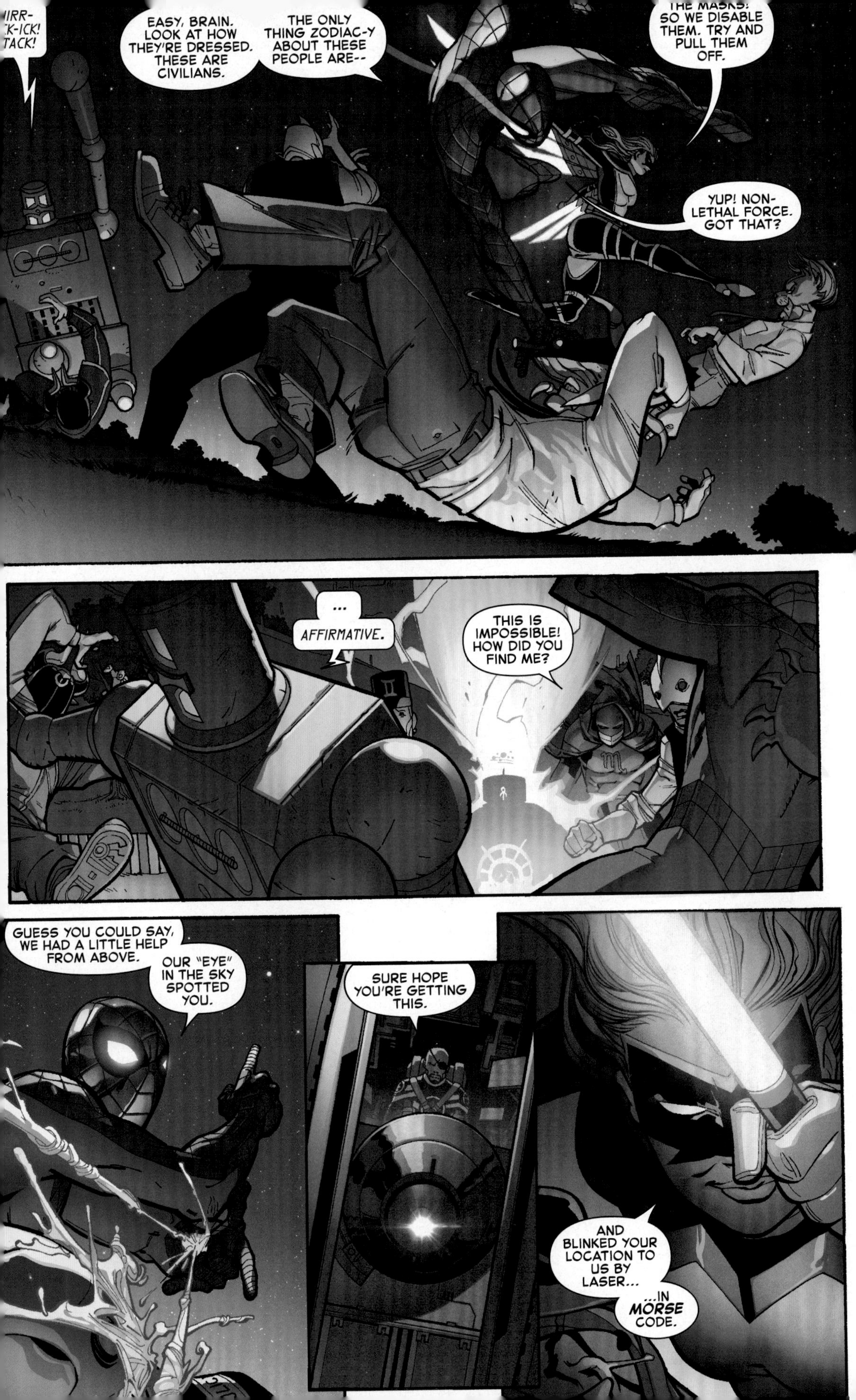
EASY, BRAIN. LOOK AT HOW THEY'RE DRESSED. THESE ARE CIVILIANS.
THE ONLY THING ZODIAC-Y ABOUT THESE PEOPLE ARE--
THE MASKS! SO WE DISABLE THEM. TRY AND PULL THEM OFF.
YUP! NON-LETHAL FORCE. GOT THAT?
... AFFIRMATIVE.
THIS IS IMPOSSIBLE! HOW DID YOU FIND ME?
GUESS YOU COULD SAY, WE HAD A LITTLE HELP FROM ABOVE.
OUR "EYE" IN THE SKY SPOTTED YOU.
SURE HOPE YOU'RE GETTING THIS.
AND BLINKED YOUR LOCATION TO US BY LASER...
...IN MORSE CODE.

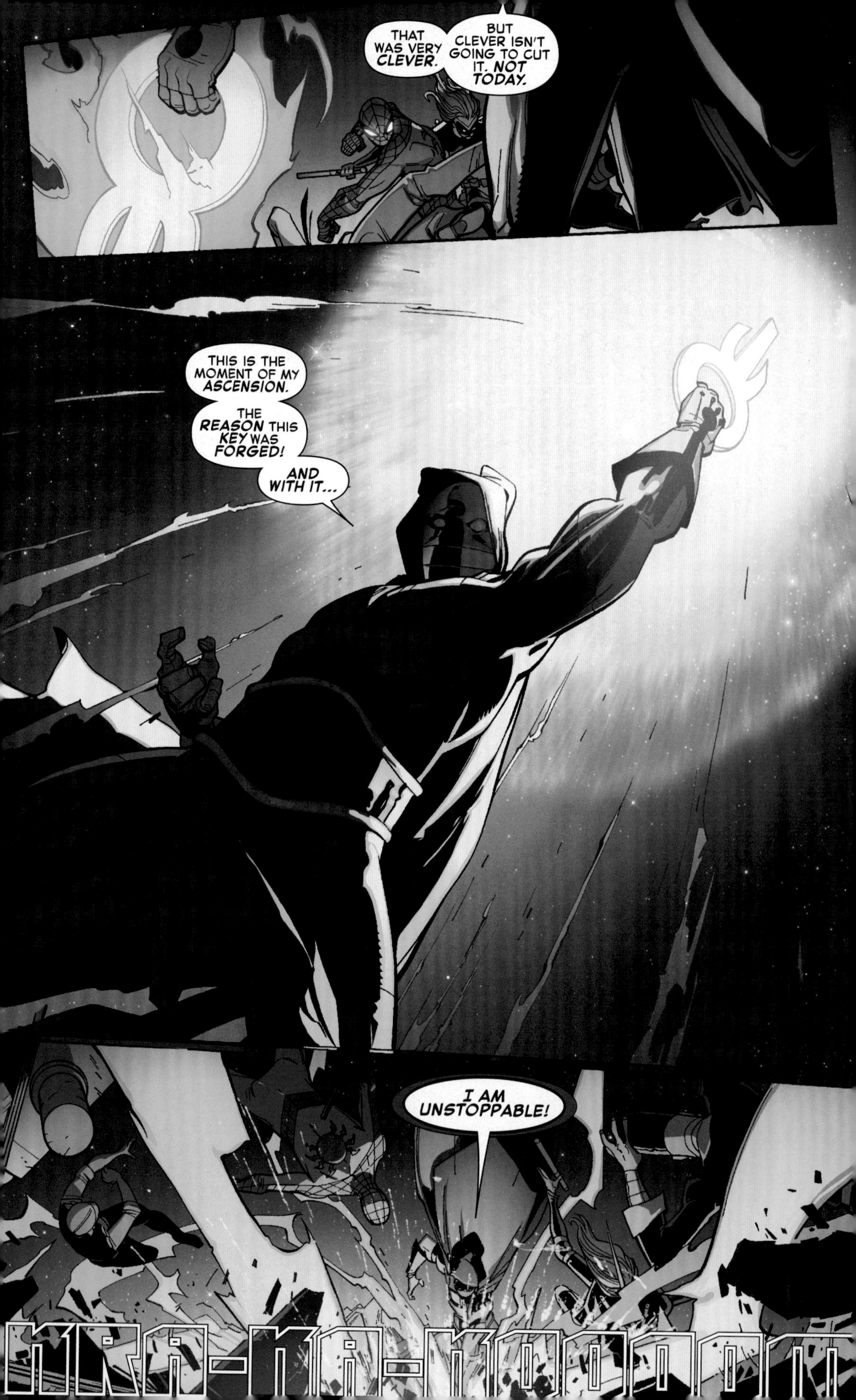
THAT WAS VERY CLEVER.
BUT CLEVER ISN'T GOING TO CUT IT. NOT TODAY.
THIS IS THE MOMENT OF MY ASCENSION.
THE REASON THIS KEY WAS FORGED!
AND WITH IT...
I AM UNSTOPPABLE!
KRA-KA-KOOOOOM

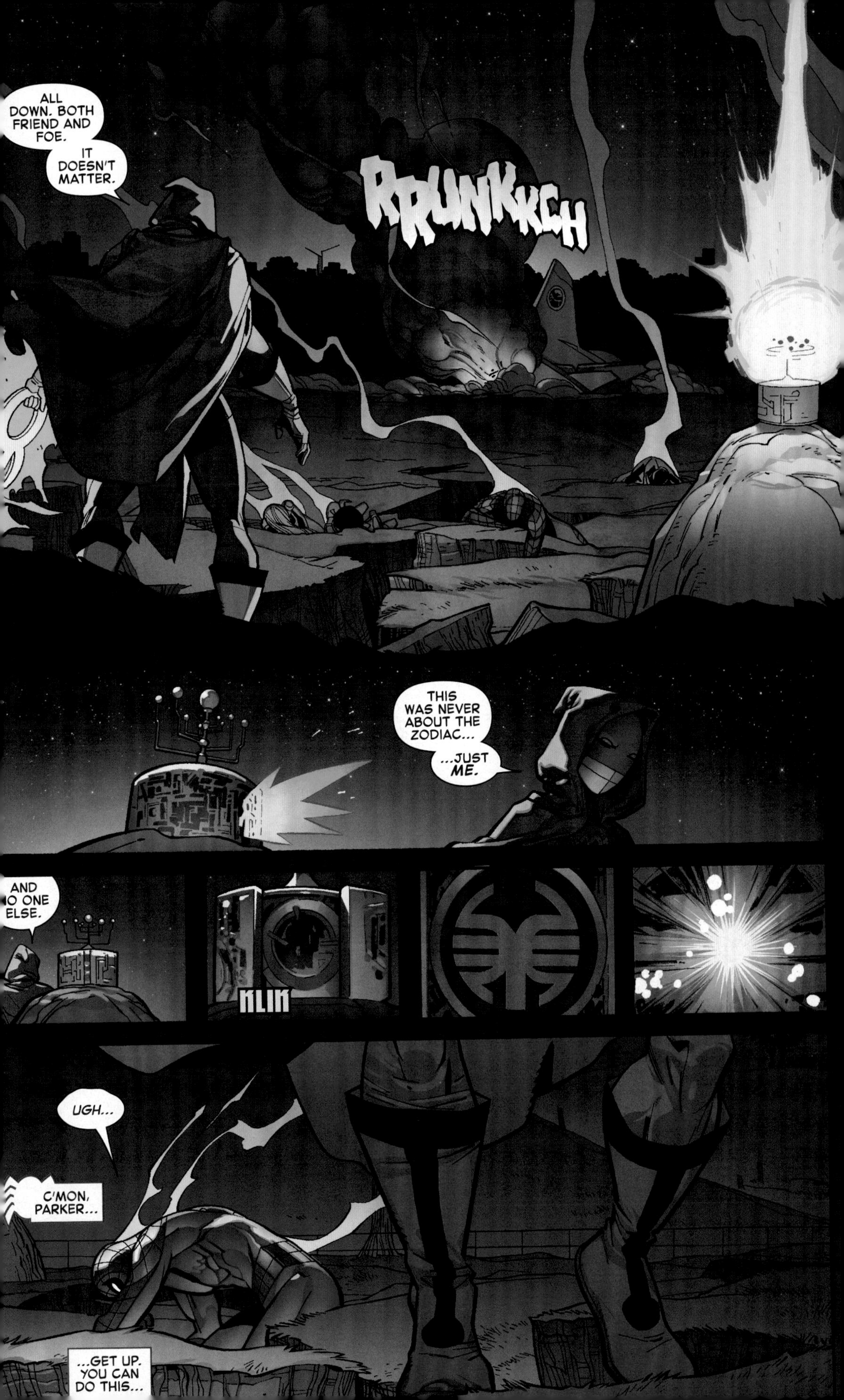
ALL DOWN. BOTH FRIEND AND FOE.
IT DOESN'T MATTER.
RRUNKKCH
THIS WAS NEVER ABOUT THE ZODIAC...
...JUST ME.
AND NO ONE ELSE.
KLIK
UGH...
C'MON, PARKER...
...GET UP. YOU CAN DO THIS...

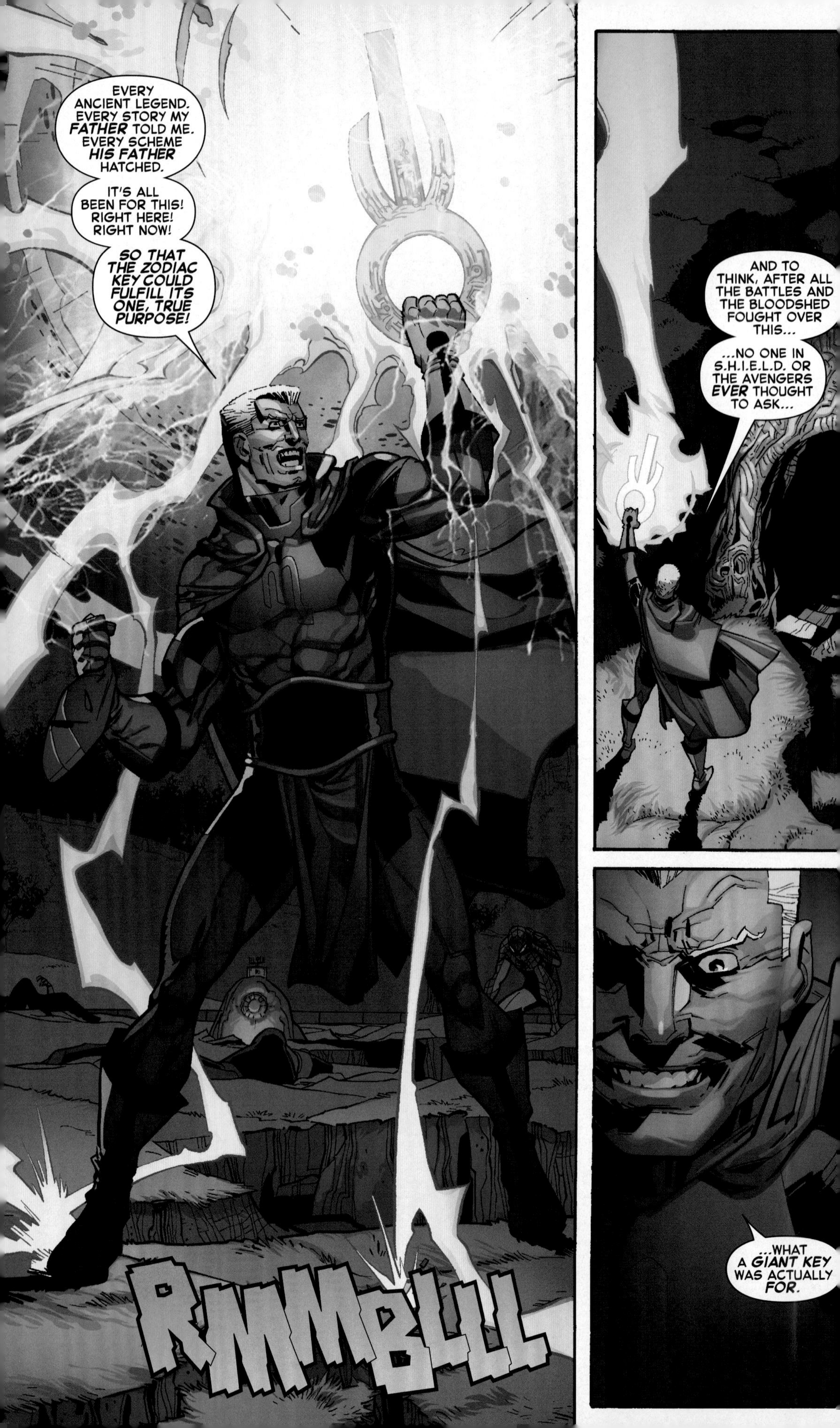
EVERY ANCIENT LEGEND. EVERY STORY MY FATHER TOLD ME. EVERY SCHEME HIS FATHER HATCHED.
IT'S ALL BEEN FOR THIS! RIGHT HERE! RIGHT NOW!
SO THAT THE ZODIAC KEY COULD FULFILL ITS ONE, TRUE PURPOSE!
RMMBLLL
AND TO THINK, AFTER ALL THE BATTLES AND THE BLOODSHED FOUGHT OVER THIS...
...NO ONE IN S.H.I.E.L.D. OR THE AVENGERS EVER THOUGHT TO ASK...
...WHAT A GIANT KEY WAS ACTUALLY FOR.

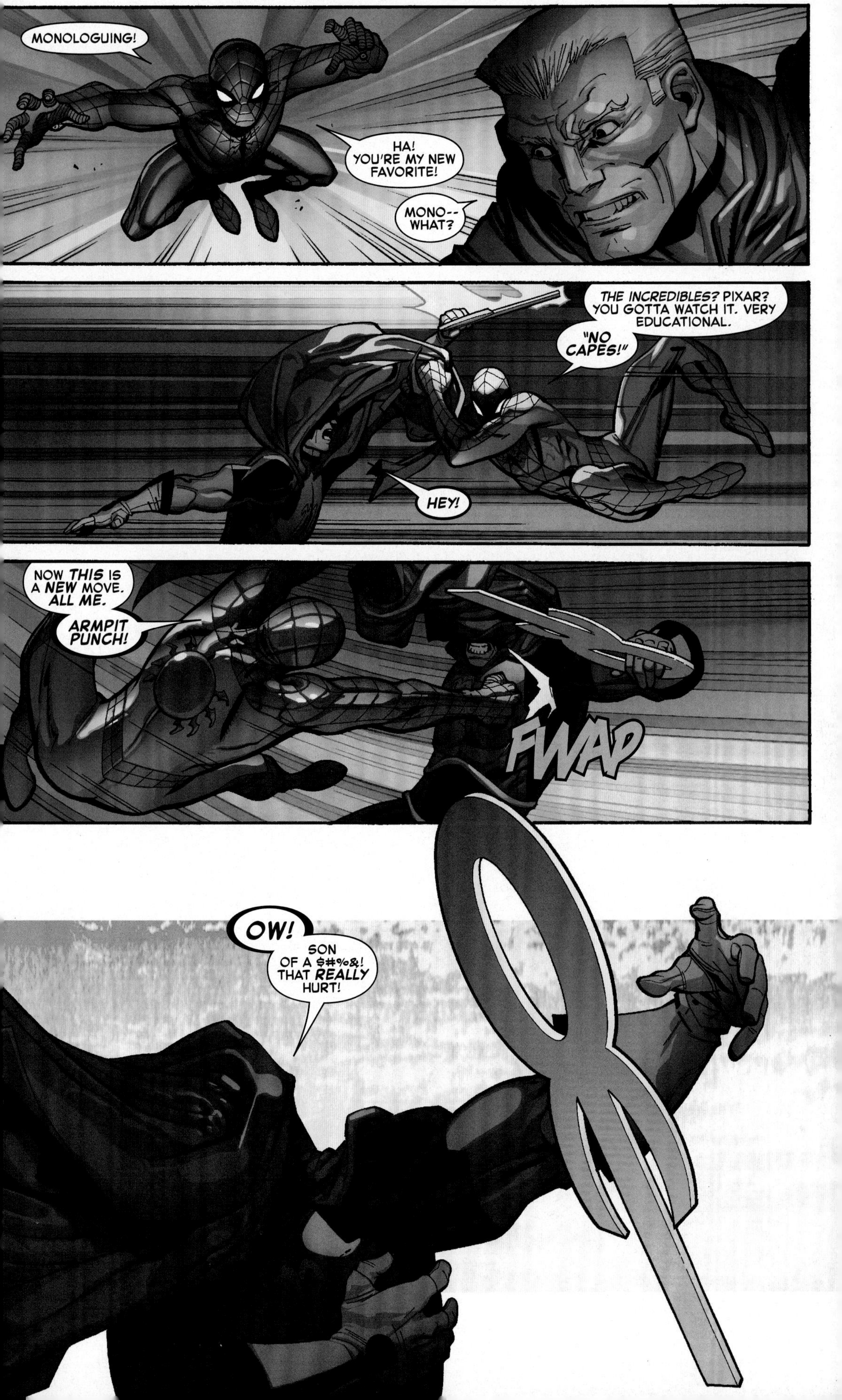
MONOLOGUING!
HA! YOU'RE MY NEW FAVORITE!
MONO-- WHAT?
THE INCREDIBLES? PIXAR? YOU GOTTA WATCH IT. VERY EDUCATIONAL.
"NO CAPES!"
HEY!
NOW THIS IS A NEW MOVE. ALL ME.
ARMPIT PUNCH!
FWAP
OW!
SON OF A $#%&! THAT REALLY HURT!

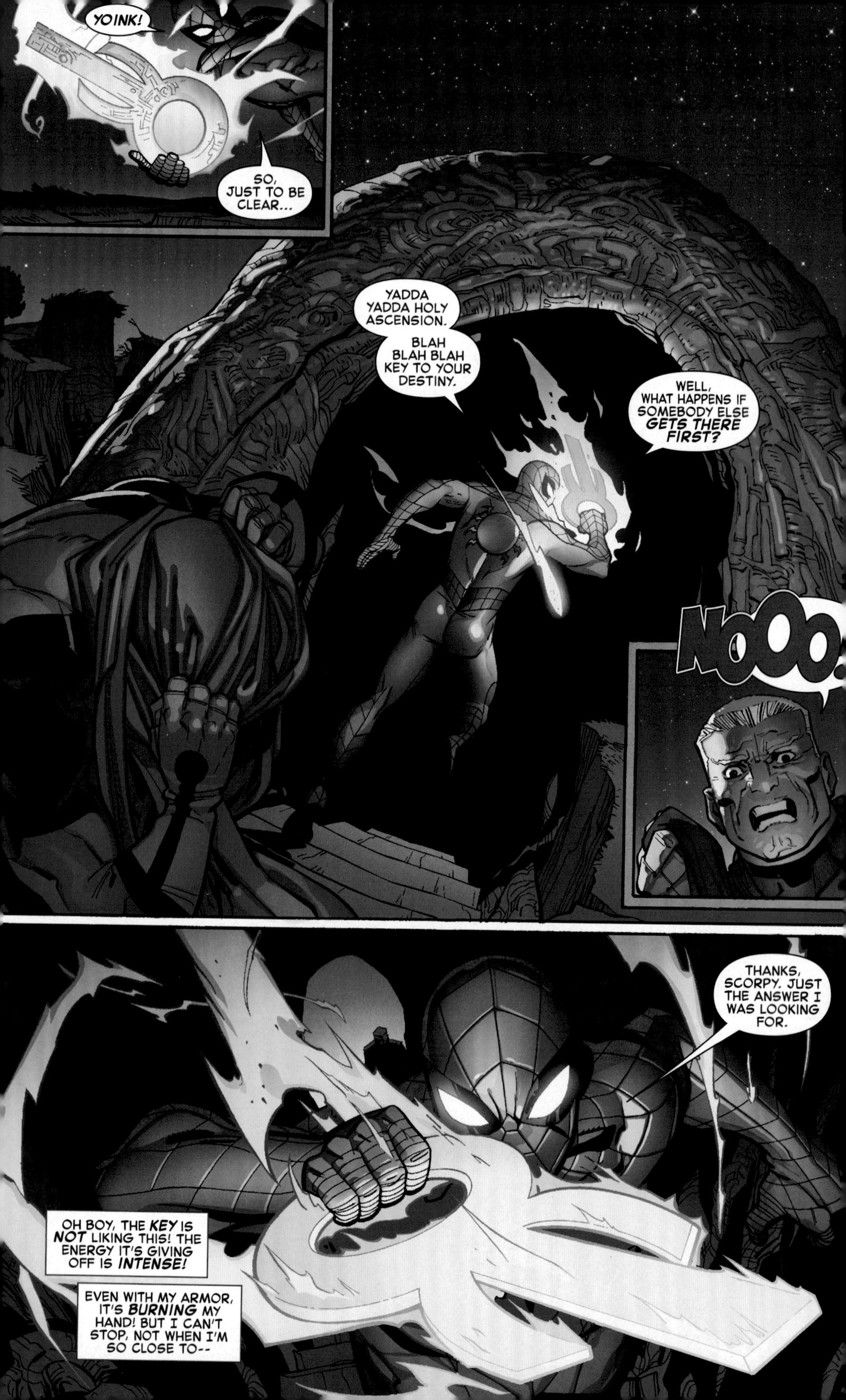
YOINK!
SO, JUST TO BE CLEAR...
YADDA YADDA HOLY ASCENSION.
BLAH BLAH BLAH KEY TO YOUR DESTINY.
WELL, WHAT HAPPENS IF SOMEBODY ELSE GETS THERE FIRST?
NOOO!
THANKS, SCORPY. JUST THE ANSWER I WAS LOOKING FOR.
OH BOY, THE KEY IS NOT LIKING THIS! THE ENERGY IT'S GIVING OFF IS INTENSE!
EVEN WITH MY ARMOR, IT'S BURNING MY HAND! BUT I CAN'T STOP, NOT WHEN I'M SO CLOSE TO--

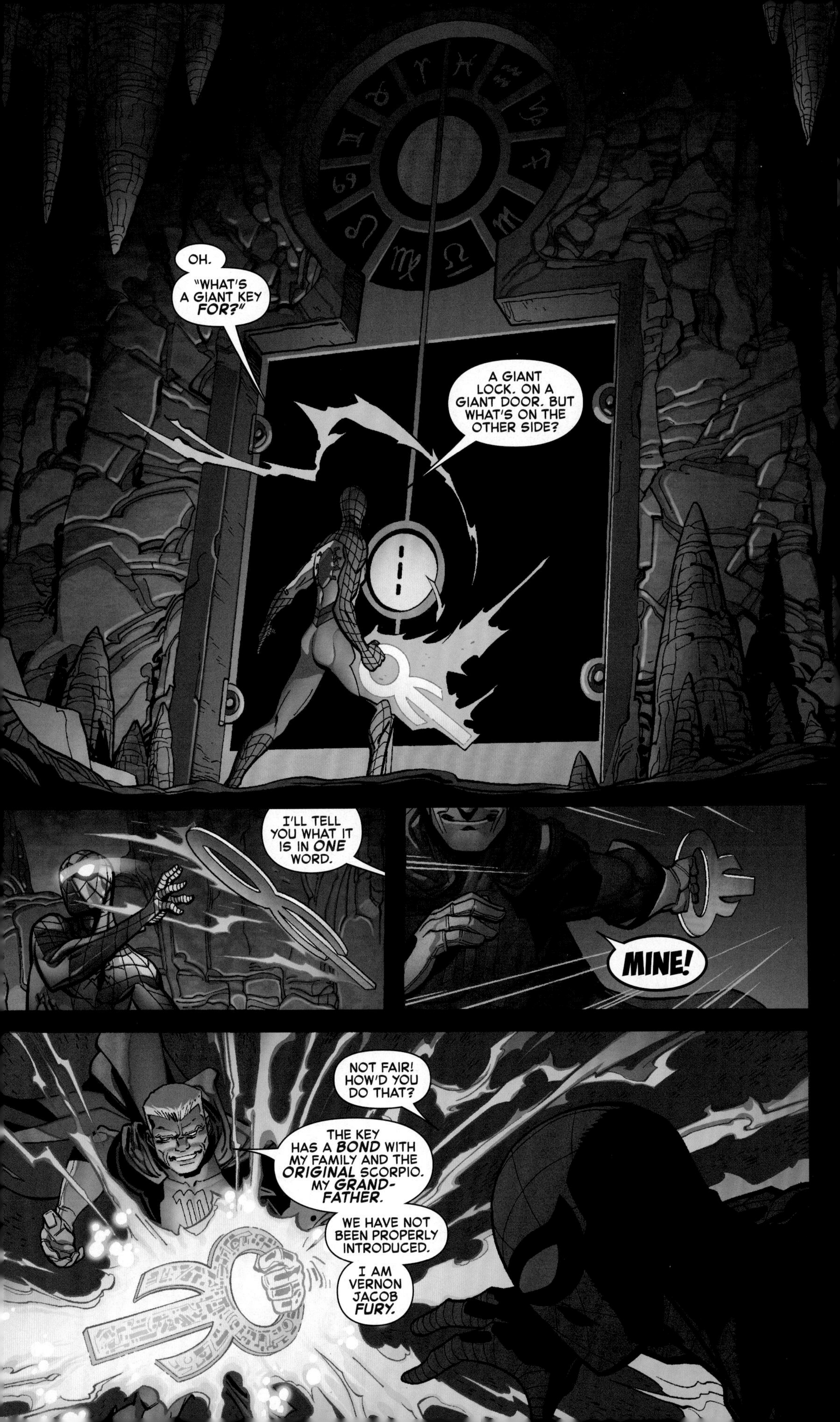
OH.
"WHAT'S A GIANT KEY FOR?"
A GIANT LOCK. ON A GIANT DOOR. BUT WHAT'S ON THE OTHER SIDE?
!
I'LL TELL YOU WHAT IT IS IN ONE WORD.
MINE!
NOT FAIR! HOW'D YOU DO THAT?
THE KEY HAS A BOND WITH MY FAMILY AND THE ORIGINAL SCORPIO. MY GRAND-FATHER.
WE HAVE NOT BEEN PROPERLY INTRODUCED.
I AM VERNON JACOB FURY.

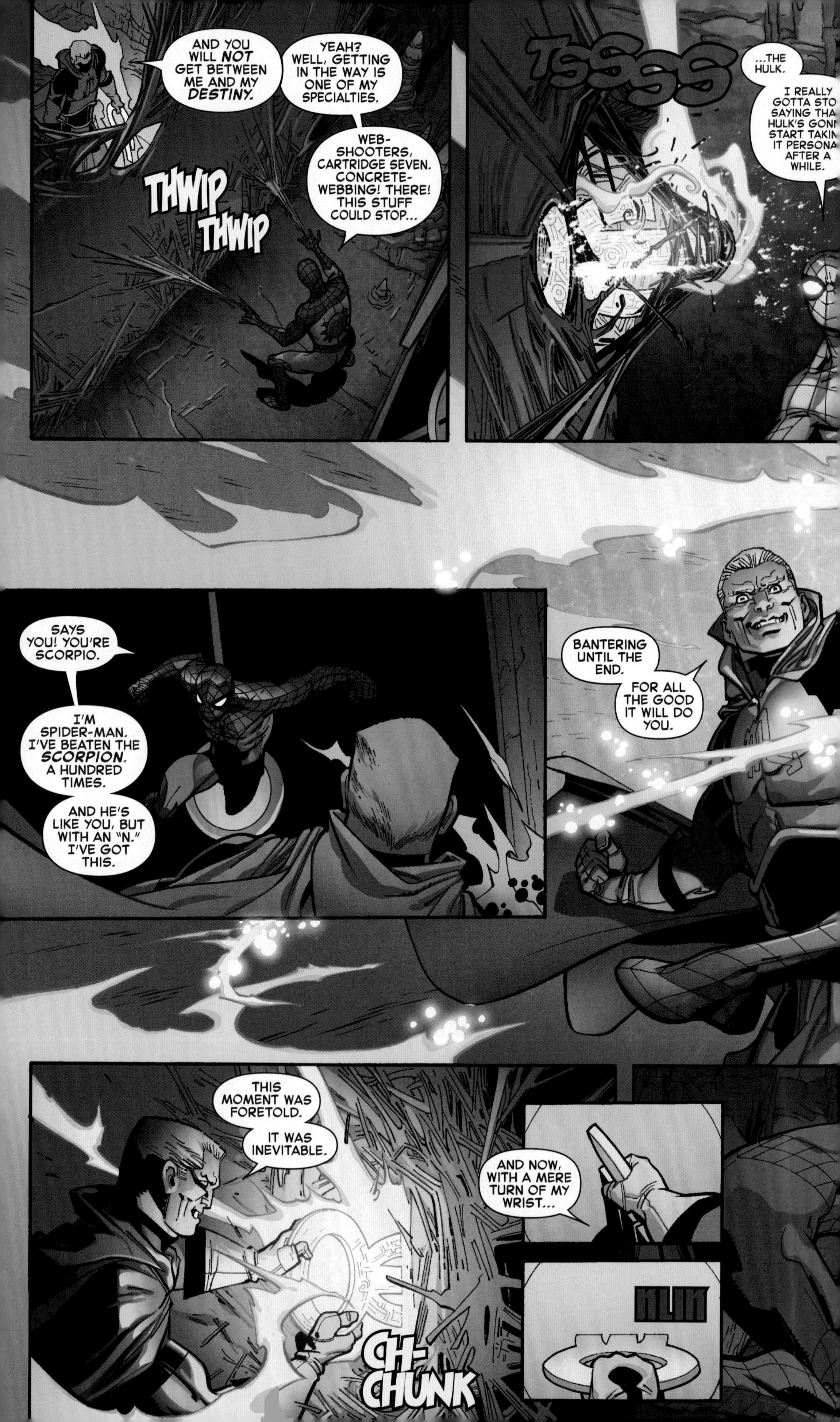
AND YOU WILL NOT GET BETWEEN ME AND MY DESTINY.
YEAH? WELL, GETTING IN THE WAY IS ONE OF MY SPECIALTIES.
WEB-SHOOTERS, CARTRIDGE SEVEN. CONCRETE-WEBBING! THERE! THIS STUFF COULD STOP...
THWIP THWIP
TSSSSS
...THE HULK.
I REALLY GOTTA STO SAYING THA HULK'S GON START TAKIN IT PERSONA AFTER A WHILE.
SAYS YOU! YOU'RE SCORPIO.
I'M SPIDER-MAN. I'VE BEATEN THE SCORPION. A HUNDRED TIMES.
AND HE'S LIKE YOU, BUT WITH AN "N." I'VE GOT THIS.
BANTERING UNTIL THE END.
FOR ALL THE GOOD IT WILL DO YOU.
THIS MOMENT WAS FORETOLD.
IT WAS INEVITABLE.
CH-CHUNK
AND NOW, WITH A MERE TURN OF MY WRIST...
KLIK

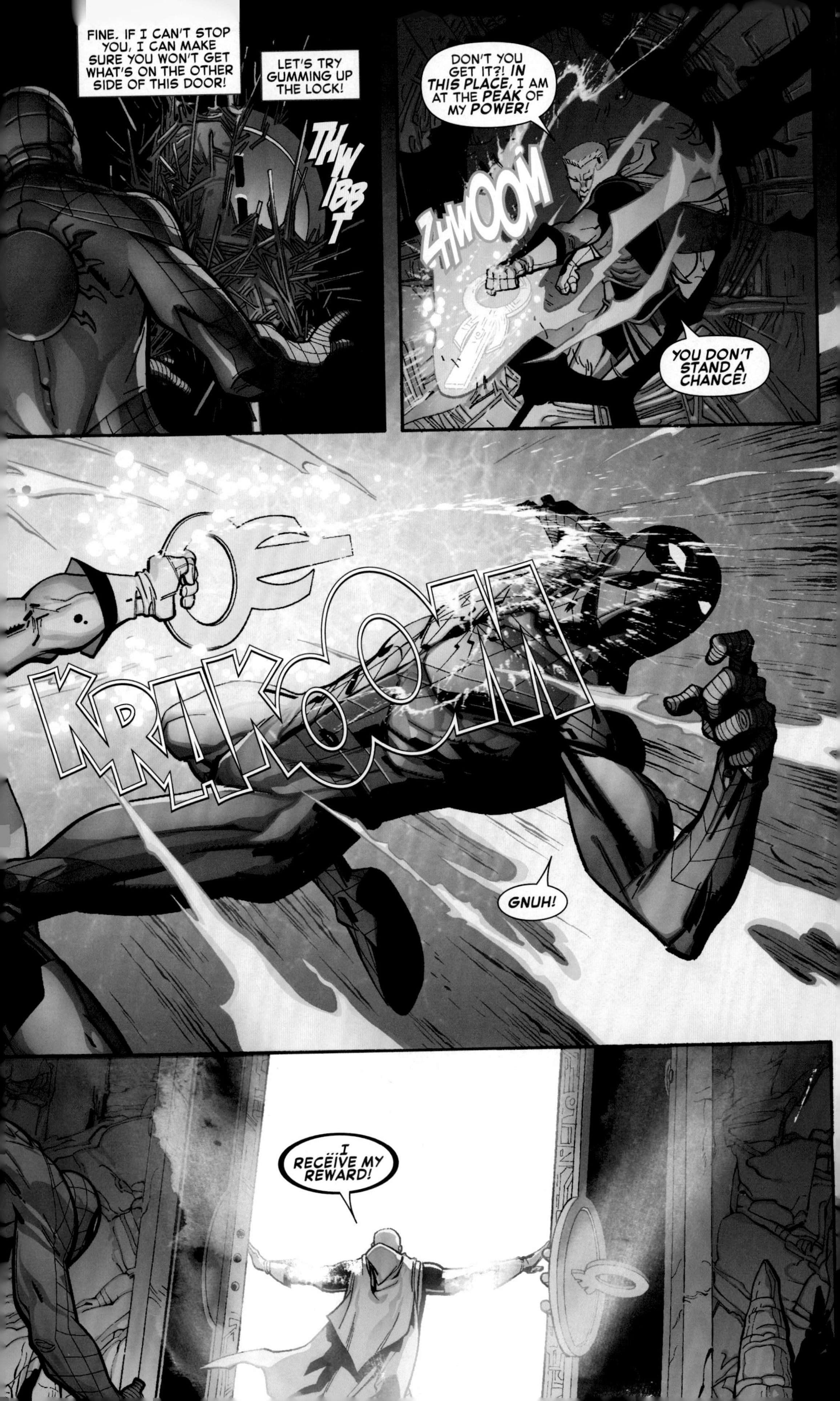

FINE. IF I CAN'T STOP YOU, I CAN MAKE SURE YOU WON'T GET WHAT'S ON THE OTHER SIDE OF THIS DOOR!
LET'S TRY GUMMING UP THE LOCK!
THWIBBT
DON'T YOU GET IT?! IN THIS PLACE, I AM AT THE PEAK OF MY POWER!
ZHWOOM
YOU DON'T STAND A CHANCE!
KRAKOOM
GNUH!
...I RECEIVE MY REWARD!

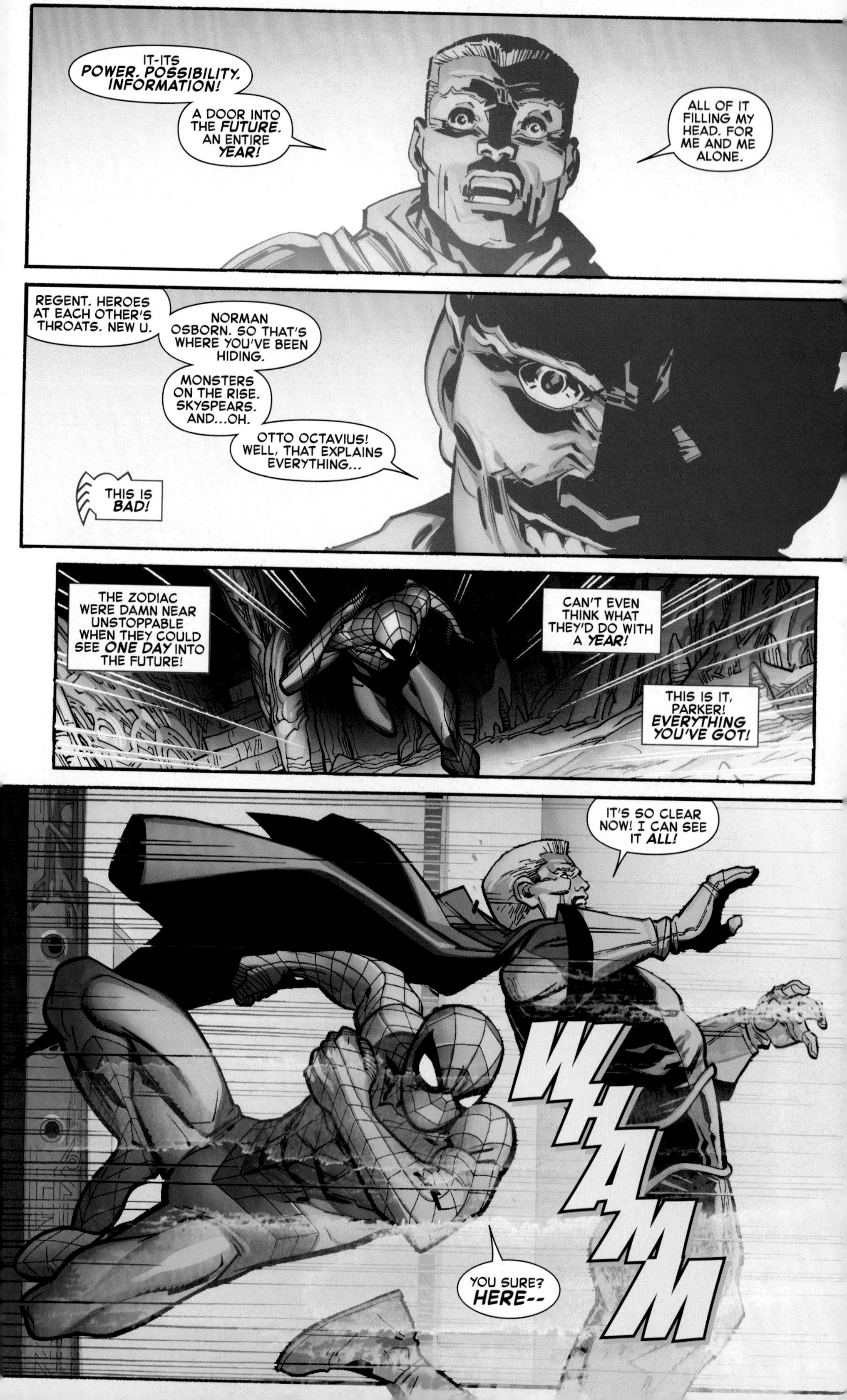

IT-ITS POWER. POSSIBILITY. INFORMATION!
A DOOR INTO THE FUTURE. AN ENTIRE YEAR!
ALL OF IT FILLING MY HEAD. FOR ME AND ME ALONE.
REGENT. HEROES AT EACH OTHER'S THROATS. NEW U.
NORMAN OSBORN. SO THAT'S WHERE YOU'VE BEEN HIDING.
MONSTERS ON THE RISE. SKYSPEARS. AND...OH.
OTTO OCTAVIUS! WELL, THAT EXPLAINS EVERYTHING...
THIS IS BAD!
THE ZODIAC WERE DAMN NEAR UNSTOPPABLE WHEN THEY COULD SEE ONE DAY INTO THE FUTURE!
CAN'T EVEN THINK WHAT THEY'D DO WITH A YEAR!
THIS IS IT, PARKER! EVERYTHING YOU'VE GOT!
IT'S SO CLEAR NOW! I CAN SEE IT ALL!
YOU SURE? HERE--
WHAM

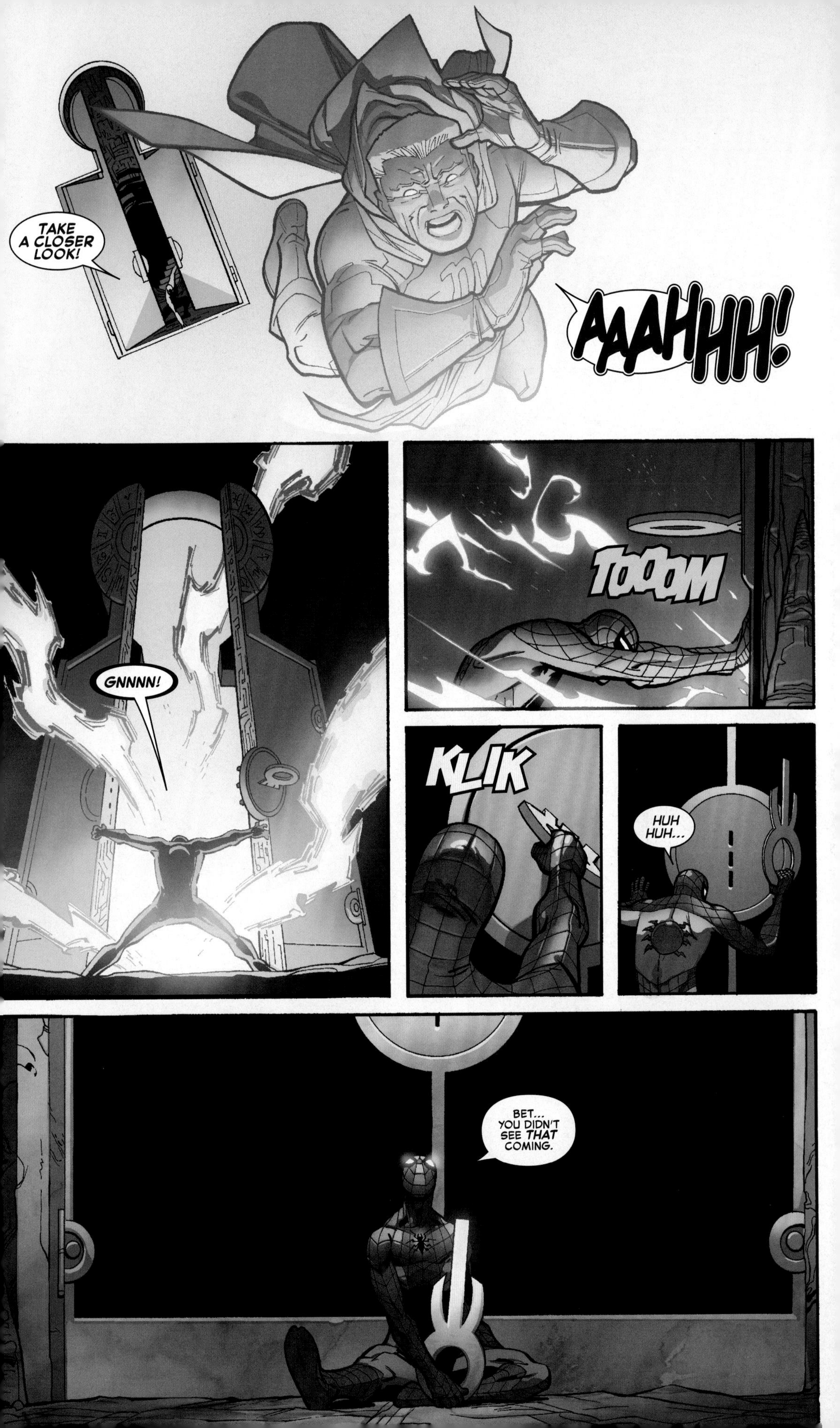
TAKE A CLOSER LOOK!
AAAHHH!
GNNNN!
TOOOM
KLIK
HUH HUH...
BET... YOU DIDN'T SEE THAT COMING.

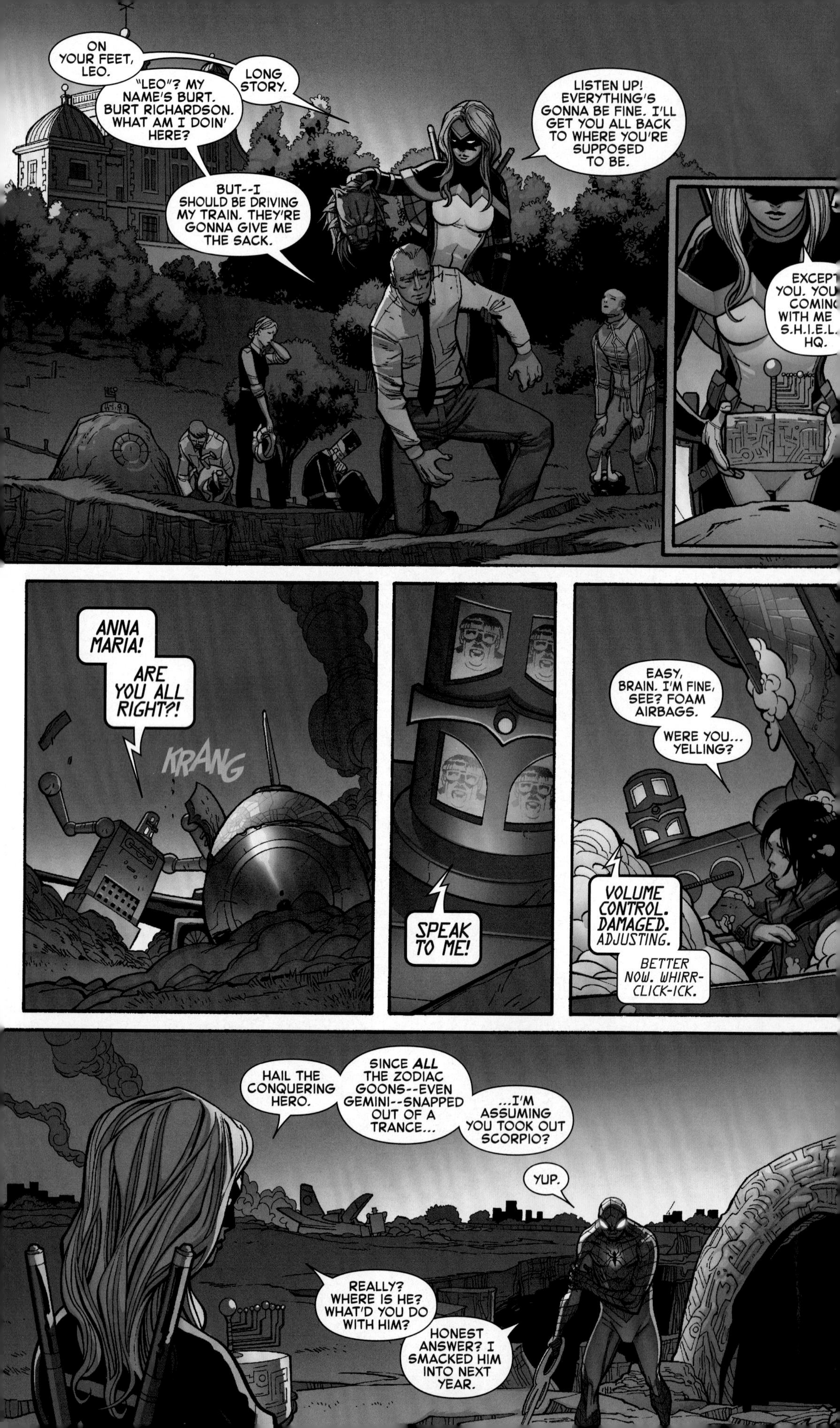
ON YOUR FEET, LEO.
"LEO"? MY NAME'S BURT. BURT RICHARDSON. WHAT AM I DOIN' HERE?
LONG STORY.
BUT--I SHOULD BE DRIVING MY TRAIN. THEY'RE GONNA GIVE ME THE SACK.
LISTEN UP! EVERYTHING'S GONNA BE FINE. I'LL GET YOU ALL BACK TO WHERE YOU'RE SUPPOSED TO BE.
EXCEPT YOU. YOU COMING WITH ME S.H.I.E.L. HQ.
ANNA MARIA!
ARE YOU ALL RIGHT?!
KRANG
SPEAK TO ME!
EASY, BRAIN. I'M FINE, SEE? FOAM AIRBAGS.
WERE YOU... YELLING?
VOLUME CONTROL. DAMAGED. ADJUSTING.
BETTER NOW. WHIRR-CLICK-ICK.
HAIL THE CONQUERING HERO.
SINCE ALL THE ZODIAC GOONS--EVEN GEMINI--SNAPPED OUT OF A TRANCE...
...I'M ASSUMING YOU TOOK OUT SCORPIO?
YUP.
REALLY? WHERE IS HE? WHAT'D YOU DO WITH HIM?
HONEST ANSWER? I SMACKED HIM INTO NEXT YEAR.

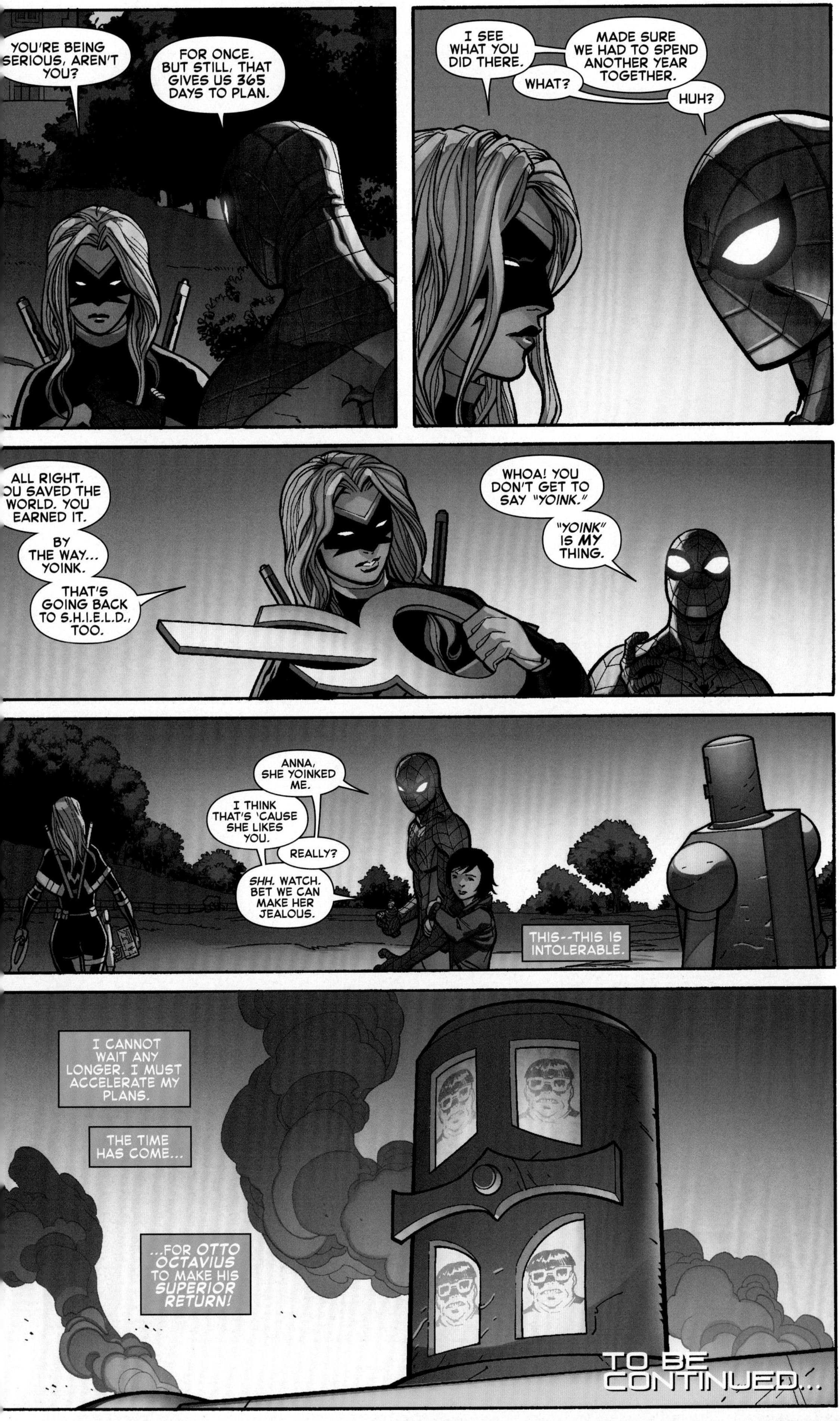
YOU'RE BEING SERIOUS, AREN'T YOU?
FOR ONCE. BUT STILL, THAT GIVES US 365 DAYS TO PLAN.
I SEE WHAT YOU DID THERE.
WHAT?
MADE SURE WE HAD TO SPEND ANOTHER YEAR TOGETHER.
HUH?
ALL RIGHT. OU SAVED THE WORLD. YOU EARNED IT.
BY THE WAY... YOINK.
THAT'S GOING BACK TO S.H.I.E.L.D., TOO.
WHOA! YOU DON'T GET TO SAY "YOINK."
"YOINK" IS MY THING.
ANNA, SHE YOINKED ME.
I THINK THAT'S 'CAUSE SHE LIKES YOU.
REALLY?
SHH. WATCH. BET WE CAN MAKE HER JEALOUS.
THIS--THIS IS INTOLERABLE.
I CANNOT WAIT ANY LONGER. I MUST ACCELERATE MY PLANS.
THE TIME HAS COME...
...FOR OTTO OCTAVIUS TO MAKE HIS SUPERIOR RETURN!
TO BE CONTINUED...

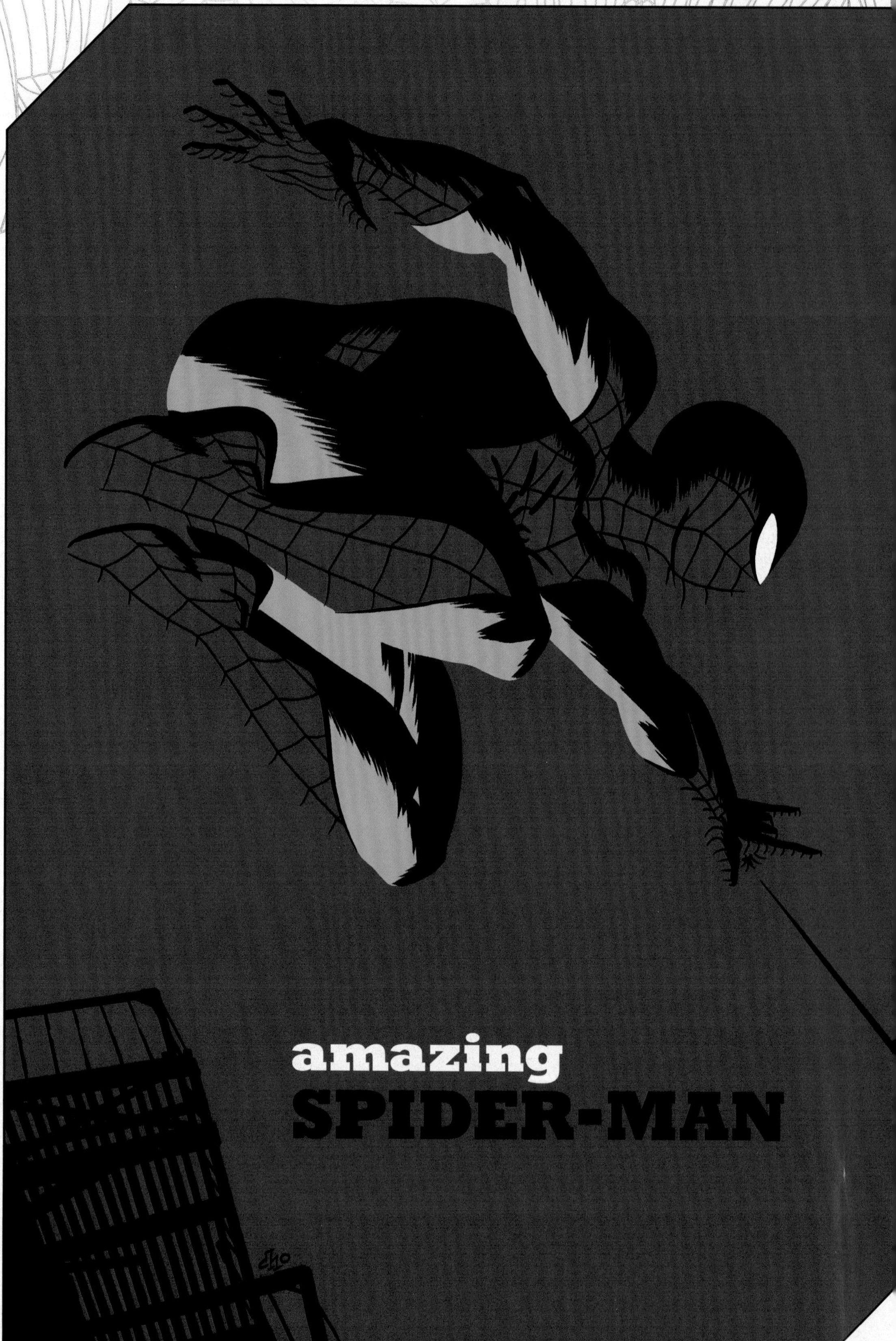
amazing
SPIDER-MAN
cho

#7 VARIANT BY MICHAEL CHO

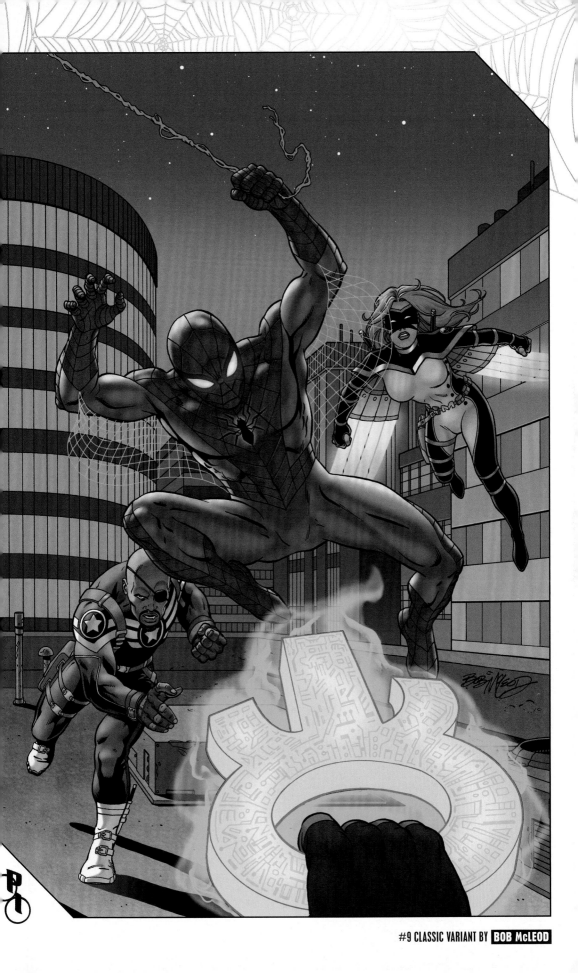

#9 CLASSIC VARIANT BY **BOB McLEOD**

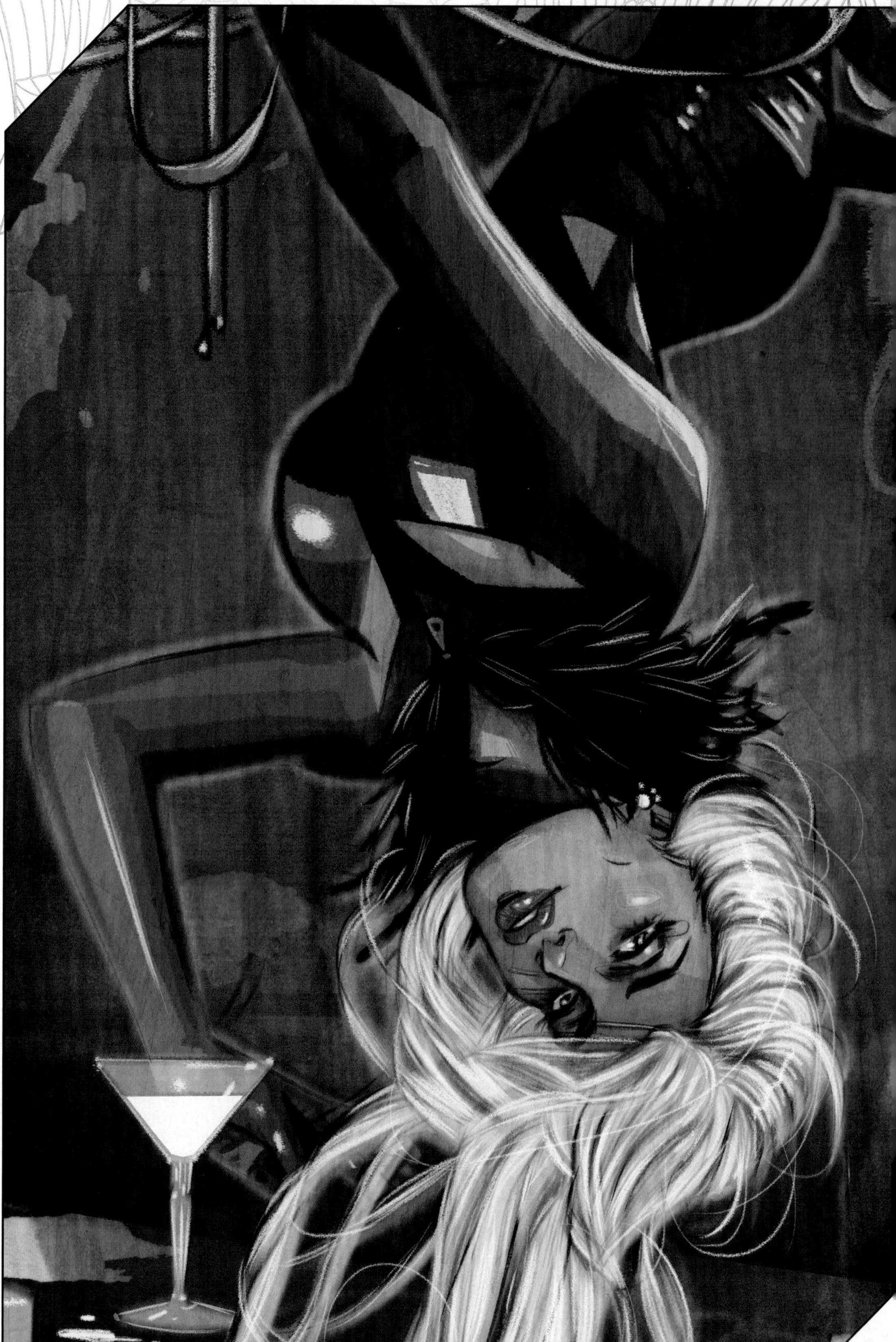

#9 WOMEN OF POWER VARIANT BY **TULA LOTAY**

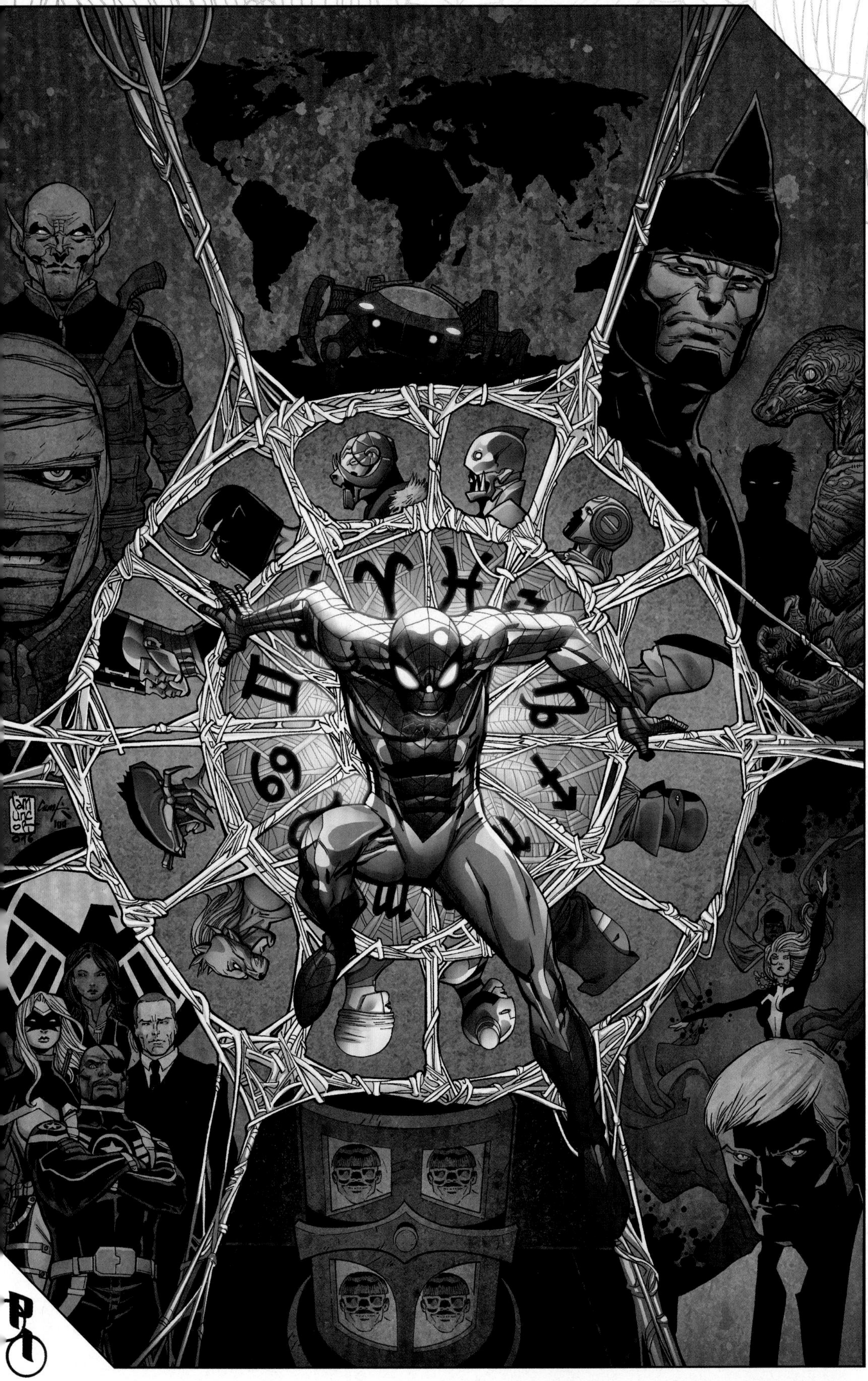

#9 STORY THUS FAR VARIANT BY **GIUSEPPE CAMUNCOLI, CAM SMITH & MARTE GRACIA**

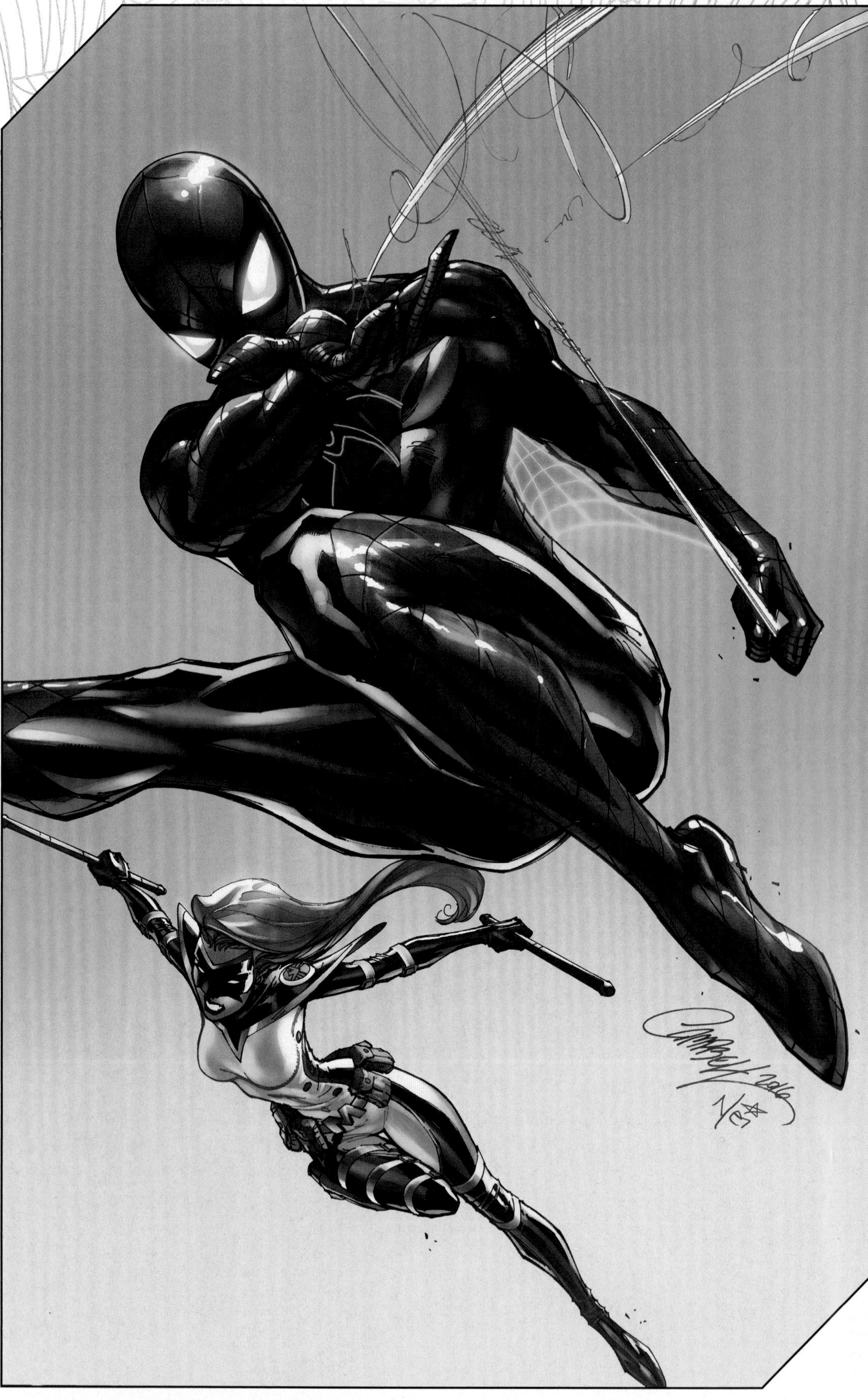

#9 VARIANT BY **J. SCOTT CAMPBELL & NEI RUFFINO**

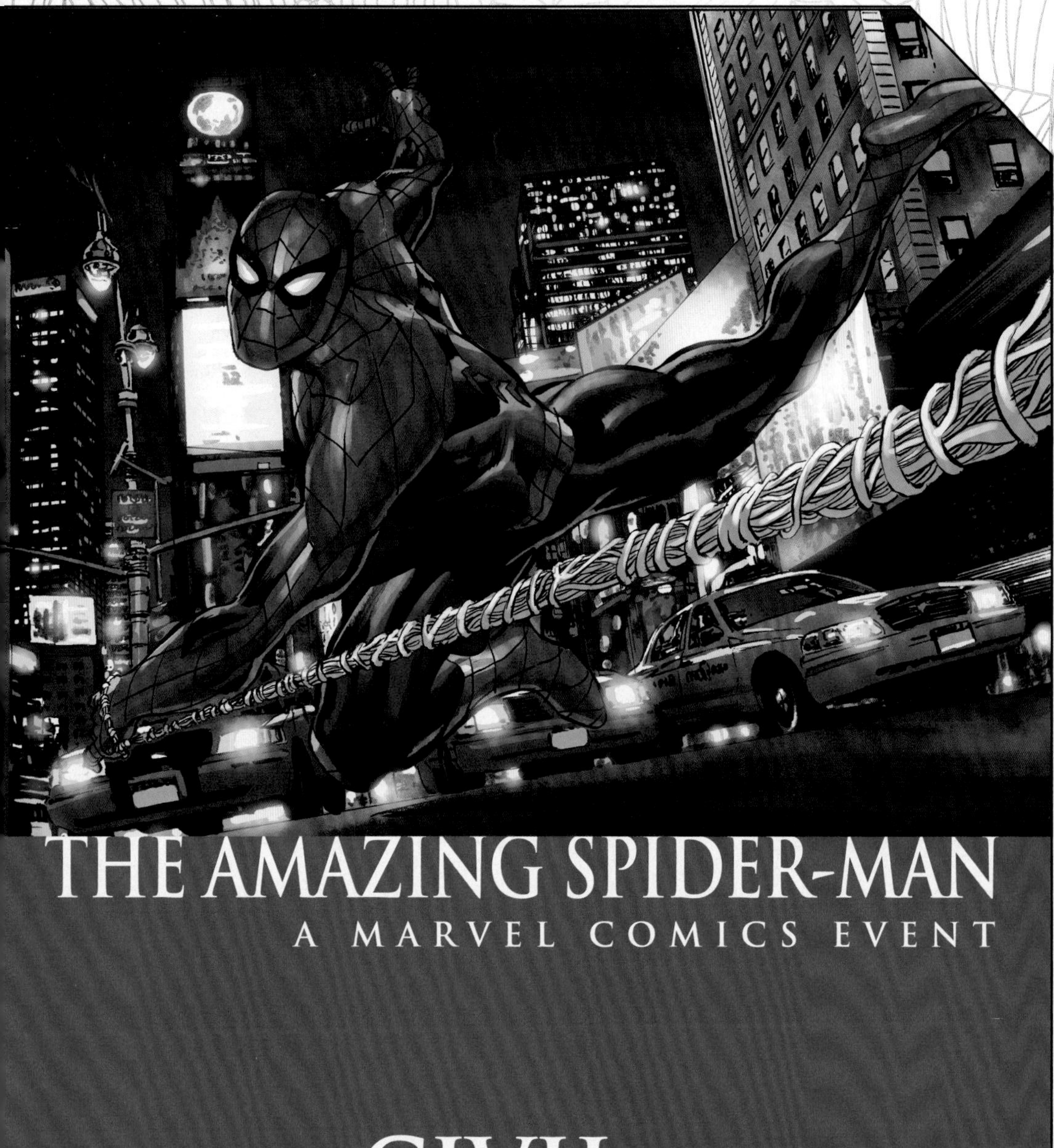
THE AMAZING SPIDER-MAN
A MARVEL COMICS EVENT
CIVIL WAR

#10 CIVIL WAR VARIANT BY **MIKE PERKINS**

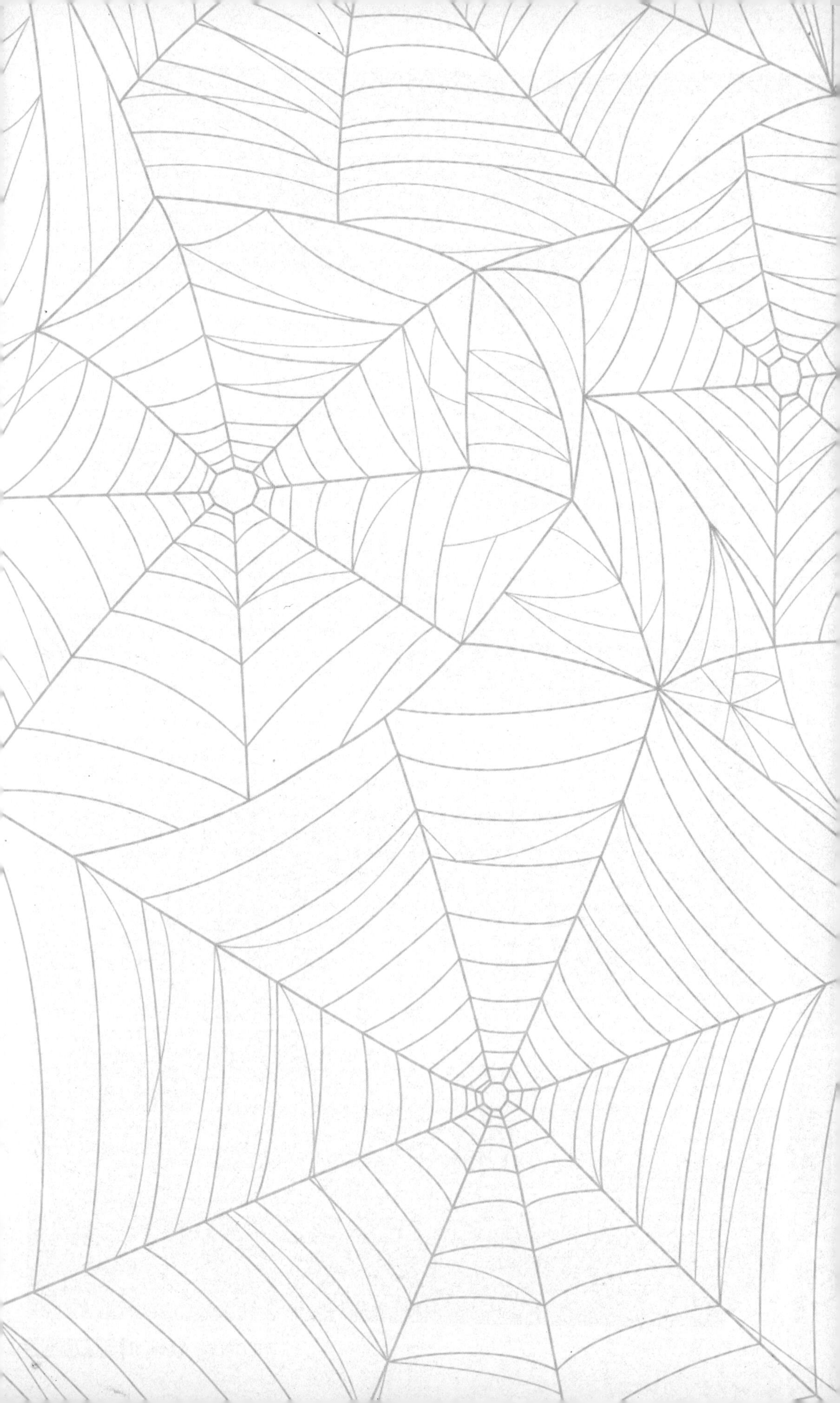